THE CHANGING PARISH

THE CHANGING PARISH

*A study of parishes, priests, and
parishioners after Vatican II*

MICHAEL P. HORNSBY-SMITH

R

ROUTLEDGE
London and New York

First published in 1989 by Routledge
11 New Fetter Lane, London EC4P 4EE
29 West 35th Street, New York NY 10001

© 1989 Michael P. Hornsby-Smith

Typeset in Baskerville
by Pat and Anne Murphy, Highcliffe-on-Sea, Dorset
Printed and bound in Great Britain by
Biddles Ltd, Guildford and King's Lynn

British Library Cataloguing in Publication Data

Hornsby-Smith, Michael P.
The changing parish: a study of parishes, priests and parishioners
after Vatican II.
1. Catholic Church. Parishes. Organisation
I. Title
254'.02

Library of Congress Cataloging in Publication Data

Hornsby-Smith, Michael P.
The changing parish: a study of parishes, priests, and parishioners
after Vatican II / Michael P. Hornsby-Smith.
p.   cm.
Bibliography: p.
Includes index.
1. Parishes — Great Britain — History — 20th century.
2. Catholic Church — Great Britain — Clergy — History — 20th century.
3. Laity — Catholic Church — History — 20th century.
4. Sociology, Christian (Catholic) — History — 20th century.
5. Great Britain — Religious life and customs. I. Title.
BX1493.2.H667 1989   250'.8822 – dc 19   88-38651 CIP

ISBN 0-415-01795-5

CONTENTS

CONTENTS

CONTENTS

FIGURES AND TABLES

FIGURES

TABLES

PREFACE

This book has emerged serendipitously from the various pieces of research which I and a number of colleagues have undertaken into the transformations which can be discerned in the nature of English Catholicism in the years of rapid social change since the end of the Second World War. Since then Catholics have attempted, with greater or lesser enthusiasm, to renew themselves and their institutions as they were urged to do nearly a quarter of a century ago by the Second Vatican Council. I am indebted in particular to Bryan Wilson who first encouraged and sponsored this attempt to identify some of the major changes in Catholic parishes and the roles of parish priests and parishioners in recent decades.

While the bulk of this book concerns the transformation of the Catholic parish particularly in contemporary England and Wales, I believe that the processes which I have tried to identify have a much wider application. In general I have been more impressed by the similarities than the dissimilarities of parish life as we experienced it in Boston, Chicago, New York, Lubbock, and Maryland in the United States, and Melbourne, Sydney, and Perth in Australia. My wife and I recall with special affection the weekend which we spent as guests in the parish of St Clement's, Lincoln Park, Chicago. A brief visit to the Philippines, and in particular to the islands of Negros and Panay in 1984, demonstrated both a similar, European model of the traditional parish and the emergence of the exciting new model of the Basic Christian Community – Community Organisation to challenge the rigidities and domesticated complacency of the older model. I am convinced that we in the western and northern parishes have much to learn about the nature of the Church from such Third World experiences and I am grateful for the wider perspectives which they encourage.

In this book I have drawn heavily not only on previous research in two London and two Preston parishes and on the fieldwork of a post-graduate student with a group of parishes in the south of England which were focusing in particular on the need for parish support for young marrieds, but also on my experiences in the parish of Merrow and Burpham over nearly a quarter of a century. My view of the Church as it struggles, not always with the greatest of enthusiasm, to renew itself, has been coloured by the everyday experiences of friendship and support, conflict and reconciliation, which have been mine there. I particularly wish to thank Fr Brian O'Sullivan for permission to quote extensively from his book *Parish Alive* (1979), which was his account of his years as the first parish priest of the newly combined parish in the 1970s.

For fifteen years or so I have enjoyed the stimulating and challenging friendship of the members of a family group in this parish. Together we have constructed our own vision of what the 'People of God', post-Vatican Church *ought* to be like. During the writing of this book I have been grateful for their critical observations on the interpretations which a sociologist might make of our common experiences. Their comments have always been a helpful corrective to any tendency to go beyond the evidence and, while I have not always followed their suggestions, I am grateful to them for their contributions and challenges. This book would have been much poorer without them and in gratitude I dedicate it to them with love: David and Frances Allen, Frank Comerford and the late Monica Comerford, Bonny and Mary D'Urso, Bob and Maureen Durston, Lennie Hornsby-Smith, and Andrew and Maureen Martin.

Some of the most challenging analyses of parish life in recent years have been offered by Monica Comerford's twin brother and former priest, Michael Winter (1973, 1979, 1985). While it will be apparent in this book that I do not always share his views, I do believe he offers an important and prophetic witness to the need for institutional reform in the Church and I am grateful to him for his friendship and stimulating challenges, especially in those matters which are the chief concern of this book: parish life as the articulation of the communal worship and mutual support of the gathered 'People of God', and the role of the priest as a religious leader who encourages the emergence and flowering of the various gifts, talents and ministries of lay people and who exercises an enabling rather than an autocratic form of authority in the religious collectivity.

During the past decade I have benefited enormously from the gentle encouragement of members of the BSA Sociology of Religion Study Group and more recently from members of the Surrey Religious Research Group. Without their support I doubt if I would have had the nerve to continue seeking sociologically adequate accounts of the fascinating transformations which are taking place in Roman Catholicism.

In the writing of this book several friends and colleagues have been especially helpful. Frs Brian Green, Tony Lovegrove, and Brian O'Sullivan, and John Fulton and Ray Lee read and commented at length and in detail on the drafts of the first five chapters. I have taken note of most of their criticisms and suggestions which were invaluable as I struggled to complete the book on schedule. It goes without saying that any faults which remain are entirely my own responsibility.

I owe a special debt of gratitude to my former postgraduate student, John Leslie, for generously allowing me to quote extensively from his Ph.D. thesis, and also to David Leege, the Director of the Notre Dame Study of Catholic Parish Life in the United States, for permission to make frequent reference to his research reports. My thanks are also due to Grace Davie for first drawing my attention to Danièle Hervieu-Léger's recent book and to Judith Glover and Catherine Dumont for helping me with the translation of some key passages. I am grateful to Ralph Lane for notes on a stimulating paper he gave at a BSA Sociology of Religion Conference some years ago.

Mrs Cotter of the Catholic Education Council could not have been more helpful in providing me with summaries of the annual parish returns for England and Wales. My thanks are also due to Michael Walsh for help in completing some statistical trend data. Some of the findings and analyses presented in these pages were first published elsewhere and I am most grateful to the editor of *New Blackfriars* for permission to use the article which comprises the bulk of Chapter 7.

I have not words adequately to thank my wife, Lennie, for her love and continuing encouragement and support, especially on the bad days when little has been written and at the times of panic as deadlines approach. She well exemplifies the hopefulness which Andrew Greeley once suggested was the particular mark of the Catholic.

Finally, while I would regard myself as a committed and involved Roman Catholic lay person wedded to the post-conciliar 'People of

God' model of the Church, I have attempted in this book to offer an analytical, sociological account of the transformations taking place in the contemporary parish. Only in the Appendix of the book have I consciously addressed questions of pastoral policy. It is now up to the reader to judge how successful that attempt has been.

Sociology Department,
University of Surrey.

19 September 1988

Chapter One

INTRODUCTION: THE CHANGING PARISH

POST-WAR DEVELOPMENTS

In this chapter the argument will be addressed that as a result of major social changes in the post-war world and the dramatic shifts of self-understanding, theological orientations, and ideological legitimations articulated at the Second Vatican Council in the 1960s — especially in the Dogmatic Constitution on the Church (*Lumen Gentium*), the Pastoral Constitution on the Church in the Modern World (*Gaudium et Spes*), and the Constitution on the Sacred Liturgy (*Sacrosanctum Concilium*) (see Abbott 1966: 14–101, 136–78, 199–308) — the Catholic parish has been transformed. The focus will be primarily on the situation in England and Wales but use will be made of comparable material wherever possible, for example the Notre Dame parish study in the United States.

Parish statistics in England and Wales are somewhat limited and largely date from the period following the Second Vatican Council and the closure of the Newman Demographic Survey in the 1960s. The pastoral statistics collated by the Catholic Education Council in their present form provide aggregate figures of the numbers of parishes, Catholic population known to the priests (generally regarded to be only three-fifths to three-quarters of the estimated numbers of baptised Catholics), and the numbers of key initiating sacraments or *rites de passage* performed (child baptisms, receptions or conversions, first communions, confirmations, marriages of various types, and deaths), as well as weekly Mass attendances and numbers of lay catechists, catechumens (under instruction in Catholic beliefs), and members of recognised Catholic associations. Surprisingly, the numbers of clergy (diocesan or members of religious orders) and

1

parish sisters, the main full-time human resource and institutional religious leadership in the parishes, is not recorded in the same series. A summary of the available statistics has been given in Tables 1.1 and 1.2. Apart from the statistics given in these tables, the annual returns also show an increase in the number of catechumens from 4,443 in 1970 to 5,314 in 1985. Over the same period the number of members of Roman Catholic associations is said to have grown from 140,766 to 147,636, though reservations must be recorded about the accuracy or significance of these data.

Table 1.1   Summary of parish statistics in England Wales, 1945–85

Year	Parishes	Catholic population	Mass attendance	Priests		Lay catechists
				Secular	Regular	
1945	1,910	2,390,000	n/a	4,122	2,135	n/a
1960	n/a	3,702,517	1,941,900	4,667	2,699	n/a
1965	2,320	4,048,415	n/a	5,033	2,775	n/a
1970	2,650	4,113,971	1,934,853	4,939	2,719	4,254
1975	n/a	4,182,210	1,790,980	4,980	2,530	4,802
1980	2,735	4,257,789	1,644,224	4,712	2,304	5,942
1985	2,715	4,186,285	1,461,074	4,545	2,173	11,451

Source: Catholic Education Council, Summary of Pastoral Statistics, 1945–85; Catholic Directories for 1946, 1961, 1966, 1970, 1976, 1981, 1986.

In the decades after the Second World War the Catholic population increased rapidly as a result of very high levels of Irish immigration and also the settlement of large numbers of Polish and other exiles. The admittedly inaccurate estimates of parish priests put the increase in the size of the population of known Catholics as high as three-quarters in the four decades after the end of the war. At the same time Catholics benefited from the growing affluence of the 1950s and 1960s and joined in the processes of geographical mobility, especially outwards from the old inner-city parishes and into the suburban areas of all the major connurbations. This period was therefore charac-terised by a huge programme of church building for the new estates. Thus in the four decades after the war the number of parishes increased by some two-fifths, though there has been a slight decrease in the 1980s due to the need for some retrenchment as a result of the fall in the number of priests. What evidence there is suggests that the average Mass attendance has declined by about one-quarter since the end of the 1950s. One of the most interesting figures in Table 1.1 is that which indicates that the number of recognised lay catechists in the parishes is more than two-and-a-half times what it was only fifteen years ago in 1970. This is one clear indication of the growing institutionalised participation in the pastoral work of the parishes by lay people and is fully in accord with the post-Vatican model of the Church which was referred to above. It could also indicate a growing sharing of pastoral leadership by priests at the parish level.

Table 1.2   Rites of passage and sacramental statistics, England Wales, 1945–85

Year	Child baptisms	Receptions	First communions	Confirmations	Marriages Total	% both RC	Deaths
1945	(73,400)	n/a	n/a	n/a	36,553	n/a	n/a
1960	123,430	14,803	n/a	80,602	46,480	50	n/a
1965	134,055	10,308	n/a	69,672	46,112	45	n/a
1970	108,187	6,069	95,382	71,956	46,105	37	36,596
1975	75,815	5,225	84,877	74,013	35,197	35	39,251
1980	76,352	5,783	68,365	54,803	31,524	34	41,715
1985	74,491	5,085	53,334	46,427	27,422	35	44,947

Source: Catholic Education Council, Summary of Pastoral Statistics, 1945–85.

The data in Table 1.2 give an indication of the scale of the everyday sacramental servicing which is performed by priests at the parish level. In 1985 the average English parish, with a Catholic population estimated by priests at just over 1,500 people and a weekly Mass attendance of around 540, celebrated some twenty-seven child baptisms, prepared twenty children for their first communions, and seventeen for confirmation. There was an average of four lay catechists to help with this task, and the priest estimated around fifty or more of his parishioners to be members of Catholic organisations and, presumably, relatively active in parish affairs. The parish had about ten marriages, in six or seven of which one partner was not a Catholic and would have had to be instructed over a period of some weeks. There were also seventeen deaths to be officiated at and two receptions into the Church to celebrate. Two more adult catechumens were 'under instruction'. These figures give some indication of the 'average' work load in the parishes, but it is clear that in many of the larger parishes it could be significantly greater at a time when the priestly workforce is ageing rapidly and declining in size.

Most of these figures indicate a significant decline following the

3

rapid drop in the birth rate, in which the Catholic population more than fully shared, from the early 1960s. Thus in the twenty years between 1965 and 1985 the number of child baptisms, confirmations and marriages declined by over two-fifths. In the same period the number of adult receptions (or conversions) declined by two-thirds. Interestingly the number of recorded deaths increased by one-quarter over the fifteen-year period since records began in 1970. This would appear to indicate an ageing of the Catholic population after the early post-war period of relatively high immigration of largely young people in the 1950s and 1960s.

The average figures, of course, hide a considerable degree of variability. Thus in England an inner-city parish might cover an area of under one square mile. (In some of the older ethnic neighbourhoods in Chicago it could be even smaller.) Parishes serving the new suburban estates would be much larger, partly because of the lower population density and partly because the proportion of Catholics in suburban areas tends to be lower. A rural parish on the Welsh border is different still; here the priest might typically serve three different churches ten to fifteen miles apart. Variations in the social class composition are also likely to have a significant effect upon the ethos of parishes. Thus parishioners in inner-city working-class areas might well tend to retain a relatively deferential attitude towards their priests while upwardly mobile professionals in the suburban estates might well expect more of a colleague-type relationship. In some of the older, rural parishes, especially those associated with landed gentry with recusant ancestry, the relationship might well be quasi-feudal with the unchallenged assumption of the leadership role, typically operated conservatively in favour of long-established local traditions, by the local landowner.

Parishes also vary significantly in terms of their ethnic composition. Some parishes are known as the first meeting place for Irish immigrants (see, for example, the role of St Anne's and the English Martyrs parishes in Rex and Moore's study of Sparkbrook, 1967: 86, 150). There are around seventy Polish parishes, and other parishes have relatively high concentrations of minority groups, for example from Italy, Spain, Goa, or the Philippines. Some of the inner-city parishes are known to be areas of transition with a transient and highly mobile population of both internal and external migrants in search of work and opportunities. Others have high proportions of 'bed-sits' for young single people. The creation of community-like relationships in such areas is well-nigh impossible. Some parishes have a concentration of hospitals, others in coastal resorts have disproportionately high concentrations of elderly or retired people. Again, there may well be distinct regional variations in parishes which reflect different historical developments, past religious conflicts, characteristic economic opportunities and patterns of industrialisation. (All the same, there is some evidence which suggests that the claims that northern parishes are quite different from those in the south-east may well be exaggerated; see Hornsby-Smith and Turcan, 1981).

The need for caution in the making of generalisations about parishes in view of the differences among them is also apparent in the Notre Dame study in the United States. While a little over one-third of the parishes there serve 1,000 or fewer known Catholics, around one-sixth serve well over 5,000. The authors report that

> on all aspects of parish life and its consequences for the religious and social behavior of its members, American Catholic parishes differ considerably by region of the country, urban-rural locale, ethnic traditions and other historical factors. It is one Church but there are many manifestations of it on the American continent. Sometimes those factors have led to the embrace of post-Vatican II changes; some have closed the door on further change. Sometimes the response to Vatican II is precisely what has given new life to a parish; sometimes it is the factor that has torn the parish asunder. And for still others, beyond the change to English and the celebration of the Eucharist with the priest facing people, Vatican II never really happened — and they are doing quite well, thank you.
>
> (Leege and Gremillion, 1984: 7–8)

The variability between parishes is even greater than that indicated since the Notre Dame study did not include Spanish-speaking parishes.

The Catholic parish is *the* key religious institution for its adherents. It is the locus of almost all their community-like endeavours: the gathering place for regular worship, the induction of its new members and frequently for the confirmation of their faith, for much of the social interaction between fellow Catholics, and the source of almost all post-school religious experiences, teaching and moral guidance. It also provides a high proportion of the available support and comfort for those in need or in situations of crisis: the sick, dying, or bereaved. In spite of some 'loss of functions' by the parish as a result of social change in recent decades, for example in the area of entertainment in an era of mass media and mass leisure opportunities, it continues to be the focal point of the religious life, such as it is, of the overwhelming majority of Catholics.

Nevertheless, the parish has its critics. It has been regarded as a mediaeval anachronism quite incapable of meeting community needs of worship, charity, witness, and apostolate. According to Michael Winter:

> the parish as we know it now is an obstacle to the kind of mission which the Church must exercise in the post-christian pluralistic societies of the English-speaking nations. So much of the corporate activity of priests and laity is expended on projects whose apostolic value has never been demonstrated clearly, such as schools, halls and large churches. The construction and maintenance of these costly buildings keeps the Catholics in a psychological ghetto of inward-looking activity, while the authentic problems of mankind are largely ignored.
>
> (1973: 66)

These are important criticisms which it is one purpose of this book to address. All the same, to adapt a phrase of the American sociologists Greeley and Rossi in the first of their studies of Catholic schools in the United States, to be for or against the Catholic parish, for example in relation to other groupings such as small basic Christian communities of friends, colleagues, neighbours, or interest groups, 'is like being for or against the Rocky Mountains: it is great fun but it does not notably alter the reality' (1966: 231). The Catholic parish is a massive social fact. It is so obvious a fact that it has a taken-for-granted character which has enabled it to enjoy substantial immunity from detailed sociological investigation.

Undoubtedly, because of its size and because it claims to include all Catholic adherents, however attenuated their religious commitment, the extent to which the contemporary Catholic parish is able to achieve community-like attributes is extremely problematic. It is the focal point of the notion of the gathered 'People of God' and not just self-selected friendship or interest groups. Inevitably, therefore, it is in the forefront of the attempts of its Catholic adherents to transcend the cleavages between irreconcilables: between 'saints' and sinners, activists and nominal adherents, regular worshippers and the 'lapsed', religious zealots and those who have adapted to the norms and values of a secular society, between those in different social classes, ethnic groups, generations and sexes, and between those on the margins of society and core members. The extent to which the rhetoric of community is realised in the religious praxis of the parish must be the subject of empirical enquiry but it is clear that the goal the parish sets itself, of managing relationships between such potentially differentiated and conflicting groups and of transcending them, is of great social significance. It is one purpose of this book to investigate the extent to which the contemporary Catholic parish is able in practice to achieve these goals.

THE PARISH IN CANON LAW

Before commencing this task, it is necessary to clarify the status of the parish as codified in the Canon Law of the Roman Catholic Church. What is the relationship between the parish and the diocese and Roman authorities? What are the rights and responsibilities of the parish priest in his relationships with his parishioners? How independent can he be in matters of pastoral practice in his parish? The canonical norms governing parishes and the roles of parish priests and assistant priests are to be found in Chapter VI of that part of the revised code of Canon Law which deals with the hierarchical constitution of the Church (1983: 92–100). Thus:

> A parish is a certain community of Christ's faithful stably established within a particular Church, whose pastoral care, under the authority of the diocesan Bishop, is entrusted to a parish priest as its proper pastor.
>
> (Can. 515 s.1)

Parishes are established by diocesan bishops after consultation with the council of priests (Can. 515 s.2). There may be more than one priest in a parish but only provided that one is the moderator and responsible to the bishop for joint action (Can. 517 s.1). Generally parishes are territorial but where it is useful might be 'determined by reason of the rite, language or nationality' (Can. 518).

The parish priest needs to have the benefit of stability so that a parish is entrusted to him 'either in perpetuity or for a specified time' and then only if the Episcopal Conference allows this (Canons 520 s.2, 522). He then exercises the pastoral care of the community . . . under the authority of the diocesan Bishop . . . so that for this community he may carry out the offices of teaching, sanctifying and ruling with the co-operation of other priests or deacons and with the assistance of lay members of Christ's faithful.

(Can. 519)

Codes for the transfer of a parish priest to another parish which rely heavily on the persuasive power of the bishop but in the last analysis on his decree are clearly laid down (Canons 1748–52) as are procedures for the removal of a priest for good cause (Canons 1740–7) and there are also codes for appeal (Canons 1732–9). In practice in this country there appears to be a considerable amount of clerical mobility. Indeed at one stage in the 1950s during Bishop (later Cardinal) Heenan's period at Leeds, the movement of priests was so much greater than usual that it was dubbed 'the Cruel See'!

The duties of the parish priest are also laid down. They derive ultimately from the theology of the Church enunciated in the Vatican Council's dogmatic constitution *Lumen Gentium* (Abbott, 1966: 14–101). Thus 'Christ's faithful have the right to be assisted by their Pastors from the spiritual riches of the Church, especially by the word of God and the sacraments' (Can. 213). Later canons spell this out in some detail. He is responsible for the proclamation of the word of God, 'especially by means of the homily on Sundays and holidays of obligation and by catechetical formation' and education (Can. 528 s.1) and he 'must direct' the liturgy in his own parish (Can. 528 s.2). Of particular interest to lay people is Canon 529 s.1 which states:

So that he may fulfil his office of pastor diligently, the parish priest is to strive to know the faithful entrusted to his care. He is therefore to visit their families, sharing their cares and anxieties and, in a special way, their sorrows, comforting them in the Lord.

He is also prudently to correct wrongdoers, help the sick and dying, 'be especially diligent in seeking out the poor, the suffering, the lonely, those who are exiled . . . and burdened', and in supporting spouses and fostering a Christian family life (Can. 529 s.1). He is charged with the administration of the sacraments (Can. 530), juridical matters, the administration of parochial property and goods, and the keeping of proper parish records and registers (Canons 532–535). Finally he has an enabling and facilitating role and 'is to recognise and promote the specific role which the lay members of

8

Christ's faithful have in the mission of the Church, fostering their associations which have religious purposes' (Can. 529 s.2).

It is one purpose of this book to explore the extent to which these prescriptions or guidelines are met in practice. First, however, it is necessary to take due account of the major social and religious changes which have taken place over the past three or four decades. These provide the social and historical context for our study.

OFFICIAL RESPONSES IN ENGLAND AND WALES

While giving due weight to the social changes which have trans-formed the Roman Catholic community in England and Wales since the end of the Second World War and which will be reviewed in the next chapter, it is important also to recognise the major initiating role of the Second Vatican Council in promoting the search for 'renewal'. Thus David Forrester (1980: 73) pointed out that fifteen years after the Council, lay people were still unaware of the official teaching on the role, rights, and responsibilities of lay people in the conciliar *Decree on the Apostolate of the Laity* and in particular that:

> The laity should accustom themselves to working in the parish in close union with their priests, bringing to the church community their own and the world's problems as well as questions concerning human salvation, all of which should be examined and resolved by common deliberation.
>
> (s.10; in Abbott, 1966: 501)

A number of attempts have been made since the early 1970s to realise these aspirations more fully. Thus in *The Church 2000*, an interim report of a joint working party of the Bishops' Conference and the National Conference of Priests set up to discuss the preparation of a national pastoral strategy, stress was laid on the importance of a 'sense of belonging' at the parish level (1973, s.86) and the role of the priest as 'guide and animator' (1973, s.94). The subsequent report, *A Time for Building*, however, spoke only in general terms of the need for a 'leadership which can inspire trust and share responsibility, which is humble enough to be always learning and yet strong enough to face every challenge' (1976, s.55) Little was said about the role of the parish especially in its relationship with a proliferation of small groups. Somewhat enigmatically it added that

The parish will remain the spiritual community into which Catholics will be baptised and married and from which they will be buried, but we forsee that the present role of priests will evolve and develop.

(1976, s.78)

In particular there is a stress on his role as 'animator of his people' (1976, s.82). In subsequent discussion about the proposals, it was clear that Catholics were divided between a 'conservationist' group who stressed the Church's changelessness and a 'furtherance' group who believed that renewal and adaptation remain incomplete (Board, 1980).

It was the latter view which predominated at the National Pastoral Congress in 1980 (Anon., 1981). In the preparations for the Congress in many parishes throughout the country, concerns had been expressed at the size of parishes which militated against 'community'. A genuine partnership between priests and lay people was called for in the promotion of the parish as a 'caring community' and regular visiting by priests was particularly stressed (1981: 53–4, 80–1). In the report of Sector A on 'The People of God' the view was expressed that 'in order to become . . . a loving, caring, worshipping community, we overwhelmingly recommend that parishes should become a communion of Christian communities incorporating small, neighbourhood, area, and special interest groups including all, the lapsed and practising' (s.8 in 1981: 130–1).

In their response to the Congress, which in retrospect can be interpreted as a high point in the influence of 'progressive', educated, middle-class and middle-aged activist Catholics in the Church (Hornsby-Smith, 1987: 139–56), the bishops expressed support for the Congress insistence

upon the parish as the natural and most effective apostolic community within the life of the Church. Whatever be its size, the parish is seen as a communion of Christian communities made up of all the faithful, whether lapsed or practising their faith, and coming together for prayer, liturgy and the eucharist, the study of the scriptures, for works of charity and mercy, or for social celebrations. Small communities of this kind are a source of strength to the parish as a whole, and must not be exclusive in themselves nor seen as an alternative to parish commitment. Much depends upon the priest in the parish as to how fully these small groups are in fact integrated into the parish community.

(s.120 in Anon., 1981: 358)

Apart from this statement of intent on the relationship between new and emergent groupings or movements within the Church and the parishes, which are more directly amenable to social control by the bishops and parish clergy as their collaborators, the bishops also advocated a 'sharing' model of the Church, encouraging the setting up of parish liturgy groups, the fostering of the spiritual life of married couples and families in parish worship, and the awareness that 'Britain has become irreversibly a multiracial, multicultural society . . . in our parishes and in every aspect of our life and mission' (*The Easter People*, ss.62, 65, 108, 175 in Anon., 1981: 334–35, 353, 381). The bishops admit that 'a thorough review of our structures and organizations in the parishes, deaneries and dioceses will have to be made' (s.32 in Anon., 1981: 320–1) if new types of collaborative relationships in the Church are to be encouraged. In order to provide a spiritual service to his people, the priest

> must be a man of prayer, conscious of the need to prepare and cele-brate the Mass worthily, with reverence, devotion and joy, to administer all the sacraments in a way which draws the most grace-filled response from their recipients. He must devote much of his energy to the regular preaching of the Word of God on which his people are so dependent for spiritual nourishment and inspiration. To this end he must continually renew himself by the study of scripture and theology, whilst at the same time trying to keep in touch with the real needs of his people. He must teach by example as well as by word. . . . The priest's communion with the Lord makes him a healer, a bridge-builder, a reconciler. He must call, form and sustain the laity in their own demanding vocation and help them in their efforts to shed the light of the gospel on their own secular world.
>
> (s.93 in Anon., 1981: 347).

Later, while considering questions of adult formation and education, the bishops reflect the tenor of the advice given by Bishop Konstant's working party which produced *Signposts and Homecomings* (1981) and state that

11

There can be no priority more urgent, no effort more worthwhile, than the slow, patient work of forming lay people for their unique and irreplaceable task . . . nothing should deflect bishops or priests from the task of calling, forming and sustaining Christians who are deeply committed to Christ and who will express this commitment in the whole of of their lives . . . our main emphasis must be on formation of adults for mission.

(s.147 in Anon., 1981: 369)

It remains to evaluate the extent to which this rhetoric, which strongly reflects the theology of the laity articulated by Pat Keegan, former president of the Young Christian Workers (Jocists) and the first layperson to address the bishops at the Second Vatican Council, is realised in the everyday routines of parish life.

The bishops note that 'Catholic lay people are beginning to take it for granted that they are consulted on matters of pastoral importance' (s.147 in Anon., 1981: 369) and that 'If we are to develop the parish as a community, there must be some way in which parishioners can respond to their priests in a genuine dialogue' in which there is a mutual exchange of knowledge, experience and attitudes, listening and response (s.151 in Anon., 1981: 370–1).

Finally, the bishops attempt to reassure the priests that the call to co-responsibility and participation does not weaken their own proper ministry of service:

You must still be the priest set apart to preside at the Eucharist, to offer the Sacrifice, to preach the word of God, to lead and form the people for prayer, witness and service. The more active the laity, the more they are formed to understand and undertake their proper role, the more they will turn to you for your spiritual leadership, for your support, and for your sacramental priesthood.

(s.182 in Anon., 1981: 385)

One of the themes which emerged from the month-long deliberations of the Synod in Rome to consider 'the vocation and mission of the laity in the Church and in the world' in October 1987 was a recognition of the place of the parish in the on-going formation of lay people (CMO, Synod Special 2). Yet the parish had not loomed large in the consultations *Called to Serve*, which were estimated to have involved around one in twenty of the practising Catholic population in England and Wales (CMO, 1986: 10), and which the bishops had initiated in advance of the Synod. Indeed, it was even reported that 'Generally people said it was faith rather than being part of a parish community that helped them in their daily lives . . . (and) faith rather than parish membership that is important for their service of others' (1986: 17, 21). The fact that most people also thought there were no ethnic minorities in their parishes or, if there were, that they were well-integrated (1986: 18), tends to conflict with evidence from black Catholics and suggest that for many Catholics the parish is simply 'there' but not a very salient institution in their lives. The development of closer and more friendly clergy-lay relationships were acknowledged as were the potential advantages of giving expression to this closer collaboration, for example through parish councils. Expectations of priests were high:

> Often in contradiction to the 'essentially spiritual role', the priest was asked to be a leader and facilitator. He should be the 'talent-spotter' who draws out people's gifts. He should work closely with people, make decisions with them and avoid any suspicion of dictatorship [feeling ran quite high on this]. He should visit them in their homes and above all he should be compassionate and caring.
>
> (CMO, 1986: 24–5)

The young English lay observer, Pat Jones, in her address to the Synod, urged that

> We need a clearer vision of our parishes as places where people are drawn into 'communio' in the life of God and with each other. . . . Within the parish the basic means of formation must be the small group, and the insights and experiences of the apostolic movements are a rich resource to be used and extended. Small groups and movements both need the ecclesial focus which the parish provides. . . . It seems that we have as yet failed to help laypeople to understand that baptism and faith involve not only personal and parish lives but also social and political choices. We urgently need formation which enables people to realise that our choices and decisions shape our society. . . . We therefore must learn how to make choices and shape politics according to the gospel.
>
> (Synod Special 1, 1987b: 330)

The renewal of parish life was one of the key themes of the first stage of the Synod selected by Cardinal Thiandoum for special consideration by the various language groups. Participants were invited to consider 'its effectiveness as a centre of community, as a source of spirituality, as a springboard for mission and as a sign, at local level, of the redemptive love of Christ offered in and through the Church'. The relationship between emergent lay movements and the local parishes was seen by many to be a source of tension with bishops concerned at the possible by-passing of their jurisdiction in their own dioceses (Synod Special 3, 1987d: 351–2).

Among the interventions, mention might be made of the observation of the Scottish Bishop Devine that there was a 'need to create the experience of communio' rather than simply asserting its importance in the life of the Church (Synod Special 2, 1987c: 340). Archbishop Worlock raised the question of whether a concentration on the renewal of Church worship and structures had resulted in a weakening concern with the renewal of the secular order (Synod Special 1, 1987b: 332) and American bishops, in particular, were forthright in their insistence that the vestiges of sexism in the Church be guarded against in both Church teaching and action (Synod Special 2, 1987c: 332). In the *Message of the Synod to the People of God* the teaching of the Second Vatican Council that the dignity of lay people derives from their baptism is reaffirmed. Among the themes addressed, the following on the parish deserves to be quoted in full:

> The parish in the diocese continues to be the customary place where the faithful gather to grow in holiness, to participate in the mission of the Church and to live out their ecclesial communion.
>
> We note with great satisfaction that the parish is becoming a dynamic community of communities, a centre where movements, basic ecclesial communities and other apostolic groups energize it and are nourished in their turn.
>
> In the eucharistic celebration, the centre of all Christian life, the faithful are especially united with Christ and are sent out in the service of the world.
>
> We exhort all the lay faithful to enter intensely into the life of their parishes by the study of the Word of God, the celebration of the Lord's Day, service on parish councils, and participation in the various forms and activities of the apostolate.
>
> (Synod Special 5, 1987e: 375)

While for Cardinal Hume the Synod left a sense of hope, for the Canadian Archbishop Chiasson it offered 'nothing of significance' but rather evidence of a fear of real dialogue (*The Tablet*, 7 November 1987). An Apostolic Exhortation from Pope John-Paul II is not expected for some time.[1] In the meantime the various debates at the Synod have identified a number of areas where it might be possible to test the reality of parish life against the aspirations of lay people and the social control concerns of the religious leadership in the Church.

Before completing this review, a brief reference might be made to the consultative document *Ministry and Mission* prepared by the Committee for Ministerial Formation of the Bishops' Conference of England and Wales (CMO, 1987a). This reviewed policy for lifelong priestly formation at the national level in the light of the contemporary social and historical context of the Church, the needs of the Church and of society, and the consequent educational requirements for priestly formation. It stresses the community roots for this and provides useful guidelines as a basis for discussion. However, in spite of the fact that this is a consultative document, at least three issues are simply excluded from the deliberations: the necessity for celibacy as an integral part of the ministerial priesthood, the possibility or desirability of women exercising this ministry, and the necessity of aspiring priests being trained in seminary-type institutions. Something is being said here about the boundaries of permitted discussion in the consultative process. At this moment in time, priests must be male celibates trained in seminaries. Lay peple can lobby for better selection procedures and more adequate provision for the life-long formation of the parochial clergy, but their share of decision-making in such matters remains strictly limited and subject to social control processes which are firmly in the hands of senior male celibate clerics.

OUTLINE OF BOOK

In order to explore the changes which have taken place in the Catholic parish since the end of the Second World War, it is useful to employ the notion of ideal-types. In Weber's classic formulation the ideal-type

> *is* no 'hypothesis' but . . . offers guidance to the construction of hypotheses. It is not a *description* of reality but it aims to give unambiguous means of expression to such a description. . . . An ideal type is formed by the one-sided *accentuation* of one or more points of view and by the synthesis of a great many diffuse, discrete, more or

15

less present and occasionally absent *concrete individual* phenomena, which are arranged according to those one-sidedly emphasised viewpoints into a unified *analytical* construct. In its conceptual purity, this mental construct cannot be found empirically anywhere in reality . . .

(Weber, 1949: 90; emphases in original)

Weber goes on to argue that in theory construction

there is only one criterion, namely, that of success in revealing concrete cultural phenomena in their interdependence, their causal conditions and their *significance*. The construction of abstract ideal types recommends itself not as an end in itself but as a *means*.

(Weber, 1949: 92; emphases in original)

In order to understand and explain the changes which have occurred in Roman Catholic parishes over the past four decades or so, it is helpful to start from ideal-type constructs of the Church in terms of its major organisational features, goals, legitimating ideology, patterns of interaction and authority relations, and relationships with other religious collectivities and orientation to the everyday secular world for both the pre- and post-conciliar periods. These have drawn on Avery Dulles' models of the Church (1976), Burns and Stalker's analysis of management structures appropriate for static and changing circumstances (1961), Winter's analysis of goal-displacement from mission to maintenance (1973), Neal's analysis of shifts of theological orientation (1970), among others, and have previously been summarised elsewhere (Hornsby-Smith and Lee, 1979: 27–30; Hornsby-Smith, 1987: 31–6).

For our present purposes the salient features of the pre- and post-Vatican Churches have been given in Figure 1.1. It is suggested that these ideal-types, in the Weberian sense, may be used to explore the changes which have taken place over the past four decades in Catholic parishes in the light of both social change generally in the post-war world and the shifting theological orientations and legitimating ideologies which emerged from the Second Vatican Council (1962–65). In outline it is suggested that the Roman Catholic Church has changed significantly in recent decades from a mechanistic, bureaucratic and hierarchically structured organisation with an emphasis on vertical, downwards decision-making to an organic, network structure drawing on the complementary contributions of all its

16

Figure 1.1 Models of pre-Vatican and post-Vatican churches

Characteristic	Pre-Vatican	Post-Vatican
Organisational features:		
management structure	mechanistic	organic
authority: location	hierarchical	'People of God'
authority: style	authoritarian	pastoral
authority: metaphors	military	servant
concern/goal	maintenance	mission
rhetoric	fortress	pilgrim
Legitimating ideology:		
relationship to change	static/unchanging	dynamic/changing
belief system: characs.	unitary	pluralistic
belief system: emphasis	uniformity	unity in diversity
External relationships:		
with other religions	anti-ecumenical	ecumenical
with secular world	differentiated/segregated	integrated/leaven

members. Less concerned with a defensive antagonism to outsiders, a rigid stress on obedience and the enforcement of a religious conformity, and a claim to unchanging beliefs and timeless structures, it has become more open to internal pluralism, ecumenical relationships and service in the wider society. It must be stressed that this does not claim to be a description of reality, but simply a point of comparison for the understanding of the existing, concrete realities and a helpful device for the interpretation of those changes which can be identified.

In previous work (Hornsby-Smith and Lee, 1979; Hornsby-Smith, 1987) evidence has been reviewed which suggests that in many respects the empirical realities of the Roman Catholic Church in England and Wales, at least in terms of its organisational features at the aggregate level and its official rhetoric, have corresponded reasonably closely with the shift in the dominant model of a pre-Vatican to a post-Vatican Church according to the characteristics summarised in Figure 1.1. Such a shift is also evident in other societies, even if there is an on-going struggle for power between the local or national Churches and the centralised bureaucracy in Rome (e.g. Coleman, 1978; Greeley, 1977; Boff, 1985). However, it is by no means certain that the everyday (or everyweek) experiences of most Catholics have indicated a corresponding shift at the parish level. Later in this book, ideal-type models of pre- and post-Vatican parishes, priests and parishioners will be offered in the attempt to test the hypothesis that the shift in the dominant official models of the Church have been reflected at the parish level.

The focus of this book will be on the parish as a key institution in the Roman Catholic Church. In Chapter 2 aspects of continuity and change in the Catholic parish since the Second Vatican Council will be reviewed. In many respects the contemporary parish has lost some of the functions, for example many entertainment functions, of its predecessor in the pre-war years. The impact of extra-parochial institutions, for example the secondary schools, was first noted by Joan Brothers (1964) in the early 1960s, and the impact of high rates of both social and geographical mobility are facts of life which inhibit attempts to create *gemeinschaft*-like characteristics at the parish level. Previous work (Hornsby-Smith, 1987) has suggested that the defensive fortress-like walls which previously defended the Catholic community from contamination by influences outside the subculture have been dissolved away in the solvent of both social and religious change over the past few decades. This has had profound effects on parish life in the 1980s.

While the main focus of this book will be the changing parish in England and Wales, it is helpful to consider changes in other countries. Thus in Chapter 3 a brief review of recent changes in the United States, Australia, continental Europe, and the Philippines is given in order to point to both similarities and variations between societies. Similar responses to the post-war processes of embourgeoisement and suburbanisation are to be found in Britain, the United States, and Australia. These countries, however, do not experience the anti-clericalism of continental countries such as France where the worker-priest movement and pioneering attempts to open-up post-war parishes to the working-class reflect attempts to cope with particular local pastoral problems. The case of the Philippines draws attention to the new strategies of *conscientisation* through the basic Christian community movement which in the future might well have great relevance in First World countries.

In Chapter 4 the question of the extent to which the contemporary parish can be said to manifest 'community-like' characteristics will be addressed. Some of the realities of everyday parish life will be reviewed here: liturgical variations, parish social and pastoral activities, ecumenical collaboration, the management of the controversial issues of justice and peace, the realities of caring mechanisms and mutual-aid giving, the vitality or ageing of traditional parish-based

18

organisations, and so on. In this chapter the quest for community and the extent to which the rhetoric is translated into religious praxis will be evaluated in terms of the three key variables of shared values, frequency of interaction, and mutual aid. The extent to which the parish can be regarded as a 'greedy' institution, consuming all the discretionary time and energies of committed parishioners, will also be addressed in this chapter. In the following chapter the way in which rival interpretations of the Church, the parish, and the roles of priest and parishioner are expressed in the parish liturgies will be explored.

In Chapter 6 the focus shifts to the parish clergy as key figures in the everyday life of the contemporary parish. An account will be offered of the priest as the key religious leader, for better or worse, in the parish. An important question is to identify the changing nature of this leadership role and the implications for his changing relationships with lay people. In the following chapter an attempt will be made to review the everyday work lives of priests in parishes from their own perspectives. Among the elements making for a frequently-expressed sense of marginality are the fragmentation of their lives and the new and additional demands on their time and energy arising from attempts to make manifest the new theological emphases on the participation of lay people in the life of the Church at every level.

The changing role of the laity as the 'lower participants' in the organisational activities of the parish will be the focus of Chapter 8. Following Etzioni's analysis of organisational compliance (1961), it will be argued that there is considerable divergence from the congruent types of compliance because parishioners have access to numerous strategies of coping with a variety of types of clerical power. The potential for conflict tends to remain suppressed and latent since those with low levels of commitment tend to withdraw from institutional concerns while committed lay people engage in processes of bargaining and negotiation about contested areas of pastoral policy at the parish level.

The final chapter attempts to bring together these various themes and see the parish as a focus of conflict, now latent now manifest, between those participants, priests and parishioners, with conflicting views as to the salience of the parish and of their rival underpinning models of the Church, parish, priest, and lay people. For those for whom it is a key institution, the parish may be a cauldron for the working out of conflicts over rival models of the Church, the nature of salvation, the priority to be attached to mission, and so on. The conflict between this-worldly and other-worldly interpretations of religion are often among the most bitter and are manifested in the struggles over issues of justice and peace. For some the parish is simply a provider of alternative sources of status, power, and other forms of gratification to those found in the wider community and there need not necessarily be any 'religious' content to their involvement. For others, commitments may be so great that it endangers domestic and other relationships with its exclusivity and greed.

Finally, the relationship of these various findings to the major debates about secularisation will be briefly considered. While some have adjusted to social change by withdrawing from institutional religion and some have reacted against the established Churches by joining the wide variety of new religious movements, it remains a significant social fact that millions of people have remained within the established Churches and struggled to change them so that they better conform to their changing vision of the nature of the Church and of its mission, of salvation and religious leadership, and of their own part in the communal activities of its members. The evidence suggests that the Catholic parish continues to be a vital institution at the end of the twentieth century.

DATA SOURCES

There has not yet been a national survey of Catholic parishes in Britain to parallel the Notre Dame study of American parishes (Leege *et al.*, 1984–88). Nor has there yet been a national study of priests comparable to that of Greeley and his colleagues in the United States (Greeley, 1972). Not only is the American Church ten times as large as the Church in Britain but the climate of opinion there is much more tolerant of and occasionally supportive of the contribution which social research can make to pastoral planning. In Britain there is a tendency for bishops to assume that they know all that there is to know about their priests and their parishes, and in a similar way priests tend to assume that they know all there is to know about their own people. The closure of the Newman Demographic Survey in the 1960s was a tragic set-back for the development of professional pastoral strategies. The fact that priests' estimates of the Catholic population are notoriously low, perhaps by one-quarter to one-half of poll or demographic estimates, is one indicator of the inadequacy of this view.

The result of the lack of official concern to investigate changes in the parishes or the changing nature of the role of the parish clergy, or why so many priests have become laicised, or how parishioners have adapted to the changes imposed on them since the Second Vatican Council and what meanings these changes might have for them, means that the empirical data base for the understanding of these processes is somewhat limited. As has been indicated previously, ideal-types of parish, parish priest, and parishioner for the pre-Vatican and post-Vatican periods will first be constructed. Then in each case comparisons will be made with two English parishes, the traditional parish in the north midlands recently studied by John Leslie (1986) and a parish in the south-east which was described by its former parish priest (O'Sullivan, 1979). A participant-observation study has also been carried out in this parish over the past decade. Apart from this main comparison, there is a limited number of academic studies which we will draw on. Other sources have been reviewed in previous work (Hornsby-Smith and Lee, 1979; Hornsby-Smith, 1987: 9–13). Frequent reference will also be made to the early reports emerging from the Notre Dame Study of Catholic Parish Life in the United States under the direction of David Leege (1984–88).

Note

1 The Post-Synodal Apostolic Exhortation of Pope John-Paul II *The Vocation and the Mission of the Lay Faithful (Christifideles Laici)* was published on 30 December 1988 after the completion of this book (London: Catholic Truth Society, Do 589).

Chapter Two

THE CHANGING SOCIAL AND RELIGIOUS CONTEXT

POST-WAR TRANSFORMATIONS

In order to understand the changes which have taken place in the English Catholic parish in the post-war years, it is necessary to review the major social changes which have taken place in British society since the end of the Second World War and also the religious changes whose legitimation can be traced to the teachings of the Second Vatican Council of 1962–65 (Hornsby-Smith, 1987). It is necessary to note at this point that remarkably little is known about the everyday lives of English Catholics in the period immediately before the transformations which are our chief concern. This was admitted by Bishop (later Archbishop) Beck in his editorial preface to the official volume which marked the centenary of the restoration of the hierarchy in England and Wales in 1850, three centuries after the Protestant Reformation. Beck admitted that:

> While accounts of notable personalities are not wanting, very little exact information is available concerning the details of Catholic history, diocesan and parochial, and of the growth and movement of the Catholic community.
>
> (Beck, 1950: vii)

In these circumstances the best we can do is to construct a picture of Catholic parish life from those fragments which have recently been published, and resort to model-building on the basis of the best available evidence in order to provide a point of comparison for analytical purposes.

With some simplification it can be argued that up to the Second World War Roman Catholicism in England could be characterised as being overwhelmingly working class and huddled together in inner-city parishes to provide mutual support in a relatively suspicious and not infrequently hostile environment. The majority of Catholics traced their allegiance from their Irish origins or ancestry so that both ethnic and religious antagonisms were compounded. As a result Catholics were often marginal people and their parishes were all-embracing social enclaves which provided them with fortress-like defences against the real or perceived attacks of a hostile, secular society.

Evidence for this interpretation comes from a variety of sources, particularly from recent historical studies of Irish settlements (Jackson, 1963: 135–51). Thus Lynn Lees describes 'the reforging of an Irish Catholic culture' in the inner-city areas of London in the middle of the nineteenth century:

A Catholic workers' culture was slowly built by migrants and priests amid the London slums. The locus of this culture was the Catholic parish, which issued an unceasing call to the faithful to reaffirm their religious and national heritage by returning to the arms of Mother Church. It drew the worshipper into a fervently nationalistic piety that bridged the gap between the secular and the sacred, the political and the spiritual, and it provided an alternative to assimilation into the English working class. Through the work of the priests, thousands of Catholics were reintegrated into local communities where raggedness and dirt did not mark them as pariahs and where Catholicism was a sign of grace rather than of superstition and error. The Roman Catholic Church functioned therefore as a major agent of social and cultural change among the migrant Irish and helped them to convert their vestiges of traditional culture into an urbanised, nationalist variant compatible with Church orthodoxy . . . whatever the initial impact of migration, the Church cushioned the shock of change for many by providing a measure of institutional and cultural continuity. . . . The parish church provided a lively social and cultural world organised to give Catholics a religious alternative to the staple forms of urban working-class recreation. Catholic London sup-ported a colourful variety of social clubs, lectures, benefit dinners, and bazaars. A form of popular recreation different from those of both the Irish countryside and English workers grew up within the Roman Catholic urban parish. In place of pubs, penny gaffs, and trade union meetings, Catholics were expected to join in the confraternities, clubs, and temperance groups of the local church. Priests organised festivals, musical evenings, church suppers, and steamboat excursions for the entertainment of the faithful, while those who wanted more active pastimes could join one of the Catholic choral societies, bands, or drill teams.

(Lees, 1979: 164–5, 190–1)

In general terms the social functions of the Catholic parish described here continued to remain much the same for the largely Irish, working-class migrants in the inner-city parishes in England up to the 1950s and 1960s. Thus Robert Roberts in his account of life in a Salford slum in the first quarter of this century noted that:

With us, of course, as with many cities in the North, until the coming of the coloured people Irish Roman Catholic immigrants, mostly illiterate, formed the lowest socio-economic stratum. A slum Protestant marrying into the milieu suffered a severe loss of face.

(1973: 22–3)

With such antagonism it is not surprising that it was not until the 1960s that 'the transition from isolation to assimilation' of the predominantly Irish Catholics of Cardiff was well under way (Hickey, 1967: 167). A similar conclusion is drawn from the study of Scottish Catholicism in the century since the restoration of the Scottish hierarchy in 1878. The impression persists that Catholics in Scotland are recent immigrants:

in spite of the fact that large-scale immigration from Ireland began to lessen perceptibly in the later nineteenth-century and that most Catholics in Scotland today are several and in some cases many generations established in Scotland. . . . The majority of Catholics have, until relatively recently, been members of a tightly-knit, inward-looking, closely co-ordinated parochial structure. This has enabled them to maintain locally a self-conscious identity of a community within a community, somewhat remote from the rest of society, sharing in it, to some extent, in necessary things but always in the last analysis self-substantiating and providing a permanent spiritual home to turn to when all else fails. In addition there is a social, secular dimension born of history. The memories of the group's own past struggles and, in industrial Scotland, its separate schools have perpetuated a tribal attitude. This has persisted even when the reasons for it have long lost their validity for its members whose main secular preoccupations are those they share, like their accents, with their fellow Scots — viz., jobs, prospects and living conditions.

(McCaffrey, 1979: 140–1)

A valuable review of Catholic parish life and clergy-lay relations in London parishes in the period from 1880 to the First World War, based largely on the surveys of Charles Booth has been given by Hugh McLeod (1974: 72–80). Elsewhere he has described how

The priests were the lynch-pins of the system. The strength of the working-class Catholic parish from about the 1840s until the 1960s depended on clerical initiative, and the willingness of Irish immigrants and their descendants to respond to these initiatives. Its double vulnerability lay, on the one hand, in the fact that these priests were insufficient in numbers and often unequal to their task, and, on the other, in the strong undercurrent of resentment that was provoked by the authoritarianism intrinsic to the priest's role. It was the priests who wielded the force of community pressure against those who wanted to marry Protestants, who accepted Protestant charity or sent their children to Protestant schools; the priest who denounced sinners from the pulpit, who squeezed from his impoverished parishioners the funds needed to build their church and school, support their priests, teachers, and parochial charities, who induced them to sign petitions and told them how to vote; who harried the Mass-missers.

Between priest and people there was . . . 'a semi-paternal relationship compounded of love and fear' (Gilley, 1971: 375–6). This priestly discipline was effective because of the widespread support enjoyed by the clergy within the Irish community, enhanced both by their devotion to their people, and by the superstitious regard that led so many negligent Catholics to send for the priest in illness. . . . The tie was further strengthened in the second half of the nineteenth century by an Ultramontane piety . . . attractive to many poor immigrants . . .

The system worked fairly well as long as priestly despotism was both practicable and acceptable. It fell into decline in the 1920s as rehousing schemes broke up the old Irish ghettos, and more especially in the 1960s and 1970s. By then the decline of clerical recruitment made the old system increasingly unpracticable and Vatican II called in question most of the assumptions that had dominated the British Catholicism of the last century and a half.

(McLeod, 1981: 130)

There is much evidence to suggest that similar functions were performed by and similar clergy-lay relations obtained in the case of various immigrant groups in Catholic parishes in both the United States (for example for Irish, Polish, and Italian immigrants in the nineteenth century; see Dolan, 1985: 158–240; Tomasi, 1975; and Greeley, 1977: 213–31) and Australia (where, however, Lewins (1978) has been critical of the ability of existing parishes to absorb successive waves of new immigrants in the post-war period).

Within the fortress the security of the vulnerable and weak religio-ethnic community was ensured and the integrity of its distinctive sub-culture (Coman, 1977: 4–5) maintained by means of an enforced community discipline which required at least weekly Mass attendance, regular participation in the varied and formidable range of parish devotions, a comprehensive programme of religious socialisation in the parish school, and an almost 'total institutional' (Goffman, 1968: 13–115) environment for recreational purposes, relaxation and social interaction with other Catholics, especially those of the opposite sex and same age group. There were strong community expectations in favour of marital endogamy. This was usually interpreted in the wide sense of marriage to a fellow Catholic, but occasionally, for example in the very tight communities in Liverpool and the relatively Catholic north-west and Lancashire, a very narrow sense of a partner from the same, often geographically small, parish. The strong disapproval of and sanctions against marital exogamy were reflected, for example, in the curtailment of any celebratory aspects in the marriage ceremony according to the requirements of the Canon Law of the time. In a review of recent work on oral histories of working-class people born in the late nineteenth century and early twentieth century, Hugh McLeod has observed that

Such weddings were in fact fairly frequent, but the couple generally met with intense opposition from one or both sides. Many Catholics saw 'mixed marriages' as treachery; and Protestants . . . often regarded marriage with a Catholic as degrading. The interviews conducted in Lancashire . . . contain many references to people shunned by relatives for a few years or permanently because they married someone of the wrong religion, to disputes over the baptism of the resulting children, or to harassment of Catholics who 'turned' by clergy and nuns.

(1986: 43; see also footnote 76, p. 49)

Writing of the period immediately before the Second World War, the biographer of Cardinal Hinsley has given a flavour of Catholic parish life when the larger parish communities were able

to indulge in a triumphalist efflorescence of faith which compacted their own solidarity while still proclaiming separation from the world outside. Week by week they continued throughout the liturgical year, the indoor and outdoor processions, rhythmically swaying their way by aisle and nave, through terraced street and suburban avenue, safely girt about by the episcopal *cordon sanitaire* of Catholic Action and the confident certainty of doctrinal belief. The serried ranks of the faithful in the sashes and regalia of their individual parish organisations thundered forth the four-square Victorian hymnody,

> Faith of our Fathers, Holy Faith
> In spite of dungeon, fire and sword . . .

. . . All life was there: colour, sound, ritual, liturgy, devotion, worship, community, not excluding ostentation, management and authoritarianism for those so minded. Never had the English and Welsh Catholic body seemed so secure, so united, so insulated . . .

(Moloney, 1985: 242)

Anthony Archer, in his pioneering attempt to convey something of the flavour of working-class Catholicism in a Dominican parish in Newcastle-upon-Tyne over the course of the last century, describes it as a 'restoration' model, to the supposed glories of mediaeval Catholicism and suffused with an ultramontanism which legitimated the centralisation of clerical authority at every level. This strategy 'incorporated the rococo Italian devotions, elaborate vestments and rather camp clothing of higher ecclesiastics which would become a familiar part of the English Catholic Church.' From the second half of the nineteenth century 'the Roman collar, "father" as a form of address, May devotions, the asperges with holy water before Mass, special mission services and emotional preaching, processions with bands and banners, the forty hours' exposition of the sacrament and the stations of the cross' were introduced and became a familiar characteristic of English Catholicism, lasting until after the Second Vatican Council (Archer, 1986: 24). As one of Archer's respondents put it: 'Religion wasn't carried into one's life. Religion consisted of going *into* church.' For the immigrant Irish communities 'for whom the Catholic Church was an effective symbol and which wanted to preserve their separate identity' (ibid.: 87), the territorial parish was appropriate enough. Rex and Moore, in their study of Sparkbrook in the 1960s, go further and stress the Catholic parish's role in promoting assimilation (1967: 150–5; 174–6). For Archer, while the aim behind the parish system had been to lay the foundations for a restoration model, transmuted in practice into an attempt to create a Catholic ghetto,

> in general, Catholics declined this proposal. They were not interested in a Catholic ghetto. For them the Church was a symbol of their own community, which was not in the first place a church community, though the Church also provided access to the sacred as a necessary and important part of this symbolic function.
>
> (1986: 103)

Nevertheless the continued isolation of Catholics from the social and religious life of the rest of the community up to the 1950s is apparent in Margaret Stacey's study of tradition and change in Banbury (1960: 62–3).

It is often suggested that Catholicism in Liverpool has a distinctive flavour and certainly the level of parish visiting recorded by Conor Ward in St Catherine's parish in the late 1950s, 'about once every six weeks' (Ward, 1965: 47), seems to be unique. All the same, in his conclusions, Ward suggests that while there was evidence of a very considerable commitment to the ideal of parochial loyalty, in practice it appeared

> to have a rather limited impact on the patterns of interaction and behaviour of most of them. . . . Loyalty . . . was . . . directed upwards towards the institution itself and not so much in a horizontal direction towards the individuals of whom the parish was composed. . . . In the sphere of specialised needs and services . . . the parish of St Catherine appeared to be a somewhat restricted unit within which to attempt to meet the needs and multiple problems of a modern urban civilisation.
>
> (1965: 115, 117)

In a related study in Liverpool, Joan Brothers has described 'the parish's laboured adaptation to change' (1964: 9). In particular she was concerned to explore the impact of the post-war expansion of secondary school opportunities and the resulting new patterns of social mobility and 'the gradual disappearance of the social homogeneity of Roman Catholicism in Liverpool' on the parochial loyalties of young people who had attended extraparochial grammar schools. She shows these local parish loyalties have no meaning for them and they resent the authoritarian demands of priests. She argues that there is a need for new and less deferential forms of relationships between priests and people. Apart from this, new social divisions are emerging between former classmates and even with families. Thus she concludes that 'Religious affiliation does not seem to be a strong enough link in social situations to overcome these divisions' (1964: 158–63).

In a pessimistic account of the social and religious changes in the Catholic Church in England, Anthony Archer has bemoaned 'the passing of the simple faithful'. Whereas the Church up to the 1950s had been an important source of identity as a distinctive subculture, the post-Vatican Church has increasingly become a vehicle for the achievement of the aspirations of articulate middle-class enthusiasts who are in open competition with older forms of clerical domination. But the liturgical changes so enthusiastically welcomed by middle-class reformers in fact articulated new forms of elitism, 'cut off many of the ritual streams that had previously nourished Catholics and covered over many of the accumulated pools in which popular Catholicism had found its strength'. While 'the new Mass proved only too vulnerable to congregational as well as clerical sabotage', it was basically classist in origin: 'its very language was that of a particular class', familiar in the courtroom and the classroom. In this sense Archer interprets the changes as new forms of class oppression and it is hardly surprising that with the dissolution of a distinctive Catholic identity, 'working-class indifference coincided . . . with the relinquishment of an Irish identity, and their subsequent failure to find anything of particular interest to them in the Catholic Church' (Archer, 1986: 141–5, 234–6). Archer's claim that 'parish and parishioners failed to provide the communitarian base envisaged by the new Mass' (1986: 142) will be explored further in Chapters 4 and 5.

PRE-VATICAN AND POST-VATICAN MODELS
OF THE PARISH

In the previous chapter it was suggested that at the Second Vatican Council a fundamentally new model of the Church was proposed. In the period following the First Vatican Council in 1870 there was a significant centralisation of organisational power in Rome, a strong emphasis on hierarchy and the decision-making authority of the Pope, and the espousal of a missionary strategy which aimed to separate or control the contacts of Catholics with other Christians (Coleman, 1978: 12). This strategy was underpinned by an ideology which stressed the static, unchanging verities of the Church which was regarded as providing a secure haven for those prepared to submit themselves to her jurisdiction. The paradigmatic change legitimated by Vatican II emphasised, rather, the 'People of God' concept and the dynamic and changing character of a pilgrim, searching Church, responding to the call to serve the needs of all people. With this new model, religious authority was to be more widely diffused among the members, the gifts of all were to be developed for the benefit of all and religious leadership was to be facilitative and enabling rather than coercive.

Figure 2.1 points to some of the implications of the two models of the Church for the parishes. With the pre-Vatican model, parishioners were typically members of an identifiable religio-ethnic (often Irish, Polish, or Italian migrant) community with a distinctive subculture in terms of ethical and behavioural norms, social and moral values, and religious beliefs. Following Etzioni's comparative analysis of organisations (1961), it could be suggested that the type of power wielded by the priest was typically coercive and decision-making 'top-down' from the pope and bishop through the priest to the lay person whose involvement in the parish was therefore likely to be alienative or calculative in terms of both immediate this-worldly concerns and costs and long-term other-worldly salvation. The interlinking institutions of home, school and parish provided an all-embracing religious socialisation and delivered a passive laity, submissive and deferential towards the 'sacred' priesthood. Lay people, therefore, could on occasion be readily mobilised in defence of what the clerical leadership regarded as vital community interests. In all matters at the parish level, however, the priest was the chief initiator, co-ordinator and decision-maker; the laity were never more than his helpmates.

30

Figure 2.1 Models of pre-Vatican and post-Vatican parishes

Characteristic	Pre-Vatican	Post-Vatican
Membership:		
defining characs.	religio-ethnic community	voluntary religious collectivity
characs. of culture	distinct subcult.	'dissolved' subculture
Organisational features:		
nature of relig. power	coercive	normative
religious authority	hierarchical	congregational
role of laity	passive helpmate	active participant
lay involvement	alienative/calculative	moral
relation to priest	submissive/deferential	collaborative
Liturgical worship:		
main characteristic	awe, reverence	participation
relation to God	mediated distance	close and direct
variability	uniform	pluriform
language	latin, separation	vernacular
emphasis	ritual	spontaneity
Exemplars:		
	Ward (1965); Rex and Moore (1967); Archer (1986)	Michonneau (1949); O'Sullivan (1979)

In the post-Vatican parish, however, membership is defined not so much in terms of the ascribed characteristics of those belonging to a religio-ethnic community but rather reflects voluntary affiliation to a religious collectivity. The distinctive religio-ethnic subculture had largely been dissolved in the solvent of post-war social change and as a result of the religious reforms emanating from the Second Vatican Council. In terms of Etzioni's comparative analysis there was a shift to normative power and hence moral involvement on the part of parishioners who were active collaborators with the priest. Religious authority was not necessarily exclusive to the priest and was legitimated by the congregation rather than unthinkingly attributed to the priest in virtue of his official position in the ecclesiastical hierarchy. Liturgical worship was pluriform, stressed the active participation of lay people using their own language, and their spontaneous, direct and close relationship to God.

It must be stressed again that these two models are not descriptions of empirical reality but ideal-types in the Weberian sense, offering points of comparison and contributing to the search for understanding of social change. The extent to which there has been a shift from a pre-Vatican to a post-Vatican model of the parish in recent decades as a result of both social and religious change is the empirical issue which this book aims to address.

POST-WAR SOCIAL CHANGES

The Second World War provides a useful starting point for the consideration of social changes in recent decades. After the ravages of the war and as a consequence of liberal and reformed international aid and trade policies, Britain, along with other western industrial nations, experienced a long period of continuous economic growth and a rising standard of living for over a quarter of a century until the major economic transformations occasioned by the oil crisis and attendant world recession in the mid-1970s. What evidence there is (Hornsby-Smith and Lee, 1979; Hornsby-Smith, 1987) suggests that English Catholics benefited from this economic advancement at least as much as the rest of the population.

Apart from their participation in the general post-war affluence and the 'revolution of rising expectations', Catholics also benefited from the 1944 Education Act which guaranteed 'secondary education for all'. In England and Wales the 'dual' system, with substantial state support for the relatively autonomous Catholic schools system, ensured its rapid expansion until the mid-1970s when the decline of the birth rate from the mid-1960s necessitated some contraction (Hornsby-Smith, 1978). Following the publication of the Robbins Report on Higher Education in 1963, there was a massive expansion of opportunities in further and higher education. Survey data have indicated that Catholics took good advantage of these opportunities. Thus the 1978 national survey of Catholics in England and Wales showed that a higher proportion of the Catholic population had left full-time education at the age of 19 and over than among the population generally (Hornsby-Smith and Lee, 1979: 171). Similar experiences of enhanced educational opportunities for Catholics has also been reported in the United States (Greeley, 1977: 69–89).

These new educational experiences had two consequences in particular. First of all they contributed to rates of upward social or occupational mobility which, in the case of Catholic men born in Great Britain, were higher than those of men generally (Hornsby-Smith, 1987: 72–7). At the same time there was evidence of geographical mobility resulting from both new patterns of Irish immigration in the affluent 1950s and 1960s, and from the general processes of urban reconstruction following the Second World War. Thus what had been a predominantly working-class community, located in particular in the north-west region, which had previously been the main point of access and settlement for Irish immigrants, and in inner-city areas in general, was now growing its own 'new middle class', upwardly mobile into the expanding professional and managerial (or 'service') classes, and geographically mobile, both diffusing generally throughout all the regions in the country and generally out of the inner-cities and into the new suburban estates (Hornsby-Smith and Lee, 1979). Similar processes are reported in the United States. Thus the Notre Dame study notes that

> the suburban parish is replacing the urban neighbourhood parish as the normative experience for a plurality of Catholics. Gone is the public nature of city neighbourhood living and in its place is the more privatized life-style of the suburb. Left behind in this move to the new world of the suburb were many of the traditions of immigrant, folk Catholicism.
>
> (Dolan and Leege, 1985: 4)

It had been anticipated that this 'new middle class' would be assertively self-confident and less deferential towards traditional forms of authority and that this would be reflected in changes in the nature of priest-lay relations and in the prevailing styles of clerical authority in the parishes. In fact what evidence there is (Hornsby-Smith, 1987: 84–6) suggested that variations in social mobility experiences were not related significantly with religious practices, beliefs, and attitudes. A higher proportion of the upwardly mobile (or the 'new middle class') respondents in the 1978 national survey of Catholics in England and Wales rated their priests as excellent on seven out of ten aspects of their work, than those in the other three mobility categories (Hornsby-Smith and Lee, 1979: 197). This provides no support for the hypothesis that the 'new middle class' would be particularly critical of priests in asserting their own new-found status. Nevertheless, the innovatory potential of this group is reflected in the fact that they scored higher than those in the other mobility categories on a scale of support for new-style ministries (for example, married or women priests). They were also the least orthodox group in terms of sexual morality and had the highest proportion of non-practising Catholics. It seems possible that both the upwardly and downwardly mobile reject some elements of the religious culture of their class of origin. Thus the upwardly mobile have in large measure jettisoned the conformity to an institutional 'Catholic' identity which is strongest among the stable working class.

The second consequence of the new educational opportunities which emerged in the post-war years was the development of a secondary schools system which was not parochially-based. In areas of low Catholic density it was not uncommon for pupils to come from ten or more different parishes. This system thus broke the pre-war system of parish-based all-age schools which had facilitated the provision of a 'total' parish-based religious socialisation with dense and close-knit ties between home, school, and parish under the dominant control of the parish clergy.

Thus Joan Brothers, in her early study of the impact of the new educational structures in Liverpool in the 1960s, pointed to some of the consequences for the parish. She argued that 'the old devotion and loyalty to the parochial settings have come to have little meaning to most of these young people who have attended (the extra-parochial) grammar schools' and that these schools are 'taking on more and more of the functions of the parish'. To the grammar school pupils and university students 'the demands of the parish priest often appear authoritarian' and 'the earlier familiarity has disappeared'. The easy relationships which previously existed in the parishes have been broken down as the upward mobility of the educated working class creates new social distinctions which are not overcome by their common Catholic affiliation. Ties between Catholics are more cultural and educational than religious and for the upwardly mobile 'the ties to the neighbourhood which [once] made the parish a social community have little or no meaning' (Brothers, 1964: 158–72). The lesson is clear: the promotion of community-like characteristics in the mobile parish is very much more problematic than it had been in the defensive period of immigrant settlement where the parish provided immediate support and served the interests of the religio-ethnic community with its distinct subculture.

Apart from the impact of post-war affluence, the expansion of educational opportunities, and the processes of suburbanisation on the parishes, mention must also be made of two more factors which have had major implications for the Catholic parish in recent decades. First, there has been a global stirring of the democratic spirit. This was apparent in the ending of the colonial period and in the contemporary struggles against neo-colonialism in Third World countries. It can also be seen in the struggles of women for emancipation and against all forms of discrimination. In industrial relations it is expressed in the struggles of workers not only for improved economic returns for their labour but also in all forms of worker participation in decision-making and the extension of industrial democracy. In family relations, too, there is increasing awareness of the exploitative nature of the traditional division of labour in household work and child rearing. Parents will be only too familiar with the struggles over appropriate guidelines which they permanently wage with their children. In sum, the struggle to be free and to participate meaningfully in all decisions which significantly affect the lives of individuals is ubiquitous and continually being reinterpreted and negotiated. Given this fact and its articulation in the post-war world, it is only to be expected that similar strivings will emerge in the Church and find their expression at the parish level in the relationships between priests and lay people, between Catholics with different religious and social ideologies, between male and female Catholics, and between older and younger generations.

Second, there is little doubt that the tremendous developments in the media in the post-war period have transformed the social significance of the Catholic parish. In the western industrial societies practically every household now has both a radio and television. In Britain watching television is far and away the most important leisure-time pursuit so that the potential, for good or ill, of this medium of communication is considerable. This is not the place to debate and evaluate the extent to which television creates new consumerist, materialist, hedonist, or secular values, or rather sensitises us to a cosmopolitan world which includes famine in Ethiopia and the complexities of world trade policies, or simply reflects the prevailing individualistic and instrumental culture in society. Suffice it to say that it has largely destroyed the important entertainment functions of parishes which were particularly important during the depression years of the 1930s, at least in the northern industrial parishes in England.

But perhaps a little-recognised function of the ubiquitous television interview is that it has exposed public authority figures, for the first time in recent centuries, to close and challenging scrutiny by ordinary people. It has raised to the level of an expectation, that those who claim authority over some aspect of our lives can be challenged in the intimacy of our homes, through the mediation of an interviewer, and that the individual viewer can claim the right to make up his or her own mind about the weight to be placed not only on the substance of the argument but also on the perceived legitimacy of those claiming our allegiance. That this might well be the case is apparent in George Scott's account of the Panorama interview of Cardinal Heenan with John Morgan in 1965. When the Cardinal answered that he would be prepared to change his uncompromising views on the matter of birth control if the Pope decided to change the doctrine, Scott interpreted this as 'an answer which stank of hypocrisy' (Scott, 1967: 260). This clearly makes the point that in the post-war world there has almost certainly been an irreversible transformation in the nature of religious authority and its legitimation. For our present purposes at the parish level, this is most likely to be found in fundamental changes in the relationships between priests and lay people and in the legitimacy which is accorded to them in their institutional role as the religious leaders of the local Church.

POST-VATICAN RELIGIOUS CHANGES

Apart from the post-war social changes there have also been major religious changes in the Roman Catholic Church which have had their most obvious impact in the parishes in the two decades since the end of the Second Vatican Council. Particularly relevant for the purposes of this present discussion was the theological shift of emphasis to a 'People of God' model in the Dogmatic Constitution on the Church, *Lumen Gentium*, (ss.9–17), the stress on the common baptism of all believers, with its potential implications for ecumenical relationships (s.10), and the full participation of the laity in the life of the Church at every level (ss.30–8). The special task of lay people was defined as the transforming of temporal affairs (s.31) in accordance with the imperatives of social justice (*Gaudium et Spes*). The 1978 survey of Catholics in England and Wales, however, showed that nearly a decade and a half after the end of Vatican II

only one-half of Catholics had heard of the Council. The proportion who said they had not heard of the Council was as high as two-thirds of the youngest age group, one quarter of weekly Mass attenders and one tenth of members of parish organisations.

(Hornsby-Smith and Lee, 1979: 73)

On the basis of this finding and also focused interviews with random samples of Catholics in four parishes (Hornsby-Smith, Lee and Reilly, 1977), it was 'suggested that Catholics evaluated recent changes in the Church at the experiential level and that there was little awareness of any ideological implications in the conciliar teaching' (Hornsby-Smith and Lee, 1979: 73).

There seems to be little doubt that the liturgical reforms which the Council legitimated were imposed on a largely unprepared laity with the exercise of a top-down style of authority which was characteristic of the pre-Vatican Church. Among the more obvious changes were the introduction of the Mass in English, the saying of Mass by the priest facing the congregation, supposedly to symbolise the full participation of the laity in the communal celebration, the introduction of lay readers for the Liturgy of the Word and bidding prayers, and the introduction of a 'handshake of peace' at Mass. The revision of the fasting regulations to encourage greater lay choice and commitment to penance led Mary Douglas to protest that 'now the English Catholics are like everyone else' (Douglas, 1973: 67).

All these changes were immediately apparent in the parishes and when a national sample was asked about the impact of the Vatican Council in 1978, it was the changes in the liturgy which were most frequently noted. At this time just over one-half of the weekly Mass attenders thought the changes introduced were about right compared to just under one-quarter who thought there were too many and one in seven who thought there were too few changes. Two-thirds or more of the weekly Mass attenders approved of the saying of Mass in English and the 'handshake of peace' at Mass and between one-half and three-fifths approved of the growing use of folk music during Mass and receiving both the host and chalice at Communion. Asked to rate the importance of Christian Unity, over three-fifths responded 'extremely important' and an additional one-third 'important' (Hornsby-Smith and Lee, 1979: 211). The full significance of this rating is unclear and requires careful interpretation.

One current trend which is a matter of some concern and to which parishes are having to adjust and plan is the decline in the number of priests and the relative ageing of the clerical workforce as a result of the decline in the number of ordinations below replacement needs, allowing for both deaths and resignations. The figures reported in Table 1.1 indicated that in the past twenty years, while there has been a 17 per cent increase in the number of parishes, there has been a

14 per cent reduction in the total number of priests in England and Wales. Using data from three English dioceses for 1976 and 1977, Winter showed that 26 per cent of priests were under the age of 45, 48 per cent 45 and under 66, and 26 per cent over the standard retirement age of 65. He observed that we are served by an ageing clergy; recruitment is declining, and there is no indication that the rate of resignations is lessening' (1979: 91).

In the Westminster Archdiocese the number of diocesan priests in parish work declined by 16 per cent between 1971 and 1981 and the number of assistant priests by 38 per cent between 1976 and 1981. In the past decade the number of retired or sick priests rose by over one-third. At the same time, as many as one diocesan priest in five continued to be involved in non-parish work, in chaplaincies, teaching, study, or administration (Diocese of Westminster, 1982).

One implication of the growing 'shortage' of priests (i.e. within the constraints of the existing model of male bachelors only) is that more priests are likely to live alone in one-priest parishes. This trend was apparent in analyses carried out on the distribution of priests in the northern industrial Archdiocese of Liverpool, with its significant inner-city decline and relatively high Catholic density, and the Diocese of Arundel and Brighton, in the affluent and expanding rural and commuter-land in the south-east with a relatively low Catholic density, over the decade 1972 to 1982. During this period Liverpool lost ten parishes while Arundel and Brighton gained two. The number of parishes with only one priest increased by one-third in Liverpool and one-seventh in Arundel and Brighton. In 1972 one-half of the Liverpool city parishes had three or more priests; by 1982 the proportion was only one-quarter. When large parishes run mainly by the religious orders are excluded in Liverpool, the proportion of priests on their own in parish work increased from one-fifth to one-third and in Arundel and Brighton from two-fifths to one-half over the decade (Hornsby-Smith, 1983). These trends are clearly relevant to such issues as the job specification of parish priests, their sources of support, and the role of lay people in pastoral ministries.

THE DECLINE OF COMMUNAL INVOLVEMENT

In the sociological literature the concept of communal involvement indicates the existence of close and intimate social relationships (Tönnies, 1957) and has typically been measured in terms of marital endogamy and commensality, that is, the restriction of marriage and friendships in the main to members of the same socio-religious group (Lenski, 1963: 23). A number of measures of the declining communal involvement of Catholics in England and Wales over the past half-century have been given in Table 2.1 (Hornsby-Smith, 1987: 183). Particularly significant for the consideration of Catholicism at the local level is the evidence for a decline in the proportion of Catholics who marry a spouse who is also a Catholic from around 72 per cent in the late 1930s to only 31 per cent for those marrying in the late 1970s. In this same period the proportion of 'invalid' marriages which were not performed in front of a priest doubled from around 15 per cent to 32 per cent and there was also evidence for a significant decline in the proportion of friendships primarily with other Catholics. These different measures indicate the extent to which Catholics have in the post-war years diffused throughout British society as a result of their increasing participation in the processes of social mobility facilitated by educational expansion and the general economic prosperity over three decades.

Table 2.1 Estimates of communal involvement over time

Indicator of involvement	Late 1930s	Late 1950s	Late 1970s
1 Proportion of Roman Catholics in England and Wales (p%)	7	10	11
2 Proportion of Roman Catholics marrying Roman Catholics (m%)	72	60	31
3 Proportion of valid marriages (v%)	85	80	68
4 Proportion of Roman Catholics with half or more friends R.Cs (f_1%)	59		
5 Proportion of Roman Catholics with half or more friends R.Cs at 17 (f_2%)	68		
6 Index of marital endogamy (m/p)	10		
7 Index of current in-group friendship (f_1/p)	8		
8 Index of early in-group friendship (f_2/p)	10		

Source: Hornsby-Smith, 1987: 1[

At the same time, it is worth noting that Catholics are still something like three times as likely to choose Catholic friendships and a Catholic marriage partner as one would expect from their concentration in the population generally. As one might have expected, younger Catholics were less likely to find most of their friends from within the Catholic community; for example, whereas the proportion of the under 35s with half or more of their friends Catholic was between one-third and two-fifths, it was between one-half and three-fifths in the case of the over 50s. There was also a slight social class gradient; two-fifths of the upper middle class compared with one-half of the lower working class found most of their friends from within the Catholic community — probably a reflection of their greater social and geographical mobility (Hornsby-Smith, 1987: 188).

There was a strong relationship between the proportion of Catholic friends and attachment to the parish though it is not clear whether the fact of having a large number of Catholic friends led to a strong attachment to the parish or whether an attractive parish led to an increase in the number of Catholic friendships. Given the amount of social and geographical mobility in British society the general level of attachment to their parish was impressive. Respondents in the 1978 national survey were asked: 'Supposing you had to move to another part of the country. How sorry would you be to leave the parish?' Overall two-fifths of those who attended church said they would be sorry to leave their parish. There was a strong age gradient with one-fifth of the under-30s compared to three-fifths of the over-50s very sorry to leave. Married Catholics, particularly housewives, and working-class Catholics also expressed stronger than average attachment to their parish (Hornsby-Smith, 1987: 188–9).

Evidence from the 1978 survey suggested that about one in eight of all Catholic adults claimed to be a member of a parish organisation (Hornsby-Smith and Lee, 1979: 45–51, 188–91). Excluding those who had very tenuous links with any parish the proportion rose to just under one-fifth. Of these the majority were also involved in a range of other organisations such as political parties or trade unions. Members of parish organisations were disproportionately female, over the age of 35, married or widowed, converts, middle-class, and Conservative voters. They were more likely than Catholics generally to rate their priests favourably and this was particularly true of office holders. They were also likely to be traditionalist in the sense that disproportionately they thought there had been too many changes since the Second Vatican Council. Of those Catholics with some contact with their parish, about one-third reported that their parish had a lot of activities, just under one-half that it had a few, and almost one-fifth almost none. Activities reported most frequently were social or sporting activities; this was followed by fund raising and women's organisations. Prayer groups or parish council work were mentioned by only 1 per cent of Catholics.

Respondents were asked a battery of eleven questions about the way they rated their parish clergy. Overall priests were rated 'excellent' on the way they do their job by one-third of Catholics who answered. Just over one-half rated them 'excellent' or 'good' on their visiting of parishioners in their own homes. There was a strong age gradient with older Catholics being twice as likely as younger Catholics to rate their priests highly. Again, married Catholics, especially housewives (who may be the group with the time and opportunity to participate more in parish activities and have greater direct contact with priests), were more favourable in their ratings than average, though in this case there were few social class gradients. There was also a strong relationship between the evaluation of the priest and the attachment to the parish though, as in the previous case, the nature and direction of the relationship remains unclear (Hornsby-Smith, 1987: 189).

Another measure of the strength of communal ties in the Catholic parish is the frequency of serious interaction between priests, as the religious leaders of the community, and their parishioners. Just over one-quarter of the Catholic respondents replied that they had had a serious discussion with a priest about religious problems within the last two years. There were the usual age and social class gradients and signs of a relative loss of contact, or weaker communal ties, with the younger Catholics and with the working class (Hornsby-Smith and Lee, 1979: 203). Finally Catholics were asked about their participation (within the previous two years) in a number of activities which reflected new styles of activism in the Church: going to a charismatic or pentecostal prayer meeting (6 per cent), attending a house Mass (17 per cent), attending a religious discussion group (17 per cent), attending an ecumenical service (13 per cent), and attending some other small group of a religious nature (19 per cent). On all these measures there were the expected age and social class gradients though, in general, the sex differences were not significant (Hornsby-Smith, 1987: 189–90).

In order to explore the nature of communal involvement further, four types were distinguished in terms of high and low measures on two variables: personal involvement (measured by the proportion of Catholic friends) and institutional vitality (measured by the reported level of parish activities). In sum the analyses that both variables were strongly associated with a wide range of religious attitudes, beliefs, and practices. In other words, increasing both the density of Catholic friendships and the perceived number of activities in the local parish were likely to increase a range of measures of the religious life of Catholics. Of the two variables, the activism of the local parish seemed to be the more important. This suggests that there are good reasons for attempting the reform of parish life. While it is true that no *direct* measures of parish activity level were available, but only the perceptions of our respondents, in the classic phrase of W. I. Thomas: 'if men define situations as real they are real in their consequences'. Clearly, therefore, it seems important to change people's 'definitions of the situation' in their parishes. It seems easier, in principle, to modify the parish activism variable since the density of Catholic friendships is likely to be dependent in part on the level of parish activities and interaction, but also to be limited by the broad patterns of social and geographical mobility which Catholics increasingly experience as they assimilate more and more successfully to British society (Hornsby-Smith, 1987: 190–6).

An important area which requires further exploration is the relationship between involvement within Catholic institutional life — parish, schools, friendships, marital partners, and so on — and Catholic involvement in the political and social life of the nation but supported by a renewed local small group and parish communal life. It seems possible that there are two tendencies which appear likely to weaken the emergence of a radical and critical involvement in the life of British society. One tendency is for Catholic institutional life to deteriorate so that a 'detached' communal involvement (both low personal involvement and low institutional vitality) is the outcome. The other tendency is for active Catholics to develop an uncritical, 'total' communal involvement (both high personal involvement and high institutional vitality) which provides high levels of affective rewards and interpersonal bonds (Stark and Bainbridge, 1980), but in a way which consumes all their interests and energies so that their critical contribution to the life of the nation is negligible by default. In these circumstances the institutional Church will have become what Coser has called a 'greedy institution' (1974).

SUMMARY AND CONCLUSIONS

In this chapter we have reviewed some of the changes which have taken place in parishes since the end of the Second World War. As a result of social change there is now a more educated laity, less prone to a passive acceptance of and deference to clerical authority. The renewal process called forth by the Second Vatican Council has resulted in a greater stress on the pilgrim People of God model of the Church and this is reflected especially in the new styles of liturgical worship which emphasise the communal nature of the celebration and the active participation of the laity. This is increasingly relevant as adaptations begin to be made in the light of the sharp decline in the numbers of priests available for parish work.

Survey data provide strong evidence of the decline of several indicators of communal involvement as the defensive walls around the fortress-like socio-religious and largely immigrant community dissolved in the solvent of post-war social and religious changes. Of particular relevance at the parish level is the evidence of a sharp decline of marital endogamy and commensality over the past four or five decades. Two alternative consequences of these changes for the social and political significance of Catholicism in the British context are postulated. On the one hand parishes might decline in vitality and as a source of social support and religious inspiration for Catholics. On the other hand they may become 'greedy' and consume all the energies of active Catholics. In both cases the result would be a failure on the part of the parish to educate and train a Catholic laity capable of and willing to address the great moral and social issues of the contemporary world.

Some of these issues can also be seen to be emerging from the analyses of the Notre Dame study. Leege and Trozzolo have pointed to 'the paradox of a communitarian Church in an individualistic culture'. Thus while 'communitarian definitions of *parish* are predominant, these are not manifested to a great degree in participation in parish-based social action, welfare, and justice activities' (1985b: 5, 8).

It is clear, too, that experiences of Catholic parishes vary significantly between different social groups. In general, however, conflicts based on social class, ethnic group, gender, or generational differences are latent rather than manifest. In the main Catholics with grievances adopt a strategy of silent withdrawal rather than overt

43

challenge to the existing distribution of power. This would seem to be particularly the case for the young or for working-class Catholics. Some indulge in forms of passive resistance, for example to authorised changes in the liturgy, while occasionally there is an 'explosion of consciousness' on the part of an articulate group of protestors such as women (more typically in the United States than in Britain as yet) or black Catholics which results in some sort of change or adaptation.

In sum the situation nearly a quarter of a century after the end of the Second Vatican Council remains one of great complexity and variability as 'progressive' priests and laity seek to establish the new post-Vatican model of the Church and parish which demands a more active and participating laity over those who, for whatever reason, remain attached to the pre-Vatican model. The current state of paradigmatic change (Kuhn, 1970) is characterised by both conflict and consensus, continuity and change, and by general processes of accommodation and adaptation on the part of both priests and lay people. Before considering the role of the parish in 'creating community', a review of changes in the Catholic parish in a number of other countries will be offered.

Chapter Three

THE PARISH IN COMPARATIVE PERSPECTIVE

INTRODUCTION

While the bulk of this book will be based on Roman Catholic parishes in England, it will be argued that whatever analyses emerge have much wider relevance in the Church. In three visits to the United States over the past decade and one to Australia, and in spite of the view held by some that there are distinct differences of religious ethos, the present writer was struck more by the similarities between parish worship, interaction, and activities generally than he was by the cultural differences. In many respects the variations between traditionalist and progressive parishes in England were far greater and of much greater sociological significance than were those between parishes which were 'progressive', in terms of their explicit attempts at reform in the light of the teachings of the Second Vatican Council, whether in England or the United States or Australia. It might therefore reasonably be surmised that research findings relating to parishes in all three countries have more general relevance and implications.

The situation in the Philippines which I visited briefly in 1984, before the overthrow of President Marcos, is very different. It seemed apparent that one could meaningfully talk there of 'two Churches': the traditional parish-based Church dominated by the rich land-owners and close to the local élites, and the emergent Church of the poor, built up around the local form of basic Christian communities (Hornsby-Smith, 1986a). In my judgement, the relatively comfort-able western parishes in the 'First World' have a great deal they could learn from such basic Christian communities if only they could *see* the evidence of new life and *hear* the hopes and fears of the poor. Since reverse influences *from* the 'Third World' are likely to increase in the future, a brief account of some attempts to become the Church of the poor in the Philippines has been offered.

This chapter, therefore, reviews cultural variations between Britain and the United States, Australia, Europe, and the Philippines. No claim is being made that the selections given here are either comprehensive or representative. The focus has been on Roman Catholic parishes and no comparisons have been made for example with Anglican parishes. The purpose of this chapter is simply to draw attention to both the similarities which do exist in the world-wide struggle to cope with both social and religious change in the second half of the twentieth century and also the unique factors which distinguish between different countries.

THE PARISH IN THE UNITED STATES

In the United States Jay Dolan has described the changing role of the Catholic parish since the middle of the nineteenth century. He stresses that the parish was both a religious and a social institution. In particular it performed important functions in bringing immigrants together, providing them with social support, especially during the early years of their adaptation to a new and often strange society, and contributed to their socialisation into a new identity as Americans. As more and more immigrants arrived and made their way to the multiplicity of neighbourhoods, the ethnic characteristics of the neighbourhood increasingly became the identifying features of the parish which itself was increasingly 'transformed into a community institution'. In the immigrant parish

the church was the most enduring and important cultural institution in the neighbourhood. As a social organization that brought people together through a network of societies and clubs, it helped to establish a sense of community. As an educational organization, it taught both young and old the meaning of America, its language as well as its culture; as a religious organization, it brought the presence of God to the neighbourhood, nurturing and sustaining the presence of the holy through worship, devotional services, and neighbourhood processions. . . . In most Catholic neighbourhoods it was the cement that bound the people together, enabling them to establish some semblance of a community life. Families were indeed the building blocks of every immigrant community, but the church was the mortar that sought to bind them together.

(Dolan, 1985: 204)

Among the most important activities of the neighbourhood parish were the processions. By this means

Catholics were marking off their neighbourhood, laying claim to it, and telling people that this was their piece of earth. . . . Such processions helped to forge a sense of solidarity among Catholics and reminded them all that this was their neighbourhood, and these were their people parading along the street with the symbols, the icons of their God.

(Dolan, 1985: 208)

While the parish continued to be a vital focal point of Catholic life up to the 1950s, with the ending of mass immigration and the cumulative process of social and geographical mobility over several generations, the nature of the Catholic parish began to change to that of 'a kind of service station where the people had their religious and spiritual needs satisfied' (Fichter, 1978; quoted in Dolan, 1985: 397). By the 1960s radical changes in many of the old neighbourhoods were taking place as established communities moved out to be replaced by people with different ethnic and religious characteristics. The result was that

City parishes took on a new look in the 1960s and 1970s. Breaking out of narrow parochial concerns, they began to redefine their mission. As one priest put it, they were 'groping for relevance'. Many became community institutions committed to serving the needs of all people regardless of race or religion.

(Dolan, 1985: 449)

The need for parish renewal if it is to face the emergent challenges in the inner cities was also expressed by another Church historian who in the late-1960s referred to

the outmoded character of the traditional parish structure. The large and expensive parochial facilities that for many years admirably served the closed society of the teeming immigrant population are quite unsuited to the open and 'swinging' social groups that have inherited these neighbourhoods; nor in all likelihood would the latter have the income to sustain them even if they were practising members of the Church. . . . In view of the radically changed conditions of urban society . . . it is hardly too venture-some to suggest that the days of the typical inner city parish whose pastor received his appointment by reason of seniority in ordination should be regarded as numbered if the Church is to fulfill her true purpose. . . . Far more in tune with the realities of the present moment would be small Christian communities headed not by a 'pastor and his assistants', but by several young priests assisted by apostolic laymen and laywomen whose energy and zeal are not frustrated by the immobility of older churchmen.

(Ellis, 1969: 170–1)

Dolan illustrates his analysis of the changing American Catholic experience with a number of studies of individual parishes, chiefly in the urban neighbourhoods of Chicago and New York. More recently McLeod has described the culture of popular Catholicism in New York in the latter part of the nineteenth century and early decades of the twentieth century. Where Dolan stresses the defeat of an older, more democratic, congregational model of the parish in the early part of the nineteenth century and its replacement by the turn of the century by a hierarchical model in which 'the Irish tradition of an authoritarian clergy and a deferential laity' had become normative (1985: 172), McLeod interprets the changes as 'the period when the champions of a fortress-like American Catholicism gained the ascendancy over those who wanted to build bridges between the Church and the surrounding society' (1986: 3). The ultramontane form of Catholicism which emerged stressed the salience of the dichotomy between the sacred and the secular and 'the deep divide between priests and nuns on the one side and, on the other, lay people' (1986: 10). It affirmed the sanctity of Church and home but relegated work, politics, and leisure to a secular sphere. The Irish Catholic community in particular had a keen sense of 'the boundary lines between insiders and outsiders' (1986: 18). During the nineteenth century a 'devotional Catholicism' was replacing an earlier interior, humanist tradition of personal piety (Dolan, 1985: 210–11). Nevertheless, there is much evidence for the persistence of privatised forms of religion and it is plausibly hypothesised that

Catholicism, apparently the most clerically-dominated form of religion, owes an important part of its capacity for survival to forms of devotion which are distinctively and uniquely Catholic, but can largely be practised without reference to the clergy.

(McLeod, 1986: 26)

In contrast to the dominant Irish pattern of parish life, Tomasi has argued that the Italian parish in New York between 1880 and 1930 functioned as a quasi-sect not only to preserve the 'sacred cosmos' of immigrants, but also as a 'strategic structure for integration', fusing 'into one community the fragmented Italian immigrants of the same American neighbourhood' (1975: 118, 124). Apart from the creation of a cultural community, ethnic shops, mutual aid societies, and other ethnic institutions emerged to facilitate the subsequent adaptation of the Italian immigrants to American society. In the Italian parish, the immigrants from a variety of different villages 'rallied around their own saints and priests to protect their self-respect and their piety' (1975: 2).

An important early post-war contribution to the sociological study of the Catholic parish was made by Fichter who distinguished five categories of parishioners:

(a) *dormant*, 'who have in practice "given up" Catholicism but have not joined another religious denomination';
(b) *marginal*, 'who are conforming to a bare, arbitrary minimum of the patterns expected in the religious institution';
(c) *modal*, who are 'the normal "practising" Catholics constituting the great mass of identifiable Catholic laymen';
(d) *nuclear*, 'who are the most active participants and the most faithful believers'; and
(e) *the leadership group*, 'an even smaller number'.

(1954: 22, 192)

Later in this study it will be suggested that some modifications to this typology are necessary in the changed social and religious context of the parish in the late 1980s. Fichter's work was valuable in pointing to the heterogeneity of the Catholic population and in demonstrating a wide range of commitment levels on the part of the five different categories of parishioner and the social correlates of differential religious participation.

Second, he also distinguished nine roles of the parish priest: communal, administrative, businessman, civic, recreational, ameliorative, educational, socio-spiritual and liturgical (1954: 123–37). Third, he suggested that there were at least seven distinct conceptions of the Catholic parish:

(a) a legal corporation;
(b) a superimposed association;

(c) an institutionalized association;
(d) a communal group;
(e) a cluster of subgroupings;
(f) a network of family relations; and
(g) a series of statistical categories.

(1954: 181–94)

Finally, Fichter replied to a number of his critics and raised several issues which have contemporary relevance, including the impact of urban change on the religious behaviour of Catholic parishioners, the power of the parish in its relationships to the wider society, the extent to which religious consensus is a necessary or appropriate principle of social integration, the range of motivations for participation in religious behaviour related to the parish, and the need for structural reform of the urban parish (1954: 195–217).

The most prolific social researcher into American Catholicism over the past two decades has been Fr Andrew Greeley. Much of his empirical work, based on surveys conducted by NORC at the University of Chicago, was reviewed in his social portrait of American Catholics (Greeley, 1977). Two themes have been consistently stressed in his writings: the enduring importance of the neighbourhood and the continuing salience of ethnicity in American society. In view of the evidence of far-reaching social change and of massive social and geographical mobility in the post-war years, referred to by both Ellis and Dolan, it is possible that his stress on the city neighbourhood is a somewhat nostalgic celebration of past, romanticised community-like experiences during the period of mass immigration. And while his stress on ethnicity is important there has been a peculiar neglect of the Hispanic Catholics both by Greeley and, more recently, by the Notre Dame researchers. This omission has been addressed in part in the work of Fitzpatrick (1971), Cafferty and McCready (1985) and the Office of Pastoral Research in the Archdiocese of New York (1982).

Overtly polemical, Greeley has proclaimed the emergence of the 'communal Catholic' who is

one commited to Catholicism and self-conscious in his attempt to understand the Catholic experience in the United States. He does not care much what the Church as an institution says or does not say, does or does not do. He is committed to Catholicism as a collectivity and as a world view (though he reserves the right to

50

interpret that world view to meet his own needs). But his expectations of the Church as an ecclesiastical institution are minimal.

(Greeley, 1976: 9)

It remains to be seen to what extent such a type exists in other societies. Greeley has argued that in order to recapture its credibility with such Catholics, the Church must be both humble and excellent, traditional and radical, relaxed and committed, intellectual and sensitive, realistic and hopeful, mature and enthusiastic (1976: 185).

In a more recent book he has reported research on the religious imagination which he sees as substantially shaped by loving, relational experiences with family, friends, teachers, and priests (1981: 235). On the basis of survey findings from 2,500 young adults in the United States and Canada he provides some evidence that experiences in an active parish, and especially the good sermon, contribute to higher scores on a 'Grace' scale which measures a 'warm, positive and gracious view of the relationships between God and the individual human person' (1981: 29, 81 – 94). This scale was shown in turn to be a more powerful predictor of religious behaviour that various propositions of doctrinal orthodoxy. For example, 'good sermons enhance the religious imagination of young people — make their imaginations more graceful — and, thus, incline them to be more likely to identify with the Church' (Greeley et al., 1981: 238 – 40).

These concerns inform the useful book *Parish, Priest and People* in which he and his collaborators offered policy recommendation for parish leadership. Their claim that 'clergy do not come into a situation in which there are isolated, rootless and anomic individuals without any existing patterns of relationships and then by proclaiming the gospel and convening the eucharistic assembly, call community into being' (Greeley et al., 1981: 53) seems unduly optimistic and dismissive of the consequences of high levels of social and geographical mobility, the isolation and vulnerability of many immigrants and young people in inner-city areas, the everyday realities of life for many people in modern society, and the enormous difficulties parishes have in constructing and consolidating community-like characteristics. Nevertheless, these authors do capture something of the changes of religious experiences which have occurred in recent decades and the implications this has for Catholic parishes:

In the past, the local Catholic community facilitated these experiences of Mystery by an emphasis on the church building itself and,

51

within the church, the real presence of Christ in the Eucharist. Although there was never a complete split between the sacred and profane, between the world outside the church building and the world within it, most Catholics understood that there was direct and immediate access to God once they walked through the doors. They blessed themselves with holy water, women put on hats, men took them off, all to signify that they were in the presence of the Sacred. Within the church one could have a reflective experience of God. . . . The Eucharist itself was, for many people, a mediated experience of Divine Reality. In and through the host Christ came into a person's heart. . . . The greater emphasis today is on the presence of God to everyday life. The focus is not so much on God's availability in the sacred precincts. . . . The always and everywhere presence of God is more stressed than his specific presence within the Eucharist or within the church building. Greater accessibility of God also means a less intense experience. One of the current challenges of local Catholic parishes is to combine a sense of sacred space with a sense of the sacrality of every space, a sense of sacred time with the sense of the sacrality of every time. This is a difficult task and one that demands great sensitivity.

(Greeley *et al.*, 1981: 75–6)

In this changing Church the use of religious authority is democratised and modernised in order to obtain consent on the part of the 'lower participants' (Etzioni, 1961). An 'order-giving model of authority' in the Church will no longer work. Rather

the local community religious leader ought to be a lovable trouble-maker, a neighbourhood type with the character to point beyond the neighbourhood. He ought to be 'a hopeful, holy man who smiles'. Precisely because of his smiling holiness, he ought to be able to challenge the people in his community for that commitment beyond the community which hope inevitably demands.

(Greeley *et al.*, 1981: 135)

They conclude that sociologically 'it seems mandatory that priests develop the talents needed to be encouragers and challengers' (1981: 146).

Six models of ministerial activity are identified: keepers of the institution, evangelical recruiters, secular helpers, pastoral helpers, liturgical celebrant, and ministry of the laity (1981: 165–9). The 'professional pastoral leader must be a multi-talented individual'. Among the skills required of the religious leader, acquired through the processes of religious socialisation and life-long continuing education, are

> the ability to proclaim the stories of the people and the stories of the tradition in an articulate way. He must be competent as a preacher as well as being competent as a listener and an agent of change. And he must be committed to a lifelong learning process. Only then will he be equipped to lead the members of a local religious community in this contemporary world.
>
> (1981: 227)

Finally, the authors note that the sociology of the local religious community has progressed little since the pioneering work of Fichter in *Southern Parish* four decades ago. This present book is a tentative contribution towards that task.

Perhaps the most comprehensive study of parishes ever undertaken was the Notre Dame Study of Catholic Parish Life in the United States under the direction of David Leege and his colleagues from the early 1980s. A mail survey of a 10 per cent sample of American parishes in 1981/82 yielded over 1,100 replies with a respectable 60 per cent response rate. From the responding parishes a representative sample of thirty-six parishes was selected from non-Spanish speaking parishes for in-depth investigation in 1982/84. In these parishes extended interviews were obtained from thirty-five parish priests, eighty-nine paid staff, 202 voluntary leaders and 2,667 parishioners, 'Catholics known to parishes and served by them' (Leege and Gremillion, 1984; Dolan and Leege, 1985; Leege and Trozzolo, 1985a). In order to provide a basis for comparison of these 'core Catholics' with 'all Catholics', 954 non-Hispanic Catholics were identified from the National Opinion Research Center's ongoing General Social Surveys for 1982–84.

In this book we will frequently have occasion to refer to the Notre Dame findings. They are based on a much more extensive data base than has yet been achieved in England. The two-volume study of the historical emergence of the Roman Catholic parish in the United States is the first major publication from this research. It claims that:

A key to understanding the history of American Catholicism is the parish. In the nineteenth century, the parish was the gathering place for the people. This is where they manifested their beliefs and demonstrated their commitment to the Roman Catholic tradition. . . . This was where the religion of the people was nurtured and strengthened; nineteenth-century Catholic education is the story of the emergence of the parish school; through their parish organisations, Catholics first learned the lessons of benevolence and social concern. It is no exaggeration to say that in the nineteenth century the parish was the foundation of American Catholicism. Without it everything else would have collapsed.

(Dolan, 1987: 2–3)

It is clear, however, that while allowing for the fact that the size, variability and immigration experiences of the American Catholic Church are in many respects unique, nevertheless there are also numerous points of similarity and opportunities for fruitful comparison with the Church in Britain and in other countries with significant immigration experiences (such as Australia) and those with either ethnic or religious pluralism (such as Holland, Belgium, or West Germany). This will be shown to be evident in the consideration of the paradox of the co-existence of communitarian symbols of Church with individualistic cultural, economic, and political values (Leege and Trozzolo, 1985b), the analyses of parish liturgies and devotionalism (Searle and Leege, 1985a and 1985b), the consideration of Church positions and policy directions (Leege and Gremillion, 1986), leaders and styles of parish authority (Leege, 1986a, 1986b), the problematic nature of parishes as communities (Leege, 1987a), and of politics and civic participation (Leege, 1987b).

AUSTRALIAN CATHOLICISM

An awareness of the transformations in Australian Catholicism as it celebrates the bicentenary of the arrival of the first convict ships in Botany Bay is also apparent in a contemporary appraisal as it looks 'towards a third century'. O'Farrell's analysis is a pessimistic one of a tired community with 'little conspicuous vitality', its former 'combative energies' having 'drained away, and the residue [having] turned inwards in arguments about orthodoxy and disputes over forms of worship' (O'Farrell, 1985: 430). With increasing internal diversity

> many Catholics sought their personal (religious) preferences outside their parishes but most stayed by necessity, habit or preference in parish situations, often to find them increasingly dominated by small groups of enthusiasts whose inclinations directed parish style. The majority acquiesced in whatever was done, but apathy and various degrees of alienation became characteristic of many who still attended their parish church. They felt removed from its spirit, which seemed to them irrelevant or not adequate to their needs.
>
> (O'Farrell, 1985: 431)

Such an account might well have been written about some aspects of English Catholicism which had also experienced the breakdown of the older, 'combative', immigrant Catholic identity in the post-war years of increasing prosperity, upward social mobility, declining religious conflict, and increasing religious indifference (Hornsby-Smith, 1987). In Australia, in addition, there were the bitter memories of the 'political schism' within the Catholic community dating from the 1950s and 1960s, but in both societies it could be argued there was a 'reduced social awareness, [a] shrinking away from public issues and [an] acceptance of the constriction of life to the devotional' (O'Farrell, 1985: 435). A vital intellectual life in the Church had been replaced by an 'introspective individualism, fashionable pieties, trendy good causes, and devotional togetherness' (1985: 437).

O'Farrell's analysis of the changing relationship between priests and lay people also has wider application. In his view there has been a 'collapse of clerical power' due not only to the increasing education and self-confidence of lay people but also to the declining numbers of priests and to their increasing professionalisation:

> the day of the religious general practitioner, the religious 'family doctor', was rapidly giving way to that of the specialist, the priest intensively trained for, and restricting himself to, some particular avenue of ministry. Priests were increasingly likely to be engaged in professional courses, involved in commissions and conferences, taken up with organising and administering some aspects of the religious bureaucratic machine — and, inevitably, less available

for the traditional social roles, visitations, parish meetings and just being at hand when needed. The result was a widening gap between priests and people, the unwanted but inescapable reverse of that closer bonding seen as imperative by the Vatican Council, and a significant departure from the historical patterns.

(O'Farrell, 1985: 441)

The importance of the Catholic parish in facilitating the early processes of assimilation by Catholic immigrants in both Britain (Hickey, 1967; Jackson, 1963: 135–51; Rex and Moore, 1967: 150–3, 173–6) and in the United States (Dolan, 1985: 158–220; Tomasi, 1975) is clear. Australia is also very much a society of immigrants and 'the Australian Catholic Church, like its American counterpart, is a migrant Church'. This led Lewins (1978: 1) to explore the extent to which the Catholic Church was sociologically able to assimilate Catholic immigrants from a large number of different countries in the post-war years. On the basis of a case study in the early 1970s of a Melbourne parish where more than half the families were Italian immigrants, he was strongly critical of the dominant 'ideology of settlement' and expectations of rapid 'assimilation' by immigrants to prevailing Australian norms. Thus among parish priests the dominant expectation was that migrants would 'fit into' the existing parish structure and 'in all instances migrants' interests were secondary to priests' concern for the welfare of the parish [and] their avoidance of conflict with other significant groups' (1978: 85). For their part, Australian laity resented the migrants' lack of commitment to existing parish institutions and their lower level of financial contributions. Their assimilationist expectations were illustrated by 'their resistance to special consideration for migrants and their resentment and antagonism towards the continuation and accentuation of migrants' national characteristics' (Lewins, 1978: 126).

But whereas Lewins concluded from his study that 'culture divides more than religion unites, thus challenging the Church's conception of itself as "the Universal Church"' (Lewins, 1978: 127), Pittarello, on the basis of interviews with twenty-eight Italian migrants, stresses diversity which

> does not work against unity, and leaves enough room to explain the difficulties Italians and Australians encounter in working together in parish committees and activities. The fact that they work together is undeniable evidence that common faith draws them towards

unity; the fact that there are disagreements in implementing pastoral activities should not astonish anyone, and is easily explained by the different religious traditions of the parties involved.

(Pittarello, 1980: 93)

THE PARISH IN CONTINENTAL EUROPE

We will next consider briefly some relevant contributions from western Europe. It has been suggested, for example, that without continental developments Vatican II would never have happened and cannot be properly understood. A full treatment of these developments is beyond the scope of this book but a few pointers can perhaps be identified. In the early post-war years Abbé Godin grappled with the missionary task of conversion, especially of the paganised urban proletariat. This task was beyond the competence of the parish alone, no matter how active it was, because 'the parish and the proletarian worlds are not merely separated, they are also utterly different' (Ward, 1949: 97). Nevertheless the missionary task is not limited to the Missions de France but needs to be complemented by the renewed and missionary parish where the task of reconciliation of political and social class antagonists can begin (1949: 225–7).

An important early response to this challenge was *Revolution in a City Parish* by Abbé Michonneau (1949), the parish priest of Sacré Coeur de Colombes. In many respects the pastoral strategies proposed were those which subsequently were to be enshrined in the teachings of the Second Vatican Council (Abbott, 1966). What is of particular note for our present purposes is the stress on the facticity of the parish with its many human, material, and legal resources as a concrete base for the Christian mission to counteract the 'materialism and sensuality' of everyday life. 'Liturgical efforts are meant to form a warm, living, dynamic . . . active community which will attract others because they find it attractive, which will stimulate its members because it is alive' (1949: 40). Particular care needs to be taken to avoid class distinctions and, in a working-class parish, to use working-class language. While a plurality of recreational, educational, and charitable activities may have some beneficial consequences, it is important not to become submerged in them but to give priority to the training of specialised apostolic groups, such as the Jocists (Young Christian Workers). The cultivation of an openness to contacts in the territorial parish is supplemented by systematic visits to every home in the parish. In the promotion of an apostolic role on the part of parishioners, 'the place of the priest is to guide, to point out possibilities, to talk over results; he is not supposed to rule and dictate, by means of an organisation that he, and not the Holy Ghost, brought into being' (1949: 102).

There is a clear appreciation of the problematic nature of comfortable priestly life-styles and middle-class parishes for the working class and for the hungry, cold and ill-clothed, and the unemployed. There is an awareness that a 'clerical culture' may set priests apart from ordinary people who will not feel at home in the Church. This has implications for the professional socialisation of priests because the result of seminary training is to be 'separated from ordinary people during all the years of our intellectual and cultural grooming [so that] when we emerge, it is into a strange and crude world' (1949: 139). There is a concern, too, in this account, that sermons should relate to the concrete everyday realities of their parishioners' lives and that there should be an openness to dialogue between priests and parishioners and that lay people should be encouraged to run lay organisations.

Whereas some tried to renew the parish as a missionary institution others regarded it as totally identified with the interests of the bourgeoisie in a class-divided society and responded with the ill-fated worker-priest movement.

> The congregation of the faithful, which in working-class districts is particularly liable to consist almost entirely of small groups of the normally non-working population — women, children and old people — has always, in its outward manifestations, had a putting-off effect on faith, rather than acting as a sign and a witness. For this reason too absence of identification with the local parish was a necessary condition for the successful ministry of a worker-priest.
> (Siefer, 1964: 56)

The traditional parish was criticised for its 'totally unbrotherly proximity at Sunday Mass of those who are strangers to each other . . . (and) constant talk of brotherhood . . . must inevitably drive from the parish community anyone used to real group solidarity' (1964: 141–2). Yet there is no way out of the dilemma for parish clergy from the dual task of ministering to all the community of the faithful, respecting their culture and affiliations, while also attempting to feel and express solidarity with the proletariat for whom the parish is an alien institution (1964: 154–5). Thirty years after the banning by the Roman authorities of the worker-priest experiment, the missionary problem which they attempted so valiantly to address remains. It may be that in the new basic Christian community movement in Third World countries the Church is finding ways of bringing the 'Good News to the poor' which seem to be beyond the capability of the traditional parish.

In her recent study *Vers Un Nouveau Christianisme?*, Danièle Hervieu-Léger sees the end of the 'parish civilisation' on the basis of Lambert's (1985) study of religious change in Brittany during the twentieth century. She describes the transformations in the rural French parish as a result of post-war social changes.

> In this 'parish civilisation', Catholicism constituted a totalitarian system of behaviour and the certainties of religious, moral, social and political faith, inculcated since infancy, in the family, at church, and at school. It furnished the guidelines which ordered everyday life, governed relationships between men and women, parents and children, rich and poor, powerful and powerless, and which determined the relationships between work, life, suffering and death. It was a unified world even if its conflicts did exist, an ordered world where religion — of fear and of mercy for the repentant sinner, of submissiveness as well as of celebration — which kept everyone in 'his place'; the religious fidelity is there experienced under the vigilant control of the clergy, as both the gateway to the other-worldly salvation announced by the Church and the means through the game of intercession and the bias of morality, for coping with life, discarding worries and attracting the harvest of heavenly favours for the family, holiness, the country, all together with the valuation and the compensation for the worries and injustices sustained day after day.
>
> (Hervieu-Léger, 1986: 57)

But this parish civilisation, which had sprung directly from post-Tridentine Catholicism, began to crumble after the shocks of the First World War. The waves of modernisation in the 1950s followed by changes in the way of life in the 1960s, finally broke the resilience of the previous society of tacit understandings and precipitated the emergence of a new type of Catholicism. The most obvious sign of the break with the past was the collapse of both optional and later

obligatory religious practices. By the early 1980s the young felt themselves overwhelmingly to be complete strangers to a religious world
which they regarded as 'old hat' and irrelevant. The liturgical year,
previously strewn with festivals, processions, devotions, and rural
rites, grew increasingly narrow. A 'desacralised' clergy, having lost
its social standing, progressively adapted to this world in which
religion had become an optional matter of only secondary
importance. Certainly religion still retained its social functions, but
only in an indirect and attenuated way. And if parishioners still
retained a few religious 'reflexes', the ability of priests to guide their
everyday conduct in the sexual, ethical, political, or educational
domains continued to be eroded.

These changes, indicated clearly by the profound transformation in
the religious socialisation of children in a context where it is no longer
possible either to impose or to coerce, is not simply a change of style,
a neglect of parish ties, but a radical transformation at the heart of
which all the 'economy of salvation' finds itself gradually redefined.
The notion of an atoning ordeal and sacrifice and the age-old and
dominant problem of sin and redemption is disappearing. The contemporary emphasis on the close personal relationship with God as a
source of fulfilment and on to the riches of relationships with others,
is shifting practical Catholicism towards a 'transcendent humanism',
offering an 'ethico-affective' and predominantly this-worldly conception of salvation (Hervieu-Léger, 1986: 57–60). In this analysis,
Hervieu-Léger is pointing to a much more deep-seated, cultural
transformation in Catholicism than is accounted for simply in terms
of an institutional shift from a 'mechanistic' to an 'organic' organisation or from a 'pre-Vatican' to a 'post-Vatican' paradigm or model of
the Church. Rather, it is important to recognise exogenous forces
which have radically transformed the nature of ecclesiastical institutions, including the parish.

A modified structural-functionalist model of change in the Roman
Catholic Church since the Second Vatican Council is used by
Coleman to account for 'the evolution of Dutch Catholicism from a
Church of the economic minority to open, post-conciliar Catholicism'
(1978: viii). Using Smelser's well-known theory of structural
differentiation (1959) and Vallier's ideal-types of missionary and
cultural-pastoral strategies (1970), he argues that Dutch Catholics
discovered an elective affinity between the new theologies of the
Second Vatican Council and their own structural needs for a decline

in the principle of separation (or pillarisation or columnisation) in a period of economic emancipation.

> These new theologies have implications for the way in which the roles of priest and laity are defined in the Church, and for the way in which they allow the appeal to experience (instead of to trans-physical fiat) as the basis for the Church's understanding of its own symbols and 'the signs of the times'.
>
> (1978: 17–18)

In particular, the priest's role shifts from that of a dispenser of sacraments and a missionary organiser of Catholic action cells with diffuse authority and prestige to that of a spiritual counsellor and 'former' of local religious communities. Similarly the roles of the laity change from those of passive hearer and doer and hierarchy auxiliary to those of autonomous Christian citizens in a pluralist society (1978: 15–16, 150). Organisationally Coleman found that there had been a considerable amount of experimentation with new 'congregational forms' specialising in different liturgies and services which were adapted to the different religious needs of different groups within the Church and that 'even within one parish team, different types of liturgical and pastoral services have been designed to cater to young, progressive, moderate, or traditional groups' (1978: 223). (The emergence of plural parish liturgies has also been noted in England: Hornsby-Smith, 1975). The unusual 'mobilisation of resources' available accounted for the speed of the transition in Holland but essentially the same problems of adaptation to the processes of structural differentiation have to be addressed everywhere in the contemporary world.

OLD AND NEW PARISHES IN THE PHILIPPINES

It is beyond the scope of this book to attempt a comprehensive review of developments in parishes in developing societies. However, in this section some brief reflections on changes in some parishes in the Philippines will be offered. As in many developing societies the Church in the Philippines is torn between its historical role of collaboration with the former colonial powers and the entrenched social, economic, and political élites of the post-colonial period, and ministering to the majority of poor, deprived, and oppressed peasants and urban workers. As in many developing societies, processes of development have resulted in widely differentiated benefits and costs for different sections of the population. The gap between the rich planters, landowners, and new entrepreneurial élites who work in close collaboration with the multinational corporations and other agencies of international capitalism on the one hand, and the landless peasants and rootless urban poor, on the other hand, have tended to widen in recent years. In consequence social tensions have increased and been contained by means of an increasingly oppressive and powerful military operating substantially on the side of the local oligarchies. In the amplifying spiral of violence, resistance, and oppression it is the poor who suffer most. In this situation the perspectives of liberation theology have been taken up by some elements in the Church. This constitutes an alternative model to the traditional parish-based model which served the interests of local élites. Frequently the alternative model is organised around basic Christian communities. Through these Church workers aim to raise the consciousness of the poor to the causes of their deprivation and to organise them to struggle against injustices which trap them in a situation of poverty and powerlessness in the face of oppression.

The conflict between the two interpretations of the role of the priest and of the parish is well told in the case of the Negros Nine, three priests and six lay workers falsely accused of the murder of the local mayor on the sugar island of Negros (McCoy, 1984; O'Brien, 1985). In the mid-1970s the Columban missionary priests began to distance themselves from the local planter élites who, as the Australian Fr Brian Gore indicated, 'want their houses blessed, their cars blessed. They want the priest to spend all his time saying Mass every day for their old ladies who then go home and harass their poor maids' (McCoy, 1984: 108). Sickened by the high levels of infant mortality and his involuntary participation in the funerals of dead infants and other manifestations of injustice, Fr Gore first refused to give a corrupt judge a funeral Mass, so 'denying them their Church, their social club with all its lovely traditions and rituals' (McCoy, 1984: 110).

Later both he and Fr O'Brien moved out of the traditional parish in the political and administrative centre where the local élites lived and up into the mountains among the peasants where they began to develop new models of decentralised parish work based on lay-led prayer groups and later basic Christian communities of thirty to fifty people (McCoy, 1984: 161). Through role play in extended seminars, the peasants grew in confidence and each local area or region sent its own representatives to the parish council.

> As their Communities gained strength and their leaders confidence, authority began to flow upward from the people to the parish council where the priest sat as just one member — a complete reversal of the top-down hierarchy in a conventional parish. In a fundamental sense, people were learning to take control of a key institution, the Church, and break their passivity, their deference before a traditional authority figure, the priest. The established pattern of Church authority from Pope to Bishop to priest was now implicitly challenged by a rise of a parish structure based on popular control.
>
> (McCoy, 1984: 162–3)

Similarly, in his adjacent parish, Fr O'Brien altered the sacramental rituals in a way which de-mystified his role and reinforced the key place of the basic Christian communities.

> The rejection of Satan and his works in *baptism* was given a new social dimension — 'Do you reject landgrabbing and usury?'; 'Are you willing to stand up for your rights?' It was no longer a 'superstitious rite saving us from the wrath of God'. *Confirmation* was to be based on 'the themes of social sin' since it would be 'ridiculous if people confessed personal misdemeanours while being totally unaware of the suffering going on all around them'. Confirmation was now done at age eighteen with the entire Christian Community, not a wealthy godfather, standing as sponsor. *Marriage* was performed in groups, on set days, for fixed fees — nobody could buy a grand church wedding.
>
> (McCoy, 1984: 169)

Clearly there is here a significantly new model of the parish, one which aims both to defend and support the poor but also to raise their consciousness of the causes of injustice and to empower them to struggle against it. The basic Christian communities in the Philippines have developed unique features which aim to combine the spiritual concerns of prayer groups with the more political concerns of activists. This is reflected especially in the BCCCOs (basic Christian community–community organisation) sponsored by the National Secretariat for Social Action, an arm of the Philippine Bishops' Conference since the mid-1970s (Hornsby-Smith, 1986a). These new structures within the traditional parish are helping to transform it in large areas where one priest has to minister to 20,000 or more people. This new model is taking the theology of Vatican II seriously in aiming to empower people to struggle against their oppression and exploitation.

My own judgement is that these new models of the parish have enormous potential for the Christian transformation of the social order provided that the leadership is not hijacked by extraneous groups. Furthermore, I believe that they are far in advance of developments in most parishes in 'First World' countries which still tend to be trapped in an older model of the parish and relatively impervious to the cries of the poor, deprived, and oppressed.

CONCLUSIONS

The aim of this chapter has been the modest one of indicating, on the basis of a number of comparisons with studies in other countries, that the essential tensions which arise in the case of a major paradigm-shift have been experienced globally in a variety of ways which have reflected different historical contexts and social circumstances. Thus the emergence of the parish in the United States has reflected its defensive functions for distinct immigrant ethnic groups organised on a neighbourhood basis in the nineteenth century. To some extent similar processes of accommodation and adaptation are clear in the experiences of Australian parishes in the post-war period of massive immigration. But in both these societies, as indeed in Britain, there have been similar post-war processes of upward social mobility and suburbanisation which have resulted in similar processes of change in the parishes in the participation of lay people and in priest-parishioner relationships. It is argued, therefore, that the general pattern of findings from parish studies in any of these countries is likely to be broadly the same in the other countries.

While the Church in continental Europe or in the Third World, in particular the Philippines, will also have experienced the global changes of the post-war period and the theological shifts of emphasis legitimated by Vatican II, these will have been worked out rather differently because of their different historical contexts and contemporary developments. Thus the parish in continental Europe, and especially France, has had to cope with a historical legacy of anti-clericalism and the overt hostility of the working class for whom the

Church is associated with class enemies. The attempt to Christianise the working class led to valiant efforts to distance the Church and priesthood from exclusively bourgeois interests. One expression of this attempt was the worker-priest movement which by-passed the traditional parish. Again, in the Philippines as indeed in other Third World countries, particularly in Latin America, the basic Christian community movement has attempted to devise new structures at the grassroots which empower those at the social base to liberate themselves from the structures of injustice which oppress them. It is suggested that in these attempts are to be found fundamental insights into the role of lay people in the Church. New strategies of lay participation developed in basic Christian communities are slowly diffusing to the older First World countries where they are contributing to the renewal of parish life.

The rest of this book is concerned to explore these processes of change in the parishes, and in the roles of the parish priest and parishioner, particularly in England as we approach the last decade of the twentieth century. We start by considering the quest for community in the contemporary parish.

Chapter Four

THE QUEST FOR COMMUNITY

INTRODUCTION

There are few words more highly regarded among Catholics than 'community'. References to 'parish community' abound. Community-talk is officially promoted and the closer a parish comes to exhibiting community-like characteristics, the more highly rated it is. There is a general awareness that whereas in the pre-war years the parish frequently provided an all-embracing or total environment for the religious socialisation of its members, with religious, educational, social welfare, and entertainment functions for all circumstances and needs, in the post-war years with the provision of secondary education for all (and hence extra-parochial schools), the high levels of social and geographical mobility, the development of the Welfare State, the improvements in home circumstances, the ubiquity of television-viewing and car-mobility (Willmott, 1986: 106), and the growth of mass, urban leisure industries focused particularly on the teenage consumer, many of these functions have been irretrievably lost. In these circumstances the quest of the parish to offer community-like characteristics has become much more problematic. As Fichter noted over thirty years ago, 'the multiple functions of the old-fashioned, solidaristic, community parish have been attentuated' (1954: 65). Later he concluded that on the basis of his empirical research, 'the typical parish is at best a secondary association and does not contain in its totality the kind of primary relations that are characteristic of the communal group' (1978: 39).

An obvious starting point for the consideration of the community-like characteristics of contemporary parishes is the ideology and practice of the early Church in Jerusalem as reported in the Acts of the Apostles (Acts, 2: 44–7; 4: 32–5). This account identifies at least eight distinct elements which it would be possible to operationalise in studies of contemporary parishes. These elements are propinquity, co-operative economy, egalitarian distribution, communal worship, commensality, commensal eucharist, shared belief and value system, and apostolic leadership. Brief reference to each element will be made in the context of the contemporary parish.

1 *Propinquity:* the faithful, members of the religious collectivity, lived closely together. In many respects the contemporary parish shares this characteristic since parishes are generally defined territorially in Canon Law (Can. 518). In practice parishes vary considerably in size from small, highly concentrated, inner-city parishes occupying much less than one square-mile, to large sprawling rural or missionary parishes. There appears to be a growing amount of 'shopping around' for parishes felt to be congenial. In the 1978 national survey of English Catholics the proportion of Mass attenders who commuted from outside the parish averaged around 8 per cent. In Liverpool and parts of Lancashire, in particular, loyalty to the parish of origin continues to be remarkably strong even where there is short-range geographical mobility, for example to a suburban housing estate. In the United States the Notre Dame study reported that 'slightly under 15 per cent cross boundaries in the selection of a parish' (Leege and Gremillion, 1984: 6). In a study of Sunday Mass attendance in Antwerp as long ago as 1971 it was found that in nine of the twenty-six churches there were more non-parishioners than parishioners, and in all but three of the churches at least one quarter of the believers were non-parishioners (Dobbelaere and Billiet, 1976: 220, fn. 34). Mobility across parish boundaries has become much easier in recent years with the spread of car ownership and also a decline in the salience of sanctions against non-attendance in the territorial parish.

In an application of Towler's typology of religious commitment (1974: 166–71) to the analysis of the 1978 national survey, the *local* commitment was operationalised in terms of respondents' stress on the salience of local 'roots' in response to a question asking why they would not want to leave their parish. One in eight English Catholics fell into this category. Half of them were aged 50 or over, much above the average (29 per cent). They were disproportionately women and working class with a high proportion of second-generation Irish and a much higher than average proportion of convert marriages and a very small proportion of invalid marriages. They had the highest proportions of regular Mass attenders, the sexually orthodox, members of parish organisations, and those with a high density of Catholic friendships. They rated their priests more highly than those with other types of commitment and were high scorers on scales of 'new-style activism', such as attendance at a charismatic prayer meeting, a house Mass or an ecumenical service, and 'new ministries', which indicated a willingness to accept married or women priests. They had attended ecumenical services more than all other categories (Hornsby-Smith, 1987: 196–8, 219–20).

2   *Co-operative economy:* the faithful owned and shared everything in common. There is no evidence of this in the contemporary parish in western industrial societies apart from a tiny handful of small, prophetic groups or the recognised religious orders.

3   *Egalitarian distribution:* the allocation of goods and services was based on the criterion of need rather than social status, position, or power in such a way that no member of the collectivity remained in want. Again, in the contemporary parish there is practically no attempt made to approximate to this criterion which is in striking contrast to the dominant western values of individualism and personal achievement in the last quarter of the twentieth century.

4   *Communal worship:* the faithful met daily in the Temple. By contrast the national survey data suggested that around 9 per cent of English Catholics attended Mass more than once a week. In the United States the Catholic Parish Life study indicated that around 8 per cent of parishioners attended Mass at least once a week (Leege and Trozzolo, 1985a: 3).

5   *Commensality:* the faithful spend all their leisure and discretionary time with other members of the religious collectivity. We have only limited measures of the communal involvement of English Catholics but it is clear that, with the dissolving of the boundaries which in pre-war years protected Catholics from 'polluting' contact with non-members of the socio-religious subculture, there has been a substantial decline in the proportion of Catholics marrying other Catholics or finding their close friends primarily among them. (See Table 2.1 on p. 39)

6   *Commensal eucharist:* the faithful performed the ritual of the

breaking of bread in their own homes. In 1978, 17 per cent of English Catholics reported that they had attended a house Mass within the previous two years. In 1974, 8 per cent of non-Hispanic American Catholics said they had attended an informal home liturgy of some sort (McCready, 1975: 3).

7 *Shared belief and value system:* the faithful were united heart and soul. The evidence is overwhelming that there is massive divergence from the official Catholic belief and value systems. In England and Wales the most comprehensive data were those from the 1978 national survey of Catholics which were used to construct a typology of English Catholics (Hornsby-Smith and Lee, 1979; Hornsby-Smith *et al.*, 1982; Hornsby-Smith, 1987). Similar data for the United States were summarised by Greeley (1977).

8 *Apostolic leadership:* the leadership of the apostles was unquestioned and extended to a general oversight of the distribution of shared resources. There seems little doubt that the parish clergy, as the local representatives of the bishop, generally continue to be the prime leaders in the parishes. In the 1978 national survey of English Catholics, three-fifths considered their priests did their job well (Hornsby-Smith and Lee, 1979: 70–1). As we shall see later, priests are increasingly sharing leadership with lay leaders but on occasion their leadership is contested where it is not regarded as legitimate by parishioners.

It is the aim of this chapter to examine critically the supposed quest for 'community' in the contemporary Catholic parish and to evaluate the extent to which the rhetoric is translated into religious praxis. For this purpose the above criteria might be reduced to three:

a) the generation and manifestation of shared beliefs and values among the members;
b) the frequency of interaction between them; and
c) the provision of reciprocal social support and mutual aid to each other.

The Notre Dame study suggests that 'community (1) develops a sense of belonging or loyalty, (2) empowers common actions, and (3) nurtures standards from outside the individual, which direct just and honorable civic participation' (Leege, 1987a: 1). It is also important to note that there is likely to be a considerable gradient in the extent to which each of these criteria are met between the parish activists (Fichter's nuclear parishioners and core leadership), the bulk of nominal or 'practising' Catholics (Fichter's modal and marginal parishioners), and the non-practising (or Fichter's dormant) Catholics.

It is an essential task to distinguish the rhetoric of community and the aspirations of the religious leadership from the empirical situation in most parishes in terms of these three variables. Given the reality of the social pressures which exist in a highly urbanised, modern, industrial, mobile, cosmopolitan society, it might reasonably be hypothesised that attempts to create community-like characteristics are unlikely to have more than a limited effect for a relatively small proportion of members. At the very least it is necessary to recognise the reality of the constraints on parishes, including the declining salience of the parish for many Catholics in the post-war years with the emergence of alternative sources of education, welfare, and leisure pursuits.

This point is stressed here because it often seems that there are quite unreasonable expectations of what the parish might achieve in the way of providing support for vulnerable groups in society. Not only is this assumption dangerous from the point of adequate analysis and hence appropriate pastoral practices but it is also likely to result in an unreasonable sense of guilt on the part of the religious leaders of the parish, both clergy and laity, at what they mistakenly perceive to be a failure of commitment or concern on their part. There is an analogy with the quite unreasonable expectations which were often held regarding Catholic schools in the past. Just as supposed inadequacies in the schools were once blamed for any deficiencies in the beliefs or practices of their former pupils, a scapegoating which diverted attention from other weaknesses in families, neighbourhoods, or parishes, so a one-sided focus on the parish will divert attention from the dominant social arrangements in homes, workplaces, neighbourhoods, and indeed society generally. Even the most active parishioners only spend a limited proportion of their spare time in parish-related activities, and for most Catholics the parish is of only marginal significance in their everyday lives. Such social facts must be borne in mind in order to make a balanced judgement of the community-like characteristics of parishes in the contemporary world.

SOCIOLOGICAL APPROACHES

Sociologists have often complained about the diffuse and ambiguous nature of the concept 'community' and Hillery is reported to have offered no fewer than ninety-four definitions (in Bell and Newby, 1971: 27–9). The ambiguous character of 'community' and its relationship to the 'private' and the 'individual' has recently been stressed by Fraser who has argued that civil society 'has had the power to determine what is, or is not, community' in terms of 'loyalties, solidarity, localism, personalism and the "face-to-face", authority, legitimacy' (1987: 797). The diffuseness of the concept is indicated in the range of references to the Irish or West Indian communities, the community of scholars, the international community, occupational, religious, or neighbourhood communities, and so on. Some sense of 'belonging' is generally considered to be important though not all regard the notion of a bounded territorial area as essential. References to community are often nostalgic and point vaguely, and often ahistorically, at some past social arrangements in pre-war or pre-industrial society in the romantic belief that social relationships were closer or warmer in rural society or before disastrous urban planning policies destroyed working-class 'communities'.

An important starting point for the consideration of 'community' is the distinction between *Gemeinschaft* (or community) primary and personal relationships which are intimate, private, close, face-to-face, co-operative, friendly, and based on shared sentiments and under-standings, on the one hand, and *Gesellschaft* (society or association) secondary relationships which are impersonal, public, contractual and rational, on the other (Tönnies, 1963, first published 1887). In terms of the well-known 'pattern variables' of Talcott Parsons, community can be considered to be characterised by affectivity, role diffuseness, particularistic relationships, and ascriptive positions in contrast to the affectively-neutral and specific roles found in society generally where allocation is supposedly based on universalistic and achievement criteria. Gannon has pointed out that American sociologists have rejected 'a linear model of *Gemeinschaft* versus *Gesellschaft*' and instead 'focused on the complex and never-ending processes of competition, conflict, accommodation, and assimilation in community life' and Janowitz has referred to the 'community of limited liability' (Gannon, 1978: 286, 291).

It is important to be critically aware of some of the potential dysfunctions of basic communities. In Belgium, for example, Dobbelaere and Billiet concluded their comparative analysis of Catholic organisations by observing that

> it appears that the *Gemeinschaft*-ideology, which is predominant in the Church, can, to a large extent, explain the lack of the values of social justice within the Church, since these are in fact more typical of a *Gesellschaft*-ideology.
>
> (1976: 257)

They also warned of the consequences of secularising processes in which 'religion, and therefore the Church, appear to have been pushed back to the private sphere, the sphere of the family, the neighbourhood and friends' (1976: 221). They concluded their analysis of the ideology of 'community' by drawing attention to 'the problem of the "closedness" of "small groups"' and observed that

> placing too much emphasis on community ideology without adjusting societal and organisational relationships would bring about an atomisation of the Church and increase the divergency between groups . . . the idealisation of community relationships implies the danger of underestimating the societal and organisational relationships within the Church by judging or fashioning everything along community standards.
>
> (1976: 223)

They stressed that pastorally, community-building should be seen as an aspect of 'communal mobilisation',

> not as an 'escape', but as a 'base for action for the penetration and the restructuring of the existing order'. . . . Community-building is meaningful only if it serves a larger structure, not if it is used as an oasis where one rejoices in the company of others and seeks there the presence of the 'Lord'. This would clearly be the end of the historic mission of Christianity: the restructuring of the world.
>
> (1976: 258)

We will return to these themes when we address the issue of the 'greedy parish' later in this chapter.

Beckford (1973: 45) has reminded us that, in general, sociologists seem to agree that the territorial parish is ill-suited to contemporary urban conditions. This view has been urged insistently by Winter who favours a shift of emphasis in the Church towards small basic communities of around thirty to forty like-minded people (1973: 57–8; 1979: 85; 1985: 139). Winter argues that

> the parish as we know it is an obsolete structure inherited from the Middle Ages. . . . The traditional parish is too large and unwieldy to be a community, yet having acquired a life of its own it acts as a parasite effectively working against what the small groups might achieve. Not only does it inhibit their proper development, it has proved dangerously impervious to the spirit of the Vatican Council, and has sufficient life of its own to take up the energy of a great many good people especially in matters like fund raising to maintain the fabric of the buildings.
>
> (1985: 131, 139)

These are interesting hypotheses. For the moment, though, it is our intention to suspend judgement and to review what little research evidence there is. On the one hand parishes are a massive fact of life for the religious collectivity and there is little point in speculating about hypothetical alternatives, at least for urban, industrial societies such as Britain and the United States. On the other hand Winter is right to point to the probable limitations of parishes in terms of (a) their inability to create 'community' and (b) the ways in which 'greedy' parishes tend to consume the energies of active members. He is also right to raise the issue of the problematic nature of the linkages between small homogeneous groups and wider Christian groupings such as the territorial parish. It is in this spirit of data-led investigation that we must evaluate the community-building aspirations and achievements of the contemporary parish.

OFFICIAL COMMUNITY IDEOLOGY

The recent emphasis on 'community' in the Roman Catholic Church can be traced back to the People of God theology articulated especially in the second chapter of *Lumen Gentium* (ss.9–17), the Vatican Council's Dogmatic Constitution on the Church (Abbott, 1966: 24–37). It is further expressed in *Gaudium et Spes* (s.32), the Pastoral Constitution on the Church in the Modern World (Abbott, 1966: 230) where the Council taught that

> from the beginning of salvation history (God) has chosen men not

just as individuals but as members of a certain community. . . .
This communitarian character is developed and consumated in the
work of Jesus Christ. For the very Word made flesh willed to share
in the human fellowship.

In the Decree on the Ministry and Life of Priests (s.6) it is stated that

the office of pastor is not confined to the care of the faithful as
individuals, but is also properly extended to the formation of a
genuine Christian community. If community spirit is to be duly
fostered it must embrace not only the local Church but the universal Church. The local community should not only promote the care
of its own faithful, but filled with a missionary zeal, it should also
prepare the way to Christ for all men.

(Abbott, 1966: 545)

The Christian community is built up around the Eucharist where
'all education in the spirit of community must originate'. Its fruits are
to be found in works of charity, mutual help, missionary activity, and
Christian witness. 'For this community constitutes an effective
instrument by which the path to Christ and to His Church is pointed
out and made smooth for unbelievers, and by which the faithful are
aroused, nourished, and strengthened for spiritual combat' (Abbott,
1966: 546). Finally, in the Constitution on the Sacred Liturgy (s.14)
it is stressed that the 'full and active participation by all the people is
the aim to be considered before all else' (Abbott, 1966: 144).
'Therefore the liturgical life of the parish . . . must be fostered in the
thinking and practice of both laity and clergy; efforts also must be
made to encourage a sense of community within the parish' (Abbott,
1966: 153).

A strong emphasis on parishes as communities was evident both in
the diocesan reports based on extensive discussion among active
Catholics at the parish level and submitted in preparation for the
National Pastoral Congress in 1980, and in the *Congress Reports* and
the bishops' response, *The Easter People* (Anon., 1981). Thus the
discussion paper *You and the Church* invited Catholics to reflect on 'the
people in the parish community' and 'the parish in the community
around it', and asked how Christians could become a praying,
teaching, apostolic, witnessing, and serving community (Anon.,
1981: 32–3). The diocesan reports suggested that 'many parishes are
too big, and their size militates against unity and community'.

The plea was for more consultation, lay involvement, and genuine partnership so that an 'explosion of life and building up of community' could take place (Anon., 1981: 53–4). There was a strong sense that parishes should be caring and ministering communities (Anon., 1981: 60–2). These aspirations were subsequently reflected in the various topic reports and in the report of Sector A on 'The People of God: Co-Responsibility and Relationship' (especially ss.6–8). In particular

> in order to become such a loving, caring, worshipping community, we overwhelmingly recommend that parishes should become a communion of Christian communities incorporating small, neighbourhood, area, and special interest groups including all, the lapsed and the practising. They should meet for prayer, social events and occasionally the eucharist, supporting one another in times of stress, sorrow and joy. Such small groups, house groups and neighbourhood groups, for prayer, study of scripture, and celebration of the eucharist, especially for the sick, the housebound and the handicapped must be seen as necessary for the building up of the parish community and as an aid to celebration. Liturgical groups should be established in parishes to work with the clergy, and as a consequence of our common participation by baptism in the priesthood of Christ, the maximum involvement and ministry of the laity, both men and women, without discrimination, should be encouraged in the preparation and celebration of the liturgy.
>
> (Anon., 1981: 130–1)

The bishops in their response (s.120)

> were glad to recognise in the voice of the Congress an insistence upon the parish as the natural and most effective apostolic community within the life of the Church. Whatever be its size, the parish is seen as a communion of Christian communities made up of all the faithful, whether lapsed or practising their faith, and coming together for prayer, liturgy and the eucharist, the study of the scriptures, for works of charity and mercy, or for social celebrations. Small communities of this kind are a source of strength to the parish as a whole, and must not be exclusive in themselves nor seen as an alternative to parish commitment.
>
> (Anon., 1981: 358)

Their encouragement of small groups and Catholic organisations was qualified by their social control concerns and by the warning that

> there can be a danger of fragmentation if they try to operate independently of the local Church and in an inward-looking way . . . (though they) can contribute much to the revitalisation of the life of the parish as a community of faith.
>
> (s.122; Anon., 1981: 359)

Finally the bishops accepted the view that if the parish is to develop as a community 'there must be some way in which parishioners can respond to their priests in a genuine dialogue' (s.151; Anon., 1981: 371). This is an interesting admission even if it continues to reflect a top-down view of dialogue. A good example of an attempt to give concrete expression to the community ideology at the parish level is given by Fr Brian O'Sullivan (1979) in his enthusiastic account of his ministry in a middle-class parish in the outer London commuter belt in the late 1970s.

In Avery Dulles' account of five different models of the Church he observes that the People of God theology illuminates the notion of the Church as community. From this point of view the Church

> is not in the first instance an institution or a visibly organised society. Rather it is a communion of men, primarily interior but also expressed by external bonds of creed, worship, and ecclesiastical fellowship.
>
> (Dulles, 1976: 51)

However, this model is not without its weaknesses and

> can arouse an unhealthy spirit of enthusiasm; in its search for religious experiences or warm, familial relationships, it could lead to false expectations and impossible demands, considering the vastness of the Church, the many goals for which it must labor, and its remoteness from its eschatological goal. As a remedy one must call for patience, faith, and a concern for the greater and more universal good.
>
> (1976: 184)

Dulles is pointing to the dangers of an obsession with in-group social relationships which detract both from a primary concern with the vertical relationship with God and from horizontal relationships with the wider socio-political world outside the religious collectivity. Thus:

the more people prize their spontaneous, local community, the more likely they are to detach themselves from the parish, the diocese, and the universal structures of the Church. The more value they set on creative liturgies and spontaneous prayer, the more impatient they will probably grow at the restrictions of canon law and rubrical prescriptions. The more they cherish the immediate experience of life together, the less interested are they likely to become in maintaining communion with the Church Catholic of all ages and places. For some Catholics, therefore, enthusiastic commitment to interpersonal community led to a true crisis of identity. They lost interest in the transcendent dimension of the Church's life, and grew impatient with the strong authority structures that are intended to safeguard that transcendent dimension from being eroded by the limited vision of particular times and localities.

(1977: 15)

Thus Dulles' personal preference is for a sacramental type of ecclesiology which 'preserves the community value, for if the Church were not a communion of love it could not be the authentic sign of Christ' (1976: 186–7).

In the previous chapter we reviewed some evidence which suggested that in spite of the goals of the liturgical reformers following the Second Vatican Council, the reality in terms of liturgical praxis in the parishes is very patchy, with only limited progress being made towards the participating 'People of God' model and some resistance, both lay and clerical, to the opportunities and demands of the new liturgies. In the sections which follow we will attempt to review and evaluate the extent to which community-building goals are reflected in the caring concerns of parishes and in the provision of social support for those in need. We will also address the charge that far from socialising or forming parishioners for missionary tasks in the everyday world of work or neighbourhood, there is a tendency for the parish to consume greedily all the spare energies of its active and committed members through its excessive demands.

SENSE OF COMMUNITY

When they were asked how sorry they would be to leave their parish if they had to move to another part of the country, two-fifths of English Catholics who were Mass attenders replied that they would be very

77

sorry. Around one-third of these gave reasons which stressed their local roots or the proximity of relatives or friends, while a further one-quarter mentioned that they liked the area or the priest or the friendliness of the parish. On the other hand the prevalence of mobility was reflected in the response of over one-fifth who said they liked change or could adapt to a new area if necessary.

In its critical self-examination in preparation for the Synod on the Laity, the parish of St Lawrence asked: 'can our parishes be called communities when the tradition of non-participation and private worship of our God (albeit publicly) remains largely unchanged since Vatican II?'. While 70 per cent responded that their parish was 'quite a good community', 'only one in three parishioners feel the clergy trust them'. A general view was that lay people were 'not being encouraged to use our gifts for the building up of the community . . . because priests want to keep us submissive to them and not equal partners' (1987: 11–13).

In the Notre Dame parish study, 'parishioners generally placed their parish somewhere between *some* feeling of community and a *strong* feeling of community' (Leege, 1987a: 4). Interestingly, there were no differences in the ratings of the subjective sense of community between priests, paid staff, volunteer leaders, and parishioners. It was also reported that in general 'parishes make their own destinies'. Thus size, unexpectedly, did not appear to be an unduly constraining variable. On the other hand, with the exception of French parishes in the United States study, ethnic homogeneity was generally found to be conducive to a sense of community. Some of the other findings from this research, which is probably the most comprehensive comparative study on parishes so far undertaken, are of considerable interest. Not surprisingly, a parish's subjective sense of community is strongly related to the sense of attachment to the parish and to measures of how sorry its parishioners would be if they had to move to another area. But

> the extent to which the parish meets parishioners' social needs is a far more important component of sense of community than is the extent to which it meets their spiritual needs . . . [A] parish may be *spiritually* satisfying and yet not have a strong sense of community but a parish could not have a strong sense of community without being spiritually satisfying.
>
> (Leege, 1987a: 6)

The importance of interaction with the priest is emphasised since the statistical analyses showed that

> frequency of conversations with the pastor is a much more important component of sense of community than are the number of close friends who are fellow parishioners . . . simple conversations that express empathy, supportiveness, courtesy, and compassion affect parishioners.
>
> (1987a: 6–7)

This is a particularly interesting finding because the general experience, in Britain at any rate, would be that there has been a substantial and almost universal decline in the visiting of parishioners in their homes by priests in recent decades. In retrospect, the six-weekly cycle of visiting reported by Ward (1965: 58) was a unique characteristic of some parishes in Liverpool in the early post-war years but it would be quite misleading to regard it as typical of the parish situation in contemporary Britain. In the national survey English Catholics rated their priests rather poorly on this aspect of their work. One consequence of low levels of parish visiting is likely to be that priests do not have such a high profile in the family life of their parishioners or the opportunities to cultivate the close friendships which are necessary for a meaningful sense of community to develop.

A number of other findings from the Notre Dame study are relevant here. First of all it is suggested that the higher sense of community in the larger urban and suburban parishes might be due to their greater tendency to celebrate their main Masses in the post-Vatican style 'with greater awareness of the community of God's people and with greater expectations for participation' and because they offer a wider range of ministries and programmes than smaller parishes (Leege, 1987a: 7). Second, a sense of attachment to a parish is most strongly related to 'opportunities for participation and service coupled especially to caring pastors (priests) and parishioners' (Leege, 1987a: 9). Third, whereas parishes with a low sense of community are particularly concerned about the past, 'parishes with a high sense of community generally worry about the Church of the future and why some people don't participate *more* . . .' Strikingly,

> parishes with the most sense of community have twice as many staff and nearly twice as many lay volunteers in their leadership structures as the . . . parishes with the least sense of community.

. . . Many of the parishes with the least sense of community have simply not found a way to get staff and laity involved in parish leadership.

(Leege, 1987a: 12–13)

In another analysis Leege has explored the relationship between the concept of community and the nature of the social boundaries which Catholics erect around themselves. Thus 'the "outsider" in a restrictive community may feel perpetually unwelcome, or the "insider" in an inclusive community may draw the conclusion that the Church is very tolerant of human foibles' (1988: 1). The results of his surveys of 2,667 parishioners in the subsample of thirty-six parishes showed that Catholics in the United States tended to apply the strictest definitions on who is a true Catholic on sexual matters, such as abortion and homosexuality, and were much more tolerant of institutional deviance such as marrying outside the Church or infrequent Mass attendance. There is a close relationship between the sense of community in a parish and the nature of the boundaries differentiating it from others:

> The parishes that express a stronger sense of community are likely to have parishioners who draw boundaries less strict on premarital cohabitation, marriage outside the Church, abortion, homosexuality, and regular Mass attendance. To a lesser extent they are also not so strict about people who commit major crimes, but *are* more concerned about Catholics who oppose desegregation. . . . People in parishes where a weaker sense of community is prevalent are more judgmental, particularly on the human sexuality issues, Mass attendance, and marriage outside the Church. Among them, however, there is little relationship between sense of community and judgments about Catholics who oppose nuclear disarmament or commit minor crimes.

(Leege, 1988: 8)

SOCIAL SUPPORT AND MUTUAL AID

In the days of the fortress Church the Catholic parish tenaciously defended the interests of the poor migrant groups as they struggled to adapt to a new and often hostile environment, frequently under the leadership of co-cultural priests, whether in Britain or the United States or Australia. Parish-based caring often took the form of ethnic minority mobilisation. In the less-harsh social and economic environment of the post-war world such basic support is not so obviously needed though the economic transformations since the 1970s have raised again the social evils of mass unemployment, urban deprivation and racism. In these new conditions the parish is having to rediscover its mission of healing and caring. Thus a recent pamphlet, which aimed to encourage the development of lay ministries at the parish level, identified a number of the social and personal problems which it argued ought to be addressed by local parishes facing the real needs of their parishioners.

> Our society has many deep problems, such as rootlessness, loneliness, marriage break-down, unemployment and impersonality, and this is the very ground where the seed of the gospel must be sown. The laity should be doing much of the sowing . . .
>
> (Comerford and Dodd, 1982: 4)

Problems particularly identified included those arising from high levels of mobility and the loss of close family ties and support, the consequences of urban redevelopment, shift work and 'factors destructive of a sense of community', a general dehumanising tendency, increasing stress, loneliness and meaninglessness. In every parish there are people living under the tensions of marital breakdown, facing agonising choices over abortion, coping with handicapped relatives or unexpected bereavement, the mentally and physically sick, and the dying.

It is chastening, therefore, to note the omission of 'church' from the category of those contributing to the neighbouring schemes studied by Philip Abrams 'because they were so rarely mentioned by respondents' (quoted in Willmott, 1986: 69). Willmott observes that this judgement needs to be qualified in that 'churches . . . can be useful sources of personal relationships that develop and become supportive'. He provides a useful overview of the different senses of community and the different forms of help which relatives, friends, neighbours (or parishioners) might provide for those in need. Where the church or parish can be seen to be a 'densely woven world of kin, neighbours, friends and co-workers, highly localised and strongly caring', characterised by high levels of interaction with others and a strong sense of identity, it can be regarded as a local interest 'community of attachment' to both place and people (1986: 83–5, 97–8). On the other hand, the voluntary character of local attachment is indicated by Janowitz's term (1967) 'community of limited liability'.

Reviewing recent literature on the social policy implications of promoting and sustaining 'informal care', Willmott distinguishes intermittent and sustaining (a) personal or intimate 'tending' care such as washing or bathing or feeding an infirm person, (b) domestic care such as cooking and cleaning, (c) auxiliary care such as shopping or offering transport, and (d) social support, including talking and listening, advice, informal counselling and emotional support (1986: 105). This is a useful classification for the evaluation of caring behaviour, as opposed to rhetoric, in parishes but it seems that there is very little in the way of empirical evidence either in Britain or the United States to illuminate and quantify the extent of community-like interaction and informal care for both its own members and those of people in need in the same locality and indeed in the wider society. Our concern here is solely with parish-based care provision and not with the long-standing involvement of Catholic institutions in child-care work, adoptions and fostering, hospitals and the more recent emergence of the hospice movement.

Tentatively it is suggested that personal and domestic care, where provided, are substantial given by close family members, particularly daughters, and there is very little provision of these types of care by parishioners. Some auxiliary care may be offered on either an intermittent and less frequently a sustained basis, particularly for the elderly and long-time housebound. This might, in a post-Vatican parish which has a well-developed sense of the value of lay ministries, be linked to the regular distribution of Communion by a team of special ministers. Occasionally senior children from a local secondary school will be involved in intermittent help, particularly shopping for the housebound. Parishioner care, where it is at all developed, is most likely to be found in the provision of social support. It may be that the charismatic movement was an important influence in the development of a heightened awareness of the ministries of healing and listening which are of particular importance for the bereaved or dying. In areas of widespread local hardship, for example in areas of mass unemployment resulting from the economic transformations of the 1970s and 1980s, some parishes might have developed self-help schemes. But there seems little doubt that the situation is generally patchy and underdeveloped so that Philip Abrams' observation about the lack of salience of the church or parish in the provision of care is likely to be substantially correct.

While we have no reliable survey data to indicate the general picture of parish-based care and support, it is possible to offer some sketches of the range and type of provision. In some parishes established Catholic organisations may offer a limited amount of social support. Three examples illustrate this. An article in the magazine of a parish south of London referred to the work of the Legion of Mary:

> the members do what lies in their scope. They visit the sick and elderly in their homes or the local hospitals. They recite the Rosary daily in Church. They take patients from their wards, to Mass in the hospital Chapel. They read to the blind. They run the Church repository.
>
> (*St Joseph's Parish Magazine*, Epsom, Summer 1984: 8)

Secondly, an article in a northern parish's silver jubilee magazine described the work of another traditional organisation, the St Vincent de Paul Society:

> The majority of the people we visit are elderly and their greatest need is for company and a sympathetic ear so we try, if possible, to visit them on a weekly basis. During the year three Social Evenings are held. . . . These are quite simple functions but for many of the people we visit they are the only social occasions they attend. Transport, entertainment and refreshments are provided. . . . Mass is said at noon on the second Sunday of each month and transport is provided for those unable to make the journey themselves. . . . [The local hospital] is also visited regularly and two or three of the patients who are well enough are brought to our social evenings.
>
> (St Julie, Eccleston, *Parish Silver Jubilee: 1961–1986*, pp. 27–8)

A retired senior executive described how in work with the SVP he

> found uncomplicated companionship and a privileged entree to a different world of problem families, alcoholics, the mentally ill and other social rejects, as well as any number of eccentrics, spongers and confidence tricksters. They all provide a valuable perspective and contrast to my own life style and a weekly meditation on the theme 'Who is my neighbour?'
>
> (McEvoy, 1987: 261)

In his account of developments in his parish in the outer-London commuter belt, Fr O'Sullivan noted twenty-eight different parish groups and organisations listed in the 1978 parish directory (O'Sullivan, 1979: 49–52). All of these would have provided opportunities for social interaction and support for the participants. Some would have provided much-needed friendship, interaction and support for those who would otherwise have been isolated or strained. Thus the Under-Five Club might provide the only available relief for an over-burdened mother of young children while the regular coffee morning for retired people may well offer them the only sustained social contact they have. Members of an active Care group visit the sick, the elderly, and the housebound and do odd jobs for them. A particular aspect of this work has been the care of the dying. The emergence of the Care team seemed to expose an unexpected number of cancer victims and led to the development of a very special form of ministry to them and their families. Since many of the Care team are also special ministers, they also take Communion to the sick and pray with them. While many of the older people originally had found the fact that lay people were taking them Communion threatening or distasteful, they soon adapted to this change in pastoral practice and now see it as evidence of the support and concern of the parish.

Other volunteers visit the geriatric wards in the local hospitals every week to play bingo with the inmates. More recently, other volunteers have provided welcome tea and other services at a local prison on a regular basis. The parish was divided up into distinct neighbourhoods and house groups and a number of these meet monthly or more often for prayer, discussion and sharing and sometimes, especially in crisis situations, have provided considerable if intermittent social and emotional support. Regular visits to newcomers in the parish or to those in need were planned. More recently regular meetings of the divorced and separated in the parish have recognised a growing need. A telephone prayer line of about fifty parishioners commits the members to pray immediately for those in crisis situations or special need.

A number of testimonies to the value of informal support given them by parishioners have recently been published in a series on 'The Everyday Lives of Lay Catholics'. One of the most moving is that of a young mother who experienced both a stillborn baby and a miscarriage within a few years. After her baby had been stillborn she described how quite a lot of ordinary parishioners came up to me to say they were sorry, which I found impressive and supportive. I did feel comfortable being part of a warm community. . . . What you need is someone to talk to . . . who is willing just to sit and listen . . . I think the trouble with Catholics is that they are so low-key; there is all this concern but they almost hide their lights under a bushel.

(Burns, 1988: 85–7)

Three single mothers also described their struggles to cope with unexpected pregnancy and having the baby despite opposition, child-rearing and coping with tiredness, money problems and loneliness, the need for social support, and the difficulties of trying to live as a Christian. While one, previously an Anglican, initially found the Catholic parish unwelcoming and intimidating, she now finds support through small-group prayer. The other two have been given considerable support and help from their parish-based One-Parent Groups which have been promoted by Family and Social Action (FSA). These have arranged outings, picnics, holidays, Christmas parties, and, in one case, a pilgrimage with a sick parent to Lourdes, but most importantly, opportunities to chat:

People listen to you when you feel absolutely desperate and say you just can't get away and your child drives you mad. You just talk; people understand and listen. . . . It's all perfectly natural and you just talk it out and feel a lot better after saying it.

(Kelly *et al.*, 1988)

Reference should also be made to the attempts to provide support at the parish level for young couples in the early years of marriage. Since research has indicated that the dangers of marital breakdown are particularly acute at this stage (Dominion, 1968: 19), a group of priests from several parishes in the South of England attempted to devise a range of parish-based schemes for providing support for newly married couples. The initiator of the scheme described the aims as

trying to promote useful occasions of meeting for couples in the early years of marriage. Isolation and loneliness were seen as crippling conditions, especially for young wives and mothers. The aim was to use some recurring occasions to enable networks of friendships to develop.

(O'Leary, 1987: 190)

The schemes were essentially parish-priest initiated and sustained and included marriage preparation for engaged couples, welcome to newcomers (especially important where there are high rates of mobility into and out from the parish associated with the state of the local labour and housing markets), pre-baptism meetings, parish involvement with baptisms and first communion preparation, Mothers and Toddlers groups, pre-school play groups, and childrens' Liturgies of the Word (O'Leary, 1987; Gibson and Hornsby-Smith, 1987). It remains to be seen to what extent such schemes are able to provide the levels of sustained social support necessary to enable young couples to adjust satisfactorily and cope with the inevitable stresses of job establishment and maintenance and the attainment of adequate housing in our contemporary society.

It might be useful at this point to refer briefly to some of the findings from the Notre Dame study of parishes in the United States. A total of 2,667 parishioners in the subsample of thirty-six parishes was asked whether they would turn to parish clergy or staff, friends, or outside professionals for help in the case of fifteen different problems ranging from the religious education of their children, counselling at a time of sickness or bereavement, marital problems to unemployment. They were also asked whether they would turn to the parish clergy or staff if help were offered and an 'opportunity gap' between the available and potential help levels was calculated for each problem. Some of the conclusions from this research are relevant to our present discussion about actual and potential social support at the parish level:

> the parish is a place for religious nurture, but it is or could be much more. . . . First, the opportunity gap is substantial for many parish services relating to severe family and personal problems. Secondly, younger Catholics of higher educational and income attainments, who are currently raising their families, have moved away from the parish and its staff as a central point of orientation for many of life's problems. Friends and professionals are the people to whom they would turn, not to parish staff . . . our data attest that the young educated parents are less attuned to seeking help in the parish, even on traditional spiritual matters. Whether the parish will be seen as the institution that should and can respond remains one of the great challenges to Catholic leaders into the 21st century.
>
> (Leege, 1986a: 5–6)

Lay people involved in the caring ministries at the parish level have often found such reflections as those of Jean Vanier in *Community and Growth* (1979) helpful to them. Vanier, who founded l'Arch, a community with people who are mentally handicapped, in 1964, offers an ideology which stresses the two elements of interpersonal relationships and a sense of belonging which is immensely attractive. Nevertheless he insists that a number of conditions have to be met if these are to grow. Among these are unity in the pursuit of its Charter, mutual trust, the faithful use of gifts and talents, especially the gift of the availability of self for service, and the recognition of interdependence, awareness especially of God's covenant with the poor, and a willingness to leave previous people and values in making a commitment to new people and values. For Vanier,

> true community implies a way of life, a way of living and seeing reality; it implies above all fidelity in the daily round. And this is made up of simple things. . . . A community is only being created when its members accept that they are not going to achieve great things, that they are not going to be heroes, but simply live each day with new hope . . . A growing community must integrate three elements: a life of silent prayer, a life of service and above all of listening to the poor. . . . Opening to God in adoration and opening to the poor in welcome and service are the two poles of a community's growth'.
>
> (1979: 68, 96–7)

This leads him to contrast Christian communities whose members believe in slow growth towards a vision of a more just society, from 'Marxist militants' more concerned with the immediate struggle against injustice. While Vanier recognises that 'there is a whole political dimension to Christian communities', he believes the way ahead is through the creation of communities which act as 'the yeast in the dough of society' so that 'if this spirit of community really spreads, structures will change' (1979: 228–30). Vanier stresses the prophetic aspect of the Christian community which

> will always be running against the tide of society, with its individualistic values of wealth and comfort and resulting rejection of the people who get in the way of these . . . a Christian community will always be a stumbling block, a question mark and a source of unease for society.
>
> (1979: 129)

For the sociologist the extent to which this ideology is in fact conducive to meeting the needs of the poor, rather than providing a legitimation for the neglect of the structural injustices which persist in society and to which some social or political response is necessary, is an empirical issue. For the moment it is tentatively hypothesised that the usual practices of 'caring' at the parish level, generally intermittent rather than sustained, and legitimated by ideologies of 'community' which shrink from the consideration of structural causes which require socially organised responses, provide little more than the amelioration of hurts experienced by parishioners in need in ways which satisfy the feelings of self-worth of the carers rather more than they find solutions to the underlying social problems.

The evaluation of the general level of parish social support mechanisms is difficult in the absence of detailed information or research. Clearly some parishes do show some concern and put their communitarian ideology into practice in tangible ways, especially intermittent social support. It is quite clear, however, that nowhere does the parish provision approximate to the early Church model outlined in the Acts of the Apostles. Perhaps it is quite unrealistic to expect that model to have relevance in modern conditions of high rates of mobility and the differentiation of work from home and family, job allocation to individuals on the basis of achievement rather than ascriptive criteria, and so on. The best that the modern parish seems capable of achieving is the amelioration of the consequences of isolation and alienation which are often the dominant characteristics of modern, urban, industrial society. Given the multiplicity of roles performed by many active Catholics, the voluntary support offered by the few parishioners may border on the heroic but there is no convincing evidence that the parish as an institution, or the parishioners who make up its membership, do or have the capacity to provide substantially more than a token witness to the Christian concept of social support. As Fr Terence Tanner has suggested:

The Church presents a rich face and although it works amongst the poor, it rarely gets its hands really dirty. There is a large population made up of the . . . lowest of the low . . . people like meth-drinkers and elderly vagrants and junkies and alkies and so on. It is very rare that the Church is seen caring about them and working for them but the Church is seen at civic receptions and the like.

(Tanner, 1980: 168)

THE 'GREEDY' PARISH

It is fifteen years since Michael Winter first drew attention to the conflict between 'mission' and 'maintenance' in his critique of existing pastoral structures, including parishes. Emphatically he insisted that the traditional parish is too large and that 'if people do not know one another they cannot be called a community' (1973: 58). More recently he has argued that it also tends to take up the energies of many core members in maintenance activities (1985: 139). Similarly, another advocate of basic communities has argued that

> a network of basic communities can give the Church the oppor-
> tunity to break free from preoccupation with the parish system, at
> present consuming nearly all its institutional energies, into a
> society now shaped as much, if not more, by community of interest
> as community of place.

> (Clark, 1977: 226)

Both critics of the contemporary parish point to the problem of the 'greedy' parish which consumes all the available time and energies of its active members so that they have no reserves left for the tasks of mission or the pursuit of social justice through struggles in the wider society to transform unsatisfactory social structures. Occasionally reference is made to a broken marriage where 'working for the Church' has resulted in domestic neglect. A justice and peace activist described a typical situation:

> the church roof needs repairing and for the past few months every-
> body has been putting their money into that. We've had an auction
> and a sponsored swim. I've given money but I haven't been
> involved at all. On one level I feel slightly guilty; it's my church
> and I should be helping. But on the other hand I feel that if we put
> all our energy into maintaining the church and fund-raising,
> there's no energy left for anything else, and that's not really what
> it's all about. That's another problem with the Catholic Church;
> we're forever trying to raise money to keep things going. I think
> the reason why I feel guilty is because I mind what people think:
> 'where was so-and-so when we had this and that?' People say: 'I've
> worked my fingers to the bone; why weren't they doing it as well?
> And then she comes along and starts preaching about justice and
> peace!'

> (Burns, 1988: 87)

The concern with plant and buildings has been illustrated in particular in the case of a parish in the London commuter belt which currently plans to build a new parish centre including a new church to seat 400 people but able to accommodate an additional 200 on special occasions, a First School for 100 children and a Nursery School for forty children, a parish hall with rooms for business, social, and special events, and a presbytery, car park, and accommodation for a caretaker for the whole complex. The estimated cost of the project in 1987 was £3.2 million of which £2.2 million was to be realised through the sale of existing properties and land. The likelihood is that in a parish with under one thousand Mass attenders a huge amount of parishioner resources of time and energy are likely to be consumed over the next few years in raising about £1 million.

In the 1978 national survey of English Catholics it was reported that around one in eight of all Catholics or nearly one-fifth of those associated with a parish were members of parish organisations. Three-fifths of these belonged to at least one other kind of organisation (Hornsby-Smith and Lee, 1979: 45–51, 188–91).This highlights the problems which arise for the activist core members of a parish. For example, a member of a parish council meeting monthly might also be a parish representative on several other committees such as the Diocesan Pastoral Council, an ecumenical liaison committee for the area, and one or more of the parish sub-committees responsible for liturgy or the co-ordination of care schemes or programmes of renewal in the parish. He or she might also be concerned to promote links with a parish in another area or with a mission parish in a Third World country. Apart from such representative roles, the activist might also be on the regular parish rotas as a steward at Sunday Mass, a reader for the Liturgy of the Word, and a special minister of Holy Communion involved also in visiting the sick. For such people the parish can indeed consume all their time and energies and leave little space for involvement in professional or political activities.

Relevant to this interpretation are the findings from the Notre Dame study of parishes. Thus David Leege notes:

Leaders are active not only in a wide range of parish organisations but are joiners in the outside community. The average volunteer leader belongs to about twice as many extra-parish organisations as the ordinary parishioner, and has more organisational involvements than either the pastor (priest) or the paid staff. . . . The volunteers have more family responsibilities, more community involvements — and more parish involvements than anyone else. . . . One-third of the volunteer leaders hold two or more major organisational responsibilities simultaneously.

(1986b: 5)

Perhaps more speculatively he offers the view which is consistent with other research on community volunteers that 'the principal reason people volunteer is that they need to be needed'. The testing of this psychological hypothesis requires the collection of data which are not currently available, at least in Britain.

Finally, it is a paradoxical result of the reforms of the Second Vatican Council that lay energies appear to have been directed more towards the participation of the laity within the Church than towards improved formation of lay people for their special task of transforming the institutions of employment and politics the better to serve the imperatives of justice and loving service. This fear was well articulated in the 1977 Chicago Declaration of Christian Concern (Barta, 1980: 19–27) and reiterated by some laity in the United States in their preparation for the 1987 Synod on the Laity:

The danger of increased lay involvement in Church ministry is a kind of 'paraclericalisation'. If the primacy of their daily vocation in and to the world is not recognised, lay people can easily become overly concerned about the internal functioning of the Church in preparation and reflection. They can also overemphasise the heroic or prophetic forms of ministry and social justice efforts organised under formal Church auspices, to the neglect of their ordinary work on the job, with the family and in the nieghbourhood.

(Droel and Pierce, 1987: 32)

The conclusion towards which the data, however limited in scope and comprehensiveness, lead us is that generally parishes function, especially for their core activists, in ways which can best be described as 'greedy institutions' (Coser, 1974). They tend to demand exclusive and undivided loyalty and commitment from these core members and seek to erect symbolic boundaries against all other forms of activity by devaluing them and asserting the pre-eminence of the religious and social activities focused around the parish and as a key to the proper living of a dedicated Christian life and ultimately to salvation. To the

extent that parishes do in fact tend to consume all the available discretionary time and energies of their members and so weaken their
ties with competing people and organisations, they can be said to
make claims as greedy institutions. While these claims may only be
realised in the case of a minority of parishioners, nevertheless these
parishioners will inevitably be the most central to the organisation
and most influential in determining its ethos.

In terms of Etzioni's concepts of scope and pervasiveness (1961:
160–74), the greedy parish aims both to maximise the scope or the
number of activities jointly pursued by members, and the pervasiveness or the number of activities for which it sets norms. However,
whereas the pre-Vatican parish aimed to maximise the number of
functions it performed, such as educational, entertainment and sometimes welfare functions as well as religious functions, with post-war
affluence and the growth of mass leisure opportunities and universal
television, and the emergence of the Welfare State provisions and
extra-parochial secondary schools, many of these functions have been
lost. On the other hand the conciliar stress on the full participation of
the laity in the life of the Church has led to the involvement of lay
people in a whole new set of roles in the institutional life of the
Church itself. Thus while the nature of the scope and pervasiveness
may have changed in recent decades, the parish continues to be
greedy in its demands for the total commitment of its members in
terms of both their time and energy resources. The criticisms of the
Chicago group seem to focus on the changing nature of the pervasiveness in the post-conciliar period. Whereas in pre-Vatican times some
attention was paid to the formation of 'lay apostles', thus aiming to
increase the pervasiveness of Catholic norms in the wider society and
especially in the realms of employment and politics, the critics claim
that in the post-conciliar period this has been neglected in favour of
parochial concerns with institutional participation.

CONCLUSIONS

In this chapter we have noted the ambiguous and problematic nature
of the concept of 'community' (Fraser, 1987) and have addressed the
issue of the extent to which the Catholic parish towards the end of the
twentieth century can sociologically be regarded to be a community
in terms of three key variables: shared beliefs and values, frequency
of interaction, and the provision of reciprocal social support and

mutual aid. In spite of attempts to promote community-like characteristics, the empirical evidence indicates in general considerable
variations in the beliefs and values of parishioners (Hornsby-Smith,
1987: 47–66); that parishes are too large to provide meaningful interaction for more than a small minority of parishioners (Winter, 1973;
1985); and that relatively little, and then only intermittent, social
support is provided to members in need. The quest for sociological
community at the parish level in modern, mobile, industrial, and
urban societies seems doomed to failure. To that extent the critics of
parishes and advocates of small basic Christian communities are
correct in their analysis. As Denys Turner has pointed out, at the
National Pastoral Congress

> quite unrealistic demands were made upon the parish to be, simul-
> taneously, a liturgical community capable of satisfying the varied
> liturgical tastes of all its members, a community capable of trans-
> cending the class and racial cleavages of society, a community
> which takes up the burdens of unemployment, handicap, loneliness
> and sickness of its members.
>
> (1983: 3)

Criticising 'merely ecclesial communitarianism' in the 'self-centred
parish' with its 'abstract gestures' and 'posturing' in its bidding
prayers, he rather advocates the 'subversive' search for 'justice in the
world through . . . seeking to make society with those whom the
world rejects', that is by having a bias in favour of an 'option for the
poor'. For Dobbelaere and Billiet, too, the lack of concern for social
justice in the Church reflects the predominance of a *Gemeinschaft*-
ideology rather than a *Gesellschaft*-ideology (1976: 257). Gannon
expresses a related point when he notes that

> the parish faces the often conflicting choice of deepening the
> religious commitment of individual members or becoming more
> absorbed into the aggregated organisational life of the larger
> metropolis.
>
> (1978: 299)

Second, it has also been suggested in this chapter that the Catholic
parish typically functions as a greedy institution, aiming to consume
all the discretionary time and energy resources of its members. In the
post-Vatican parish the nature of pervasiveness has shifted and critics
have convincingly argued that it has tended to stress the extension of

lay roles within the institutional Church rather than concerned itself with increasing the pervasiveness of Christian witness in the wider society.

Having reviewed the nature of parish 'community' in general terms, we will proceed in the next chapter to consider the specific area of parish liturgies which aim both to celebrate and to develop and sustain community.

Chapter Five

PARISH LITURGIES

INTRODUCTION

The liturgy of a parish is perhaps the most obvious indicator of the extent to which it manifests community-like characteristics. Attendance at a Sunday Mass gives an immediate impression of the nature of the authority-style of the priest, the extent to which he actively promotes lay participation, the warmth of social relationships between parishioners, and the openness of the welcome given to strangers. In this chapter we will consider variations in contemporary parish liturgies and how these might be interpreted using the ideal-types of pre- and post-Vatican parishes discussed in Chapter 2.

The liturgy is the public, formal worship of the Church and 'consists in the celebration of the Eucharist and other sacraments, together with the Divine Office and certain other ceremonies' (McCabe, 1985: 34). In the Vatican Council's Constitution *Sacrosanctum Concilium* the liturgy was regarded as 'the outstanding means by which the faithful can express in their lives, and manifest to others, the mystery of Christ and the real nature of the Church' (s.2 in Abbott, 1966: 137). It is considered to be an exercise of the priestly office of Jesus Christ (s.7 in 1966: 141) and

> the summit toward which the activity of the Church is directed; at the same time it is the foundation from which all her power flows. For the goal of apostolic works is that all who are made sons of God by faith and baptism should come together to praise God in the midst of His Church, to take part in her sacrifice, and to eat the Lord's supper.
>
> (s.10 in 1966: 142)

95

The liturgy, however, does not exhaust the entire activity of the Church and the Christian's spiritual life is 'not confined to participation in the liturgy' but is likely to include both local popular devotions and forms of private prayer (ss.9, 12–13 in Abbott, 1966: 142–3). In Lenski's terms participation in the liturgy would be a measure of associational involvement while devotionalism would measure the importance of private or personal prayer (1963: 23, 25).

We are concerned here only to identify some aspects of change in parish liturgies, chiefly in the celebration of the Eucharist, rather than with aspects of personal spirituality. In Figure 2.1 we postulated a contrast in terms of liturgical worship between pre-Vatican and post-Vatican parishes. Thus in the former there would be a strong element of awe and mystery in the transcendent presence of God who would be approached only through the mediation of the 'sacred' person of the priest. Social distance would be maintained both physically and symbolically by such means as altar rails and with the priest facing the altar and with his back to the congregation. The ritual of the Tridentine Mass was uniform in all parishes and there were few variations beyond those recognised between 'low', 'sung', and 'high' Masses and the distinctness of the priests' enunciation of the sacred words. Mass was said in an esoteric language, Latin, which largely served to separate the 'sacred' priesthood from the subordinate laity and to emphasise the special expertise and status of the clergy. In the pre-Vatican liturgy the emphasis was on the objectivity of the sacramental system (Leslie, 1986: 15).

In contrast, the post-Vatican parish would stress the active participation of lay people in the Eucharistic celebration, with lay readers for the Liturgy of the Word, offertory processions from the people, the exchange of a sign of peace, and special ministers for the distribution of Communion. Their relationship to God is direct with the priest presiding over the worship of the gathered local community, using the everyday language of the people and their own bidding prayers of petition. A pluriformity of liturgies reflects the plurality of people's needs and cultures and allows for the spontaneous and creative expression of worship. The priest faces the people gathered round the one table and there are no physical or symbolic barriers between them.

As we noted above, only half of English Catholics in 1978 admitted to having heard about the Vatican Council nearly a decade and a half after its concluding session. This lent support to the view that

Table 5.1   Approval of recent changes in the liturgy (%)

	England and Wales		USA
Recent change	NPC delegates (1983)	All Caths (1978)	All Caths (1974)
1 Saying the Mass in English instead of Latin	90	62	82
2 Folk (guitar) music during Mass	76	54	64
3 Lay people distributing Communion at Mass	72	26	45
4 The 'handshake of peace' at Mass	n/a	60	77
5 Reducing the number of things like devotions, novenas, and benedictions	22	35	37
6 Receiving Communion under both kinds (the appearance of both bread and wine) at Mass	84	52	n/a
7 Non-Catholics receiving Communion at Roman Catholic services	30	43	n/a

Sources: Hornsby-Smith and Lee, 1979: 211; Hornsby-Smith and Cordingley, 1983: 44; McCready, 1975: 11.

Catholics evaluated recent changes in the Church at the experiential level and that there was little awareness of any ideological implications in the conciliar teaching. Attitudes to recent liturgical changes (Table 5.1) both in England and Wales and in the United States indicated a fair measure of support, in particular for the saying of the Mass in English and for the 'handshake of peace'. Catholics also largely approved of folk (or guitar) Masses and receiving Communion under both kinds. There was surprisingly strong support for non-Catholics receiving Communion at Mass (though this is not officially permitted) but lay people were more equally divided in their response to the decline of more traditional devotions. Some disquiet at the reduction of status differences between priests and lay people is indicated in the relatively low support for lay special ministers of Communion. In general there were strong age gradients in the responses with older Catholics being much less enthusiastic about the changes. The data from the survey of activist delegates to the National Pastoral Congress demonstrates their relative progressiveness when compared to Catholics generally (Hornsby-Smith *et al.*, 1987).

Overall the results are similar among Catholics in the United States though it seems clear that English Catholics lag some way behind in terms of their acceptance of the recent liturgical changes. The Notre Dame study of parish life has provided some important data relating to the celebration of liturgies in the United States in the early 1980s. Of particular interest are the results of the intensive observations of seventy Masses in a sample of thirty-six non-Hispanic parishes (Searle and Leege, 1985a, 1985b). Given earlier findings that Catholics defined their religious beliefs in individualistic rather than communitarian terms, the researchers considered it hardly surprising that the congregations they observed 'seldom appeared to act as a *gathered* assembly' (1985a: 3). In the post-conciliar period there has been a decline of traditional ritual forms.

> The legalism which used to protect the Mass to some extent from idiosyncratic alterations seems largely to have waned. In its place enthusiasm and good-will have to substitute for a sense of the rite. As a result, important elements of the Mass structure are sometimes omitted or distorted by misunderstanding. Often the freedom given to the local community to plan and adapt the liturgy results in poor or altogether inappropriate selections of prayers, readings, and especially music.
>
> (1985a: 4)

The researchers argue (in my view correctly) against a form of liturgical determinism. Rather

> while the liturgy provides an important focus for a parish community's sense of identity, that identity cannot be provided by the liturgy alone. . . . Liturgy often mirrors what is happening in the parish community. . . . Generally parishes where the people are least satisfied with their liturgies are ones where the conciliar goals are not evident in the celebration.
>
> (1985b: 4–5)

Finally, as is apparent also in Britain, changes of parish priest (pastor), where these involve radical shifts of leadership style and pastoral policy in such matters as lay participation and liturgical emphasis, are likely to lead to considerable frustration and decline in morale on the part of parishioners.

The early results from the Notre Dame study suggest, therefore, that while there has in general been a significant shift away from the ritualistic Latin rite of the pre-Vatican parish, there now exists a much wider spectrum of liturgies both between parishes and within them in terms of variations in the liturgical styles at Masses celebrated at different times from the Saturday evenings to the Sundays.

While we do not have comparable data for England and Wales, there is some evidence to indicate that similar variations in liturgical styles and their attendant ideological underpinnings can be found. This will be illustrated below by comparing the liturgies in a traditional parish in the north midlands with a progressive parish in the south-east.

LITURGY IN A TRADITIONAL PARISH

In looking at parish liturgies it is argued that attention must be paid to both structural constraints (the physical layout of the church and the normatively prescribed liturgical routines which are enforced by the presiding priest) and the consciousness of the worshippers who interpret, modify, and attribute meanings to those routines. John Leslie, whose study of a parish in the north midlands of England is drawn on here, has stressed that

> worshippers are no social dopes driven either by irresistible social forces or structures of the unconscious mind to employ the images, symbols and metaphors of the rite in a particular way.
>
> (Leslie, 1986: 183)

Leslie goes on to point out the consequences of the traditional belief that the sacraments had an effect in themselves.

> They could not, therefore, be vitiated by unworthy ministers or by the feelings, attitudes and dispositions of those present. Against this background sacramental reality could be easily established by the validity of the sacramental rite, that is by the observance of the appropriate regulations in canon law. On the other hand sacramental grace was an individual and private matter. It depended on the individual recipient's disposition. Naturally there was a great deal of uncertainty about the extent to which supernatural help, that is grace, had effected any change in individual lives. The validity of the sacrament, therefore, was unaffected by a lack of evidence of its having borne fruit. The practical effect of this theological orientation was to de-emphasise the participation of the laity and to define sacramental efficacy as largely the accomplishment of the priestly minister. There was also a tendency to separate the worshipper's ritual action from his/her involvement in the world outside.
>
> (1986: 186)

99

These considerations are apparent in Leslie's account of the 'liturgical praxis' in an English north midlands parish in the early 1980s. Important recusant roots in 'Saxonshire' were preserved as a result of its remoteness from pre-industrial communications routes before the present Gothic parish church was built in the middle of the nineteenth century. Leslie found close ties of marriage and kinship among several of the key lay activists in the parish which served both to reflect and to reinforce the stability of the parish and to maintain the traditional relationships of social distance between the priest and lay people. The physical structure of the church is also a constraining factor:

There is a very clear and obvious separation of the sanctuary and choir areas from the nave of the church. Stone steps and roodscreen divided the one from the other. Two side chapels with altars and statuary were placed in the 'lay' part of the building. . . . Due to alterations carried out in the early 1970s the roodscreen no longer interrupts the view of the choir and high altar. The pulpit, too, has been removed and a modern stone altar with its reading desk has been placed in the choir area. The choir at the 10.30 a.m. Sunday Mass . . . have continued to occupy the loft, which they share with the organ at the west end of the nave . . . the present arrangement has the effect of separating the choir from the congregation.

(Leslie, 1986: 269)

Leslie describes how it is possible for 'obedient' traditionalists to conform to the letter of the law in conformity to the post-Vatican liturgical norms while in practice undermining the spirit of the reforms.

In this North Midlands parish, Mass is said with the priest facing the people and it is in English, apart from the Latin Credo, Gloria, Sanctus and Benedictus, which are sometimes sung at the principal Sunday Mass, but few of the options for encouraging lay participation and involvement have been taken up. Prayers are read at speed and the congregation does not answer the responses with any degree of enthusiasm and is not encouraged to do so. Bidding prayers, although usually read by a male lay reader, are taken directly from a book of such prayers. They are never composed by the priest, reader or other parishioners and are unrelated to events or 'needs' in the parish. Only at the 10.30 a.m. Mass is there any singing; even then the choir sings alone from a loft at the west end. Few people appear to know the hymns and there are no hymn books. . . . Hymns on the Mass leaflets are not always the ones the choir sings and few contemporary hymns are attempted.

Often . . . parts of the Mass are said quietly by the priest while the choir sings. Some of the prayers require a response on the part of the congregation. . . . Only the server makes the responses on these occasions.

The bread and wine are not taken to the altar by members of the congregation, which is now a common liturgical practice, they are always taken by the servers from the credence table. Many boys are allowed 'to go on the altar', but only those over ten years of age are allowed to serve.

No women ever read the lessons. Even nuns are not invited to do so. Despite the fact that there are large numbers of communicants, there are no extraordinary ministers of the Sacrament. Consequently, Holy Communion is given at speed. The practice of receiving in the hand is actively discouraged and people must kneel at the altar rail to receive. A paten is usually thrust between the communicant's mouth and his hands whether he is receiving in the mouth or in the hand. There is no Kiss of Peace in the Mass, which is optional and in England usually means shaking hands with those nearest to you and saying 'Peace be with you'. Visiting priests have caused confusion and embarrassment by inviting the congregation to 'offer each other the sign of Peace'. This is a significant omission because the practice involves the priest's contact with members of the congregation in that he too has to shake someone's hand. By omitting it the priest maintains his social distance and emphasises his separation from the laity . . . [In sum] it seemed as if the old rite had simply been rendered into English with the entrance rite and the last gospel omitted. The priest reads the English prayers, including the Canon, as many priests had (previously) read the Latin, at speed and without expression. It was rather like a form of magical incantation.

(Leslie, 1986: 274–75, 278)

In his description of the saying of Mass in his research parish, John Leslie has drawn attention not only to the routine liturgical practices but also to the ways in which the priest maintains social distance from lay people and discourages their full participation. In his sermons the priest offers a legitimation for the traditional practices. For example, using selective accounts of historical developments he argued against the practice of receiving communion in the hand when it was first officially permitted by the hierarchy of England and Wales. The heavy emphasis he places on the sacramental presence of Jesus and sacred areas of the church has resulted in relatively formal demeanours and interaction being maintained

> Talking to other members of the congregation, even greeting them, beyond the porch area is actively discouraged. The parish priest has spoken against such pollution on a number of occasions. The clear physical boundaries within the building serve to reinforce the sacred/non-sacred division.
>
> (1986: 278)

LITURGY IN A PROGRESSIVE PARISH

A parish in the outer London commuter belt provides a contrast to that studied by John Leslie. Its parish priest during the 1970s has vividly described the processes of development stimulated by the parish liturgy committee so that 'our liturgy has come to life' (O'Sullivan, 1979: 24). An early study indicated that a plurality of liturgical styles was favoured by a majority of the parishioners and appeared to lead to significant increases in the average attendances at Mass. It was argued that such pluralism, linked to a process of 'shopping around' for most favoured liturgies, should be welcomed and encouraged as being 'healthily complementary rather than . . . divisively competitive' (Hornsby-Smith, 1975: 524). The aspirations of the parish liturgy committee at this time are apparent in Fr O'Sullivan's enthusiastic description of the emerging liturgy in the 1970s:

> It is varied, it is profoundly significant to all who take part and above all it has helped to deepen and to enrich unity in diversity for the people of the parish. If you were to come to a typical Sunday Mass you would first of all be struck by an air of expectancy and even of excitement as the congregation gathers. There is a great deal of friendly greeting outside the church and inside it as people assemble. Stewards at the door welcome the new arrivals, making sure that he has the necessary hymn book and supervise the placing of people as the church fills up. It soon becomes evident that the

congregation is involved at every possible opportunity in our celebration. The young girls of the parish prepare the church and the altar for the Mass. A rota of over thirty boys take it in turn to provide the servers. Another rota of fifty names provides the readers who will proclaim the word of God to the people. These men and women of every age group have undergone a training course to help them in the use of the practical techniques of public reading, but above all to help them to understand the significance of their ministry. After the penitential rite at the beginning of Mass the children under twelve are led from the church into the adjacent hall where they have their own liturgy of the word adapted to their own understanding and experience, but based, as is the adult one, on the reading of the bible and an explanation of the significance of what has been read. They return to the church at the offertory and join in the presentation of gifts, bringing anything they may have made, painted, or coloured during their own liturgy of the word in the hall.

(O'Sullivan, 1979: 24)

After describing how the introduction of the sign of peace at Mass was initially met with a certain amount of suspicion, Fr O'Sullivan observes that

this greeting of peace created the contact which had to be followed up afterwards. If the person in the pew next to you was a stranger, because you had greeted them during Mass with a handshake you could not ignore them when you were leaving the church together; so that in this way it helped to break the ice and to help people to make contact and deepen the community experience. Now when we greet each other we all know each other and so the greetings are warm and happy and people move about stretching across benches kissing, embracing, shaking hands and evincing every sign of true friendship, love and acceptance. It would be difficult for a visitor to feel that he was still a stranger after being greeted so warmly.

At communion some of the sisters and more than forty of the lay people in the parish assist the celebrant in the distribution of the host and the chalice. This too met at first with considerable suspicion but like the greeting of peace, has proved to be of enormous importance in stressing the participation element, underlining that priest and people are one in the celebration though each performs his or her own special task. That lay people should participate in this most intimate aspect of the celebration of Mass is a very dramatic way of portraying this sense of shared ministry.

. . . The music . . . is [also] varied and appeals to as many tastes as possible and is always planned carefully so as to harmonise with the theme of the day, the theme of the scripture readings or the festival.

After the Mass is over it is not uncommon to find the congregation still gathered in the car park as long as twenty to thirty minutes after the end. At least once a month we gather in the hall for coffee and conversation.

(1979: 25)

Even when due allowance is made for the fact that the aspirations of progressive clergy and like-minded parish activists are not shared to the same extent by many parishioners, the above account does indicate a very different model of the Church, clergy-lay relations, and appropriate liturgical approaches from that described by John Leslie. There have been some changes in this parish over the past decade, not only because there has been a change of parish priest, but also as a result of a very substantial growth in the number of new housing estates served by the parish. There is, therefore, an on-going need to induct large numbers of newcomers who have not experienced over a period of some years the long process of religious socialisation into an acceptance of the new liturgical styles and the development of expectations of a more participatory role for the laity.

The general position at the end of the 1980s, however, remains substantially the same as that described by Fr O'Sullivan at the end of the 1970s, and the following contrasts with John Leslie's traditional parish can be noted. First, the physical design of the new church serves to reduce the strength of the boundaries between the sanctuary and the body of the church. Symbolically, social distance between the priest and laity has been attenuated. Second, the choir at the main 10.30 a.m. Mass is located adjacent to the sanctuary and their leader faces the congregation to encourage them to participate in nearly all the sung parts of the Mass and the hymns. Third, it is now extremely rare for any part of the Mass to be sung in Latin. Fourth, large numbers of both men and women regularly read the scriptures and bidding prayers. Fifth, these bidding prayers are compiled each week by a different group within the parish and they are closely related not only to the readings from scripture but also to contemporary needs and concerns, for those within the parish, and for issues of justice and peace such as the victims of terrorism or famine, war and disasters throughout the world, and so on. Sixth, the priest always says Mass clearly and audibly and full participation in the responses by all those present is both encouraged and expected. Apart from the Sunday liturgies, there generally are no altar servers at the weekday Masses. Seventh, at all Masses there is always an offertory procession from the back of the church in which two or more parishioners bring up the gifts of bread and wine and the chalices for the distribution of the consecrated wine at the Communion. Eighth, Holy Communion is received under both kinds at all Masses in the parish. Perhaps four-fifths of parishioners receive the host in the hand and around the same proportion also receive the chalice. At the 10.30 a.m. Mass there will typically be five special ministers. The priest and one lay person will distribute the hosts while on each side of the altar there will also be two other lay people offering the chalice. Ninth, in this parish the sign of peace is invariably given and people are frequently asked to introduce themselves to those adjacent to them in the pews. By such means as this and with stewards at the entrance porch, strangers or newcomers are usually spotted and made to feel welcome. Finally, there is a relatively relaxed atmosphere in the church with a consider-able amount of conversation, especially after Mass among the activists involved in the planning of the various parish events.

LITURGICAL CONFLICT

From these descriptions of two parishes in England in the last quarter of the twentieth century, it is clear that there are considerable dif-ferences in their 'liturgical praxis'. These differences are caused by a variety of factors including their different social and religious contexts and histories, the religious orientations of their previous and current priests, and the social characteristics, mobility experiences, and religious predispositions of past and present laity. The two parishes considered appear to approximate to the models of pre- and post-Vatican parishes save that as far as the liturgies were concerned, the traditional parish has gone some way towards implementing the reforms of the Second Vatican Council but with little enthusiasm. Thus the priest now faces the people and says the Mass in English but in other ways he behaves in such a way that the spirit of the reforms is frustrated, the full participation of lay people impeded, and his social distance from them maintained.

One of the paradoxes of the post-conciliar Church is that many of the programmes of renewal, and particularly liturgical renewal, which purported to encourage the full participation of lay people in the life of the Church, were in fact introduced with pre-Vatican forms of religious authority. In other words they were imposed on an unsuspecting and unprepared Church by the religious leadership with the result that prolonged and agonised protests, the formation of defensive pressure groups to safeguard the treasures of the past, and a great deal of dragging of feet and downright clerical or congregational sabotage (Archer, 1986: 143) were the inevitable consequences. This now seems to be recognised, and, in a paper on *The Content of Liturgical Formation* prepared by the National Advisor for Liturgical Formation for the Bishops' Conference of England and Wales, it is confessed that an emergency situation has developed and that 'we have allowed liturgical reform to proceed without giving people the formation which should have accompanied it (Boylan, 1980: 1).

The liturgical conflicts of recent years have been reflected in an emerging sociological literature. Thus Hesser and Weigert have suggested a conceptual framework for the comparative study of liturgies, including intra-denomination liturgies such as those described above for both a traditional and a progressive parish. They suggest that

> liturgy can be related to changes in credal, experimental, organisational, authority, and socialisation dimensions of religion, as well as to processes in the larger society such as industrialisation, urbanisation, nation formation, or the emergence of quasi-religious ritual.
>
> (Hesser and Weigert, 1980: 224)

In terms of the variables they suggest the following contrast can be made between the liturgies in traditional and progressive parishes.

In the traditional parish the service is likely to be shorter, the verbal input is likely to be monopolised by the leader (priest), and the singing monopolised by the choir. The ritual language is likely to include some Latin, be formal in style, focus exclusively on the Deity, and place a strong emphasis on exhortation and possibly reprimand. The gestures of the clergy are likely to be formal, there are few other 'performers', and they are exclusively male. The design of the building directs attention exclusively forwards towards the altar and the priest and there is a tendency for the congregation to be dressed relatively formally.

In the progressive parish, on the other hand, the length of the service will frequently be significantly longer, with the priest sharing some of the verbal input with lay readers and with the choir leading the congregation in joint singing, responses, and chants. The language employed in the liturgy is almost exclusively the vernacular. It tends to be less formal, more conversational, and at times distinctly 'jokey' in comparison with the traditional parish. There also tends to be a relatively greater stress on reflection and possibly praise. The gestures of the clergy are likely to be more 'deliberate' than 'formal'. There are likely to be several other performers including altar servers, stewards, collectors, offertory gift bearers, and special ministers at the main Sunday Masses, and a majority of these is frequently female. The spacial design of the relatively new church, with relatively narrow depth and relatively large width and with benches on either side of the sanctuary, aims to stress the participation of the laity in the communal celebration. Finally, there is a tendency for the congregation to be dressed relatively informally as if to stress the involvement of everyday matters in the central act of worship.

Conflicts over liturgical reform have been reflected in the sociological literature. In the report of the 1978 survey of English Catholics, it was observed that

> working-class Catholics are less happy with recent changes (than the educated and articulate middle class), suspicious of the shift of emphasis from ritual to participation, defensive about their loss of a privatised autonomy in a mass congregation, and suspicious of proposed new forms of ministry, possibly because they represent new and alternative sources of authority to which they will be expected to respond.
>
> (Hornsby-Smith and Lee, 1979: 127–8)

A similar view has been expressed by Flanagan who claimed that 'the new rite became a liturgical charter for the further domination of the middle class' (1980: 4). Archer regarded the reforms as being 'based on the recovery of early liturgical models rather than the needs of the people' and as the brainchild of 'ecclesiastical bureaucracy and the international liturgical scholarship'. They were 'the epitome of middle-class taste of the 1960s' but as such they cut off many of the ritual streams that had previously nourished Catholics and covered many of the accumulated pools in which popular Catholicism had found its strength.

(1986: 141)

Not all would agree with Archer's analysis. Some consider he over-romanticises pre-war working-class Catholicism and fails to value the reforms which, as one priest put it, enable 'them to grow out of a wooden-headed response to an authority which prefers them not to grow up'.

Apart from the social class implications of the reforms, some have interpreted the debate simply in terms of a conflict between tra-ditional ritualists and progressive anti-ritualists. Thus Mary Douglas in her well-known discussion of 'the bog Irish', considers there has been an underestimation of the expressive function of ritual and the importance of the drawing of symbolic boundaries between the sacred and the profane in the reformed Mass (1973: 59–60, 69–71). Kieran Flanagan, in a number of papers, has taken this view further. For him the plurality of liturgical styles allowed by the reformers has resulted in 'a gaggle of competitive assemblies' which 'have eroded the central worshipping identity of Church membership' (1981: 20). He contrasts two ideal-types of liturgies: 'spiky privatisation' and 'convivial puritanism'. The former refers to

a traditional reliance on full ceremonial effects, a belief in letting symbols and actions speak in a standardised, sequential movement that faithfully observes the rubrics. It is a high form of liturgy . . . [which] offers little compromise in its belief in the efficacy of ritualistic practice. Gothic, elaborate music, bells, and smells, it provides a visual image of heaven expressed within the limits of an earthly liturgy. The laity are passive, and private spectators, free to construct their interior reactions without an obligatory effusiveness that characterises participation at other rites. Intrusion is dis-abling, and the fixedness of the relationship between the clergy, the servers, and the choir allows the laity to do their own extension through the symbolic frame ceremonially supplied.

(1981: 37)

In contrast

puritanical assemblies of God are often a humanistic escape for congregations of the middle class, fleeing from the powers of symbols, to the communal cultivation of self in relation to a behavioural transcendence, a coming within the group.

(1981: 56)

Both Archer and Leslie reject the claims of Douglas and Flanagan that there has been a process of deritualisation with the introduction of the recent liturgical reforms. Thus Archer suggests that

at its best, this hardly allows for the possibility that some of the former might want to change or develop their symbols and that some of the reformers might be ritualists too. At its worst this argument can fall into the trap which takes either the romantic or patronising form of supposing that Irish or working-class culture . . . must remain always the same.

(1986: 136)

Leslie tellingly comments that 'while the use of incense and holy water will be regarded as ritual actions, embracing a fellow worshipper in a Kiss of Peace will not' (1983: 57).

In a recent paper, William Dinges has examined the extent to which liturgical conflict can be interpreted as social conflict between rival élites within the Church and to recent shifts in identity, power and authority, and alterations in social relationships, for example between clergy and lay people. Like Archer he has located pressure for liturgical reform among strategic élites and the 'emerging knowledge class of liturgical experts and scholars' with horizontal forms of peer-group legitimacy. Clerical responses have ranged from adaptation and withdrawal to passive and/or active resistance. Unlike essentially lay-initiated organisations that emerged to counteract 'modernist' influences in the post-conciliar period, Catholic traditionalism, focused around the campaign to oppose liturgical reform and to preserve the Latin Tridentine liturgy, in the United States and probably also in Britain, was largely a clerically inspired social movement concerned to uphold traditional, hierarchical and juridical ecclesiastical authority. In sum,

conservatives who opposed the agenda of professional liturgists saw in the reforms both a 'de-sacralising' of Catholic ritualism and a *process* that shifted the legitimation of authority from apostolic hierarchy to that of bureaucracy, expertise, and professionalism. In endorsing such a shift, Catholicism mirrored the prevailing cultural consensus and thereby eroded its hierarchical and transcendental claims. The Church appeared, once again, to be 'socially constructed' and subject to the legitimating norms of the modern world . . . [Thus] opposition to liturgical reform in the Catholic Church is as much an expression of social dislocation, role status loss, and interest group conflict as it is a catechetical or psychological problem.

(1987: 153–4)

LAY RESPONSES

Some survey findings about the responses of English Catholics to liturgical change in the late-1970s were reported above. Further evidence is available from focused interviews carried out with random samples of Catholic electors in an inner-city and a suburban parish in each of the London and Preston areas in the mid-1970s (Hornsby-Smith, Lee, and Reilly, 1977; 1985). In general it was found that Catholics welcomed the liturgical changes which had taken place in the Church since the Second Vatican Council. To a very large extent many preferred the replacement of Latin as the Church's liturgical language by English simply because they could now understand and appreciate better what was going on. 'I can follow it better', and 'I feel more part of it' were common observations. One person commented that 'the Latin didn't register in the same way', while another remarked: 'We just knelt there and hoped for the best . . . the priest could have been saying anything really.'

For some the advantage of this change was that it held the attention of their fidgety children better. Others, particularly older working-class Catholics, appreciated the use of English for they felt that their lack of education had prevented their following the Latin Mass in the way that others, more privileged perhaps, had been able to. In the words of one such person: 'For the likes of me that didn't understand the Latin, the English is much nicer.' There is in such observations a hint of underlying matters of power, status, and social control which point to the validity of Dinges's analysis referred to previously.

Some who had converted to Catholicism on marrying a Catholic particularly appreciated the changes. As one observed: 'I was beginning to get frustrated with the Latin Mass and I was so pleased when the change came because the Mass began to mean more.' On the other hand, the opposition to the new Mass had something of a nostalgic quality. People felt that there had been a break with the past and a loss of tradition which 'was there for thousands of years'. Many people, including a number of non-practising Catholics, reiterated the view-point which they had been taught as children that the Latin Mass was the same for every Catholic throughout the world. There was therefore a feeling, on the part of many of the people interviewed, that a distinctive feature which helped to set them apart as Catholics had been lost. The Church, in this view, was being moved towards Protestantism. Coupled with this was a strong feeling that the sense of awe and mystery and beauty which was associated nostalgically with their memory of the Latin Mass had been lost, leaving it 'not like a Mass at all'.

In this connection, and in contrast to those who favoured the new Mass because of its greater appeal to the young, there was a condemnation of developments like folk music during the service. For these people this represented a needless pandering to the young. Many of these feelings were expressed by a spinster in her mid-60s who had left school at the age of 14 for domestic work and was currently employed part-time as a rent collector and who had lived in her present house all her working life:

I wasn't happy with all these changes. There was something peaceful about the Latin Mass. I liked the incense, the singing and the organ playing. Now there is no incense, nothing, even at Midnight Mass. These folk songs they have now, they remind me too much of what you get on the wireless. To me it isn't church. It pleases the kids; they've got to be catered for, but we're doing too much for the youngsters. The Mass is not as solemn as it was. It sounds like a fairground now. The priest says it makes the kids more 'aware' but we had to learn the Latin and we soon got to know it. Even if it were just in English, I wouldn't like it; it's going all Protestant.

Interestingly, few of the non-practising Catholics interviewed in the four research parishes cited liturgical changes in the Church as a reason for their present lack of practice and there were no signs of unrest or conflict in the parishes on this issue as early as the mid-1970s. In many ways the supporters of the changes and those who opposed them were very similar in their social composition. That there was little coherent opposition to the changes seems to stem from the fact that people have not taken up positions of ideological opposition to the post-Vatican Church. By the same token there was

111

also little evidence of ideological support *for* the changes, at least among ordinary Catholics in the four research parishes, though such support was more evident among parish activists.

Few 'ordinary' Catholics wished to be seen as 'traditionalist' or 'progressive'. Generally this was because the majority of those interviewed were unaware of any theological re-orientation in the Church and did not know why the changes had been introduced. There was little sense that the transition to new liturgical forms symbolised a fundamental shift in the self-awareness of the Roman Catholic community. The changes were simply liked or disliked. Not surprisingly, ordinary Catholics showed little commitment to or conversely rejection of the new principles that are supposed to govern the Church.

This present book is being written some twelve to fourteen years after the interviews reviewed here. Whereas in the 1970s the Second Vatican Council appeared to activist Catholics to have been a watershed in the life of the Church, a whole new generation of young Catholics has grown up for whom the Latin Mass and pre-Vatican liturgies are ancient history. Their formative socialising experiences have been different and their current expectations are couched much more in terms of those experiences as their point of departure. Many, perhaps the great majority, of Catholics who were initially shocked or dismayed by the 'Protestantism' of the reforms, have become acclimatised to them or at least to a discrete or undemanding version of them. The consequence must be a decline in the general level of opposition to the reforms and the marginalisation of those who continue to regard them as a sociological disaster or a betrayal of timeless rituals and symbolism.

The findings from a consultation carried out in a commuter parish south-east of London in preparation for the Synod on the Laity (St Lawrence's, 1987) provide a salutary reminder that the aspirations of the reformers have in many cases, perhaps the great majority, still not been realised. One of the strongest conclusions was that:

> people want to be *involved*. . . . Liturgical groups [are] needed to bring the liturgy *alive*. It is too restricting — we need greater freedom of expression. . . . The liturgy should not be hedged in by stifling legalism. The gospel message is that we should be free. If the children's needs can best be satisfied by stepping outside the

present rigid barriers in the liturgy — then that is where we should be prepared to go.

(1987: 21)

The report also concludes:

> sadly public worship, apart from obligatory Sunday Mass, is poorly supported. Generally this worship is organised by the clergy for a people who do not respond. . . . Liturgy and worship is an area which cries out for renewed vitality. It is the spiritual needs not the physical ones that are not being met. These can only be met when the correct balance is achieved in the relationship between priest and people. Neither can do without the other, nor replace the function of the other.

(1987: 20)

Finally the report also showed graphically how great is the alienation of young people on matters of liturgy and worship, in spite of the attempts of reformers to provide a plurality of liturgies with 'relevance'. In this parish three-fifths of those aged 15–24 years (compared to 7 per cent of those aged 25 and over) affirmed 'I go to Mass because I am obliged/made to go' and over half of those in the younger age group felt they were spectators at Mass compared to under one-fifth of those in the older age group. Two-fifths of the younger age group also found the Mass 'boring' and 'repetitive'.

The limited research findings it has been possible to review in this chapter support the view that there are wide variations in the extent to which different parishes have attempted to operationalise the teaching of the Second Vatican Council on liturgical matters. The near-uniformity of the pre-Vatican Roman liturgy has been replaced by a plurality of liturgies both between and within parishes. Furthermore there is evidence of a considerable variation in the enthusiasm with which the liturgical reforms have been adopted. It is also clear that some priests have been either active or passive resistors of the reforms. While the priest remains a key figure in the determination of liturgical styles at the parish level, it is also clear that large numbers of Catholic lay people are happy to have a quiet life and discharge their religious obligations with the minimum of fuss. For Catholics, it often is of no great consequence what style of liturgy is employed. For parish activists, on the other hand, such issues are often the focal point of an on-going struggle for dominance. The outcome of this struggle varies from parish to parish and in this sense 'parishes make their own histories'. In this process the key figure is the priest and it is to the examination of his changing role and the nature of his social control in the parish that we now turn.

Chapter Six

THE PRIEST AND PARISH LEADERSHIP

INTRODUCTION

A few years ago the pioneering Jesuit researcher Fr Joseph Fichter, reminiscing about his life's work, observed: 'as I continued my research on the Catholic Church I became ever more convinced that the key people, the agents of change in Catholicism, were the fulltime professionals in the service of the Church' (1973: 161). The view taken here is that this needs to be elaborated in two ways. First, the parish priest can be regarded as a gatekeeper and adjudicator of what enters or leaves the parish, for example in terms of liturgical or pastoral practices and priorities. This is partly because he often has a near-monopoly over both access to information, for example new pastoral messages from the bishop or statements published by the Vatican, and the paths for its dissemination within the parish, by such means as open meetings and discussions or making available relevant papers or reports. In spite of any increase in the participation of lay people in the life of the Church in recent decades, the priest remains in a very powerful position by virtue of both his juridical status and the deep-rooted normative expectations there are concerning his decision-making rights and power and his relationships with his parishioners.

Second, it is important to note that a gatekeeper can both open the gate to or regulate the flow of new influences, or shut them out and exclude them altogether. Either way, in the preservation of things as they are or as the initiator of change, the role of the parish priest is crucial. However a third point might be added. Frequently the laity are quite happy to leave things as they are because they are comfortable and unchallenging and have resulted in a quiet and undemanding life. It would be quite misleading to assume that in the case of parish reform since the Second Vatican Council a consistently enthusiastic and progressive laity has been consistently frustrated by a traditional clergy who wielded the power of the gatekeeper to keep out, as far as possible, any of the new ideas and practices which were being advocated.

The reality has been more untidy than that. On occasion a charismatic progressive priest has been able to drag a more-or-less reluctant parish towards a post-Vatican model. In this he might have been aided by the crucial support of a committed group of progressive activist laity. On other occasions he might have had to struggle against a strategy of resistance and downright sabotage on the part of an obstinate and entrenched laity. In other parishes initiatives which have begun to take root and pastoral styles which have started to emerge have abruptly been terminated at the diktat of an incoming priest with an alternative model of the Church and of the roles of priest and lay people. In still other parishes things remain substantially unchanged and unchanging as a result of the connivance between the priest and a core group of parishioners in what they see as their mutual interests. In this chapter we will consider the changing role of the priest and in particular the way he exercises leadership in the parish.

It has been argued that the parish priest is inevitably a subject of criticism because 'the expectations as to the role behaviour of the p.p. are multitudinous, multifarious and even contradictory' (Schreuder, 1961: 111). It cannot be inferred from the research data, however, that there is a significant cleavage between priests and their parishioners, at least in England and Wales. In the national survey in 1978 Catholics were asked to rate their priests in their parish on four-point scales (from excellent to poor) on each of eleven aspects of their work. Between one-quarter and one-third did not know how to answer these questions and on the priest's 'understanding of my own personal problems' the proportion was over two-fifths. This might be taken as one indication that the extent to which Catholics know their priests and are known by them is somewhat limited. All the same, English Catholics gave their priests fairly high ratings on many aspects of their work. Table 6.1 compares weekly Mass attenders with non-attenders, those in high and low social classes, and the youngest and oldest groups. Overall priests were rated 'excellent' or 'good' on the way they do their job by two-thirds of Catholics who answered.

Table 6.1 Evaluation of priests in parishes by Mass attendance frequency, social class, and age (% excellent or good)

Aspects of priest's work	Mass attendance		Social class		Age		
	Within week	Over year	AB	DE	15 – 24	65 +	All
1 Their ability to manage the affairs of the parish	82	26	59	60	44	75	59
2 The way they treat their parishioners	74	29	55	58	44	78	55
3 Their sermons	65	14	44	51	30	63	46
4 Their involvement in the local Catholic schools	70	32	46	57	47	66	55
5 The way in general that they do their job	83	36	66	63	54	81	63
6 Their knowledge of what is going on in the world	77	28	55	59	47	71	57
7 The amount of visiting they do to parishioners in their own homes	51	24	39	39	34	58	40
8 Their knowledge of what is going on in the Church	88	40	70	69	61	78	69
9 Their understanding of the problems of married people	58	15	38	41	22	59	39
10 Their understanding of my own personal problems	54	14	37	38	18	66	36
11 Their understanding of the problems of the young	64	18	36	47	28	62	44
UNWEIGHTED N = 100%	491	253	212	249	184	100	1023

Source: Hornsby-Smith and Lee, 1979: 208.

On the other hand, only one-half of weekly Mass attenders rated them at this level on their visiting, an indication, perhaps, of the general decline in parish visiting in recent years. On both questions there was a strong age gradient, older Catholics being much more likely than younger Catholics to rate their priests highly. Converts rated priests much more highly than 'cradle' Catholics and active Catholics, such as members of Catholic organisations, especially office holders, rated them much more highly than non-members (Hornsby-Smith and Lee, 1979: 184, 191). Also noteworthy are the relatively low ratings for priests' understanding of personal problems and the particular problems of married people and the young. Finally, well under one-half of Catholics rated their priests favourably on their sermons. According to Greeley in the United States,

> the sermon is the single most important parish activity in affecting the attitudes towards Catholicism. . . . [At the parish level] nothing else matters if the sermon is not good. Sermons have an independent influence of their own . . . as strong as family and nature and Catholic schooling.
>
> (Greeley, 1981: 81, 83)

Interestingly, in a comparative study of priests, women religious and lay people who attended the National Pastoral Congress in 1980, few differences between the three groups were found across a wide range of religious beliefs and social and moral attitudes. It was concluded that:

> whatever cleavages there might be within the Church in this country, they are not between lay people . . . and the clergy or religious, but more probably between 'progressives' and 'traditionalists' at every level in the Church.
>
> (Hornsby-Smith and Cordingley, 1983: 26)

Although for historical reasons there is relatively little anti-clericalism in Britain, the United States, and Australia, the changes in the Church in recent decades have had a profound impact on the parish clergy. Like other occupational groups which have experienced significant reductions in their claims to a monopoly of expertise or to a legitimated social distance from their clients, they have often reacted anxiously and defensively to the changes. Perhaps this is one reason why no national survey of parish clergy has yet been attempted in Britain and why a professional judgement until now has been that there is little likelihood of achieving a satisfactory response rate to any such enquiry. One measure of this was that in a comparative study in three areas in the early 1970s, only 47 per cent of Catholic priests responded compared to 78 per cent of Anglican clergymen and 93 per cent of Methodist ministers (Ranson, Bryman and Hinings, 1977: 172). The situation is rather better in the United States largely because one-man researchers such as Fichter (1973: 160–98) braved intense institutional resistance in the early 1960s. Apart from Fichter's own study of *Religion as an Occupation* (1966), Greeley has reported on a major survey of a random sample of 6,000

American priests and all the 276 bishops and 208 major religious superiors in the winter of 1969/70. In spite of evidence of status-anxiety in the occupational group, Greeley reported that

> we have discovered no evidence that the Catholic priesthood is in a state of collapse. . . . There are many strong and positive forces at work in the priesthood. . . . On the other hand, the priesthood has certain very serious problems, most of them centering around the highly volatile subjects of power and sex which indicate trouble and conflict in the years ahead . . . the priesthood has both more assets and more problems than most other professions.
>
> (1972: 315)

The data base, then, for the study of the priest in his role as the religious leader of the parish is somewhat limited, so that we will have to rely to a large extent on the interpretive analysis of case studies in parishes which approximate to the ideal-types of pre-Vatican and post-Vatican parishes which we discussed above in Chapters 1 and 2.

However, before we proceed to the consideration of the changing role of the priest, it is appropriate, first of all, to note the sociological distinction between the priest and the prophet. While in Catholic theology all the baptised are said to share in Christ's threefold office as priest, prophet, and king (*Gaudium et Spes*, ss.10–13), sociologically there is value in the distinction, deriving from Max Weber, between the priest as the official functionary in the religious organisation, concerned with the 'cult', and the prophet, who in an individual capacity is the 'bearer of charisma'. Thus:

> the personal call is the decisive element distinguishing the prophet from the priest. The latter lays claim to authority by virtue of his service in a sacred tradition, while the prophet's claim is based on personal revelation and charisma. . . . The priest . . . dispenses salvation by virtue of his office. Even in cases in which personal charisma may be involved, it is the hierarchical office that confers legitimate authority upon the priest as a member of a corporate enterprise of salvation. But the prophet . . . exerts his power simply by virtue of his personal gifts.
>
> (Weber, 1966: 46–7)

Elsewhere, Weber sees priests as 'the primary protagonists and representatives of . . . sacred norms . . . striving for a firm regulation and control of life' (1966: 22) and, as an ideal-type, as the 'functionaries of a regularly organised and permanent enterprise' and characterised by 'special knowledge, fixed doctrine, and vocational qualifications' and by rational training and discipline (1966: 28–9). Thus:

> the crucial feature of the priesthood [is] the specialisation of a particular group of persons in the continuous operation of a cultic enterprise, permanently associated with particular norms, places and times, and related to specific special groups.
>
> (1966: 30)

That the parish clergy conform closely to the Weberian ideal-type can be seen by a cursory review of the appropriate parts of *The Code of Canon Law* (1983). These point to the specific requirements for the training of priests in seminaries (Cans. 232–64), the procedures for the enrolment or incardination of the cleric in a particular Church or diocese (according to Cans. 265–72), and the cleric's rights (such as the power of ecclesiastical governance) and duties according to Cans. 273–89. As we have previously noted in Chapter 1, the pastoral care of a parish is entrusted to a parish priest under the authority of a diocesan bishop and he is required to perform a number of specified functions on behalf of the institutional Church according to Cans. 515–52. It is as an official in a hierarchically structured organisation that the parish priest has inevitably to be concerned with 'maintenance' functions as well as show concern for 'mission'. The role of the parish priest has been described as 'to oversee and coordinate the ministerial gifts of the baptised and to preside at those public moments when such gifts and services are corporately expressed through ritual' (Nathan Mitchell, quoted in Greeley *et al.*, 1981: 177).

THE CHANGING ROLE OF THE PRIEST

It is not necessary here to repeat all that said above in Chapter 2 about the major social and religious changes of the past four decades which have transformed the nature of the Church, its institutional life at the parish level, the characteristics of the membership, and their social distance from and relationships with the parish clergy (see also Hornsby-Smith, 1984). Although we have relatively little systematic research data to document the changes, it is possible to construct models of both pre-Vatican and post-Vatican parochial priests in order to generate hypotheses about the transformations which have taken place in priest-lay relationships at the parish level and in the prevailing characteristics of the leadership styles of priests. Figure 6.1 summarises the main features of these ideal-typical priests which have drawn heavily on Moore's analysis of the paradigm shift in the Church (1975) and Reidy and White's study of traditionalism among priests in New Zealand (1977)

Figure 6.1 Models of pre-Vatican and post-Vatican parish priests

Characteristic	Pre-Vatican	Post-Vatican
Personal:		
favoured virtues	obedience, docility, institutional loyalty	confidence, flexibility, spontaneity, innovative
view of priest	sacred man, set apart	co-responsible ministry of service
Theological orientation: (relative emphasis)		
view of God	transcendent	immanent
nature of Church	visible organisation	community of believers
	static fortress	dynamic pilgrim
	pyramid of power	community of service
paradigm of priesthood	sacred and mediatorial	quasi-democratic
	ordained to celebrate	authorised by People of God
main emphasis	ontologically superior	priesthood of all believers
missionary emphasis	conversion	development of people
relationship to secular world	submission to God	mastery of world
posture towards secular world	defensive against	open to dialogue
	intransigence	accommodation
relationship to other Churches	distant to hostile	warmly ecumenical
	exclusive	inclusive
Pastoral practice:		
liturgical style	traditional	pluralistic
leadership style	sole initiator	facilitator, co-ordinator
	authoritarian	democratic
	didactic	enabler, empowerment
	routiniser	innovator
relations with laity	distant, aloof	close, friendly
	master	servant
general attitudes	traditional	adaptive
emphasis	orthodoxy	orthopraxis
priorities	maintenance	mission
Exemplars:		
	McLeod (1974) Leslie (1986)	O'Sullivan (1979)

Pre-Vatican and post-Vatican priests

In the first place it is likely that the seminaries will be looking for different strengths in their applicants and aiming to socialise the seminarians into a different cluster of attributes than was the case thirty or so years ago. In the earlier period priests were trained in seminaries which approximated to Goffman's 'total institutions' (1968) as Moore (1975: 47–55) and Anthony Kenny (1986) have indicated. In general terms the pre-Vatican priest was socialised into the virtues of obedience, docility, and loyalty, and he regarded the priest as a 'sacred' figure, a 'man set apart' from others for the purposes of leadership in the Church and particularly at the parish level. The 'inherent dignity' of the priest 'separated him from the laity, over whom he was infinitely superior' (Moore, 1975: 46). In contrast to this model, the post-Vatican ideal-typical priest has been subjected to a less coercive seminary regime and has been encouraged to develop a certain spontaneity and flexibility such as will suit the different leadership role envisaged as enabler and empowerer. In Moore's analysis of the 'shift from the sacred and mediatorial paradigm of priesthood to the competing quasi-democratic, secularised paradigms' of the post-Vatican period, the stress on the sacralisation of the priesthood, set apart from 'the world', has been replaced by a stress on 'priesthood as a co-responsible ministry of service' (Moore, 1975: 30, 43).

In the study of the delegates to the National Pastoral Congress (Hornsby-Smith and Cordingley, 1983; Hornsby-Smith, 1987: 143–5), a battery of alternative images of God, the Church, the priesthood, the purposes of mission, and relationships with other Churches and with the secular world generally, were developed. On the basis of these images and again in ideal-typical terms, a pre-Vatican priest is likely to have a clear image of a transcendent God, a strongly institutional model of the Church (Dulles, 1976), to regard himself as having been ordained to offer up the Mass on behalf of the faithful and as authorised to administer the sacraments, and to have a missionary call to bring 'non-Catholics' to conversion to the 'one, holy, Catholic and apostolic' faith. He is also likely to have an 'other-worldly' view of religion and an ideology of submission to God's will. He is apprehensive about both other Churches and the secular world generally and is active in the maintenance of defensive walls around an exclusive Catholic parish, seeing this as guarding his parishioners against seductions from outside.

Reidy and White (1977) suggest that this 'traditional' ideal-typical world-view corresponds to Berger's posture of intransigence and sect-like entrenchment in contrast to a posture of accommodation in the face of the realities of a pluralist religious situation (Berger, 1973: 156).

The post-Vatican priest, by contrast, has a greater awareness of the immanence of God and sees the Church not as an unchanging institution but in terms of the pilgrim People of God, forever on the move in the face of new challenges and constantly in need of reinterpreting its mission. He does not regard himself as having been set apart but rather sees himself as the religious leader and representative of the parishioners he has been sent to serve, all of whom share in the common priesthood of all believers. He sees his missionary task more in terms of encouraging the development of people in their growing awareness of God's infinite mercy and love. He encourages pastoral initiatives, spontaneity and service within the community of believers, all of whom are encouraged to contribute their talents to the shared task of mission. While he still has a presidential role, his management style is 'organic' rather than 'mechanistic' (Burns and Stalker, 1961). Warm and open ecumenical relationships with other Churches are encouraged and he adopts an accommodative posture towards the secular world which is not shunned but rather engaged in dialogue.

The liturgical styles of the two priests will reflect their different orientations along the lines discussed in the previous chapter. The pre-Vatican priest will be a traditionalist in liturgical matters and a minimalist in terms of his response to recommended reforms. Thus he is quite likely to sabotage attempts to introduce reforms which depart from the way the liturgy has always been performed or which modify his central controlling role. He regards himself as having been given ultimate decision-making powers in the parish and as being the only legitimate authority and sole initiator of any new pastoral practices. Where he deems it expedient he will use his gatekeeper's role to filter out information, whether from the bishop's pastoral letters or in the Catholic press, which is likely to promote or legitimate any change from existing practices. In Merton's terms (1957) he is a ritualist and routiniser. He remains aloof from laity and maintains a distinct social distance from them. In the last analysis he regards himself as their superior. Finally his pastoral concerns are primarily with the preservation of orthodoxy of belief and the maintenance and indeed extension of the plant which has been entrusted to his care.

The pastoral practices of the post-Vatican priest are quite different. He is more flexible in his approach and encourages a certain pluralism of liturgical practices for different groups within the parish. Rather than considering himself to be the sole focus of action and decision-making in the parish, he develops an awareness of the range of gifts and talents which lay people have and his concern is to facilitate the growth of all of them. His concern is with the 'empowerment' of everyone in the parish. He is not dominated by traditional ways and is prepared to allow experimentation and innovations. His relationships with lay people are close and friendly and he regards himself as being, in principle, at their service. His primary concern is not the maintenance of orthodoxy so much as the realisation in Christian praxis of the imperative to transform the world in which we live so that it better approximates the values of the Kingdom of God. This concern is reflected in his pastoral focus on mission and he encourages his parishioners to take over the maintenance functions of the local parish.

Priests and professionalism

It is frequently suggested that as a result of social change in recent decades the priest has lost some of the social functions he previously performed when he may have been the only person in the parish with any post-school education. Furthermore, as a result of the major shifts of theological orientation at the Second Vatican Council, and in particular the strong emphasis on an enhanced role of the laity as the People of God and the relative neglect of the role of priests, the priest has become marginalised in the Church. Hence there is said to be a crisis in the priesthood which has manifested itself in the huge numbers who have left the priesthood and in a general lack of confidence in relation to an increasingly educated and independent laity. In response to this view it could be argued that just as the modern family has lost some functions but gained others and also been expected to achieve far higher standards than previously, so with social and religious change and the emergence of the 'caring' professions, the priest has lost some functions, gained new ones, and is required to achieve higher standards than previously, for example in liturgical celebrations and the promotion of a sense of community service.

Whereas it has been said that in the nineteenth century the priest was 'often the patriarch of his parish, its ruler, its doctor, its lawyer, its magistrate, as well as its teacher, before whom vice trembled and rebellion dared not show itself' (Dean Church quoted in Ranson *et al.*, 1977: 61), it is now often argued that priests have become more marginal to society. Thus in their account of *The Fate of the Anglican Clergy*, Towler and Coxon (1979) pointed out that the priest's monopoly over specialised skills, which is one of the marks of a profession, has been steadily eroded as the educational level and participation of the laity have increased. This has left 'the clergyman as the spokesman rather than the supernaturally authorised leader, and (substituted) presiding ministers where formerly there were sacred ministers' (1979: 39). He has become a

> jack of all trades. He occupies a unique position, but the uniqueness of his position has nothing to do with unique skills, or even with unique competence. . . . He does not have a job at all in any sense which is readily understandable today. . . . As a result the clergyman finds himself marginal to society.
>
> (1979: 53–4)

Unfortunately there is no comparable study of priests in Britain but there is no reason to suppose that the findings would be significantly different. Catholic priests are likely to respond to their changing role in the same way as Anglican clergymen. According to Towler and Coxon:

> The clergy show many signs of trying to escape from their uncomfortable marginality. Some quit the ministry for jobs in teaching or in the welfare services, while others go half way by involving themselves in voluntary organisations . . . or by doing a little teaching on the side. Some try to find a specialism peculiar to the clergy in 'pastoral psychology' or 'clinical theology', or through management training courses. Some renounce their public status altogether and confine their activities to the faithful remnant, retreating to within their local church and congregation. Very few just stand and, as it were, allow the waves of marginality to break over them.
>
> (1979: 54)

Diana Leat on the basis of interviews with a random sample of thirty ministers and priests of various denominations in a large town south of London examined one response of the clergy, regarded 'as a cognitive minority' (Berger, 1971: 18; 1973: 156) to their perceived marginality. This was pastoral counselling, which they saw as a means of 'putting God over . . . in a modern way'. Although pastoral and secular counsellors described their aims in the same way, she found that 'the acceptance of the principles and means of counselling represents an attempt to adapt and make relevant to the dominant world-view the traditional pastoral aims' (Leat, 1973).

Against the views of Towler and Coxon, Fichter has argued robustly in his discussion of 'the myth of the hyphenated clergy' that historically priests have always performed a wide variety of roles and the same is true today. A priest does not become a layman by specialising occupationally, whether as sociologist or lawyer or physician or whatever. Rather,

> the professionalisation of the clergyman is the development of expertise in a specialised function, and this function *is* his 'holy calling'. Furthermore, to be a professional means to have a total commitment, to be dedicated and devoted and even 'consecrated' to one's life work . . . ideally speaking, the clergyman is the super-professional, the paragon of consecrated dedication to his vocation.
> (1974: 49–50)

To some extent, while it may be true that not all priests need be parish clergy but may legitimately specialise in any number of professional areas, nevertheless in the case of the parish clergy this begs the question as to exactly what it is that they are specialised in or committed to. And there is a great deal of evidence world-wide that for many priests the answer has not been very clear; hence the sense of crisis and marginality. In the first place there is a lack of consensus in the literature about the extent to which the clergy can be considered to be a professional occupation.

A number of researchers have operationalised Hall's five dimensions of professionalism (1968: 93): the use of a professional organisation as a major point of reference, a belief in service to the public, a belief in self-regulation, a sense of calling, and job autonomy, in order to investigate the extent to which the priesthood has become professionalised in recent years. Thus Struzzo, in a study of 166 priests in the Archdiocese of Washington, DC in 1969 used a nine-item index of professional autonomy to test the hypothesis that the greater the degree of professionalism attained by the priest, the more he will tend to resolve authority conflicts in non-compliant ways . . . in terms of traditional canonical and magisterial norms established by the hierarchy of Church officials.

(1970: 93–4)

In all four areas considered: stance on birth control, liturgical experimentation, offering communion to non-Catholics at Mass, and the readmission to the sacraments of the divorced and remarried, the evidence showed that 'the more professional a priest is, the more he tends to deviate from the institutionalised norms of the hierarchy in resolving pastoral issues' (1970: 102). In a study of Anglican clergy, Methodist ministers and Roman Catholic priests in England in 1972/73, Bryman and his colleagues found that the priests were 'the most professional in terms of vocation and service orientation' Ranson *et al.*, 1977: 56), a finding which gave support to earlier work by Gannon (1971), but that there were doubts about both the adequacy of Hall's scale and the resultant factor structure and also the extent to which the clergy could be regarded as supporting the attitudinal qualities of a profession (Bryman, 1985). Jarvis (1975), on the other hand, following Etzioni (1969) has argued that the parish ministry is best conceptualised as a semi-profession since it has no theoretical knowledge base or monopoly of skills or special area of competence and because occupational control is exercised by non-professionals.

Finally, Goldner and his colleagues (1973), who surveyed the priests in a major US diocese in 1970, regarded the crisis in the priesthood as one example of a process of deprofessionalisation generally. Distinctions of social prestige between all professionals and their clients or lay people have been reduced as a result of the general rise in educational standards, and this has been accompanied by increasing demands for the 'inclusion of the laity' in the control processes of all professions, including medicine and education. In the case of priests the professionalisation of social welfare has resulted in a reduction in the frequency of interactions with the priest. One response, particularly among younger priests, is that of 'interpersonalism' or 'building a Christian community'. Goldner observes that leadership roles in such interpersonal experiences are more dependent on personal characteristics and 'charisma' than professional skills. Again, these adaptations are not unique to priests. Even more challenging is the view of these authors that such processes appear:

> to represent an anti-institutional movement within Catholicism. Interpersonalism . . . represents, for many, a retreat from unsuccessful efforts to provide a better world by reforming organisations or societies. It is a move outside of the structural, political, power and distributive issues of the world and back to those emotive states involved in interpersonal relations.
>
> (Goldner *et al.*, 1973)

Whatever the limitations of the concept of professionalism, evidence which will be given in the following chapter will indicate the utility of the contrast between the hierarchical organisational control of the bureaucrat by his superiors and the peer-group control by the professional colleague group in the case of the relationships between parish priests and their assistant priests.

The testimony of a senior priest

Before leaving this discussion of the changing role of the priest, it is instructive to note the observations of a senior parish priest on the increasing stresses experienced by the parish clergy.

> One stress, for instance, is that many people in the parish still have expectations based on the old model of priesthood of the pre-Vatican II Church, where the priest ran everything, did everything, organised everything, consulted nobody, and all he was expected to do was to visit his flock and you judged his quality as parish priest by the number of times you were visited. There are still many people who expect that and it's quite impossible. . . . Another expectation . . . by many other parishioners [is] to be the modern parish priest who consults about everything and has delegated authority throughout the parish. That, too, presents its problems. . . . We are confronted with division very often in the parish because we consult. . . . The amount of paperwork (including diocesan meetings, deanery meetings . . .) has multiplied enormously and that is a great strain on many priests who have no notion of how to handle an office, or even, indeed, how to use a secretary, even if they've got one, because of lack of training in those simple techniques. We have the stresses of having to try to get things like (special adult education) programmes going and find

128

leadership in our parishes for that, and in many parishes there is apathy and people don't want to be involved, don't want to be given leadership roles. More and more people will turn to the priest these days for counselling rather than spiritual direction or confession, as . . . in the older days. Here again, there can be stresses on a priest who perhaps isn't used to counselling, hasn't been to any training in it. . . . There are higher expectations, too, with regard to the sacramental ministry. Liturgy is a much more demanding thing. Saying Mass for me today is a far more exhausting process that it was when I was first ordained, not only because I'm thirty years older, but because in those days you had no personal projection in it at all. You went through the Mass like a robot that had been wound up and most of it was silent; you had your back to the people; you sort of muttered and mumbled. . . . Now you've got to project every word you say. You are facing the people, you have got to lead them in worship in a much more demanding way. . . . And if you did three Masses on a Sunday morning, the physical strain alone of that is a stress, plus the fact that there are . . . maybe three entirely different liturgies. . . . So just the sheer concentration of that can leave a man chewed up like a piece of string at the end of a Sunday morning. Not to mention that he then goes on and does three baptisms and has a confirmation class and perhaps has a united service with the Anglicans in the evening. There just isn't enough time in the day. That's just Sunday . . . but the week can be equally full.

(Taped interview, June 1988)

Reflecting later on some of the changes he detected in priests he suggested that priests were a great deal more open to new ideas, for example about scripture, now than they had been thirty years ago. He also considered priests were 'much more prepared to bend the rules if not break them'. This was 'because priests are talking more to the people and listening to them, and so naturally they are compassionate because they're not dealing with the people as just a flock of silly sheep that's got to be told what to do and where to go and where to do it'.

PRIEST AND PROPHET?

Twelve years after the end of the Vatican Council an English seminary student reflected on the changing role of the priest and specified the job description given in Figure 6.2. It is interesting to note the emphatic assertion of the importance of prophetic witness in this model of priesthood. In Catholic theology no necessary contradiction is seen between the roles of the priest and the prophet. The parish clergy, like the People of God generally (*Lumen Gentium*, Ch. 2), participate in Christ's three-fold office as priest (to worship God), prophet (to be a living witness), and king (to rule the fellowship of believers). Thus the Second Vatican Council taught in the Decree on the Ministry and Life of Priests (*Presbyterorum Ordinis*, s.1) that 'by sacred ordination and by the mission they receive from their bishops, priests are promoted to the service of Christ the Teacher, the Priest, and the King' (Abbott, 1966: 533).

Figure 6.2 Job description for parish priest

WANTED

A MAN (*sic*):	to be a priest, which is basically to be a sign of contradiction to the world.
TASK:	to disturb the comfortable and comfort the disturbed.
LOCATION:	where two or three are gathered in the Lord's name.
BASIC REQUIREMENTS:	an ability to learn and to teach;
	to give, to heal wounds;
	to be a member of each family yet belonging to none;
	your friends must be drug addicts, prostitutes, gangsters, homosexuals, vandals, thieves;
	you must be able to teach, initiate social awareness and advance social development;
	you must be able to console, solidify and stand up and be counted.
SALARY:	as little as possible.
PROSPECTS:	starvation; nakedness;
	being misunderstood and misquoted;
	you will be lonely or even unwanted;
	if you function properly you will be an embarrassment to people.
N.B.:	if half interested — forget it;
	if fully interested — think again!

Source: Student at St John's Seminary, Wonersh.

This theology has been enshrined in the revised Canon Law. It is significant, however, that 'only clerics can obtain offices the exercise of which requires the power of order or the power of ecclesiastical governance' (Can. 274 s.1). The law defining the rights and duties of parish clergy is given in Part II on 'The Hierarchical Constitution of the Church' in Book II on 'The People of God'. Chapter VI deals with 'Parishes, Parish Priests and Assistant Priests'. In Weberian terms the authority of the priest is clearly legal-rational and indicated in Canon 519:

> The parish priest . . . exercises the pastoral care of the community entrusted to him under the authority of the diocesan bishop, whose ministry of Christ he is called to share, so that for this community he may carry out the offices of teaching, sanctifying and ruling with the co-operation of other priests or deacons and with the assistance of lay members of Christ's faithful.
>
> (Can. 519)

The duties of the parish priest are specified especially in Canons 528–30. These include the celebration of the sacraments and prudent pastoral correction and care. For present purposes, the code relating to his teaching functions is particularly relevant:

> The parish priest has the obligation of ensuring that the word of God is proclaimed in its entirety to those living in the parish. He is therefore to see to it that the lay members of Christ's faithful are instructed in the truths of faith, especially by means of the homily on Sundays and holydays of obligation and by catechetical forma-tion. He is to foster works which promote the spirit of the Gospel, including its relevance to social justice. He is to have a special care for the Catholic education of children and young people.
>
> (Can. 528 s.1)

The Code proceeds to enjoin the priest to lead the faithful to prayer, strive to know them well, prudently to correct them, solicitously to care for the sick and dying and diligently to seek out the poor, suffer-ing, lonely, and exiled. Finally, we might note the address of Cardinal Hume to the National Conference of Priests in 1979 in which he referred to his dream of a new form of exercising priesthood built on a deep life of prayer, a sense of community, not so 'churchy', and more radical and prophetic (Forrester, 1980: 75).

How can we interpret this sociologically? According to Weber the roles of priest and prophet are quite distinct and typically in conflict. Where

> the priesthood . . . can be said to be characterised by the presence of certain fixed cultic centres associated with some actual cultic apparatus . . . (and) his professional equipment of special

knowledge, fixed doctrine and vocational qualifications . . . rational
training and discipline . . . [so that] the crucial feature of the priesthood [is] the specialisation of a particular group of persons in the
continuous operation of a cultic enterprise, permanently associated
with particular norms, places and times, and related to specific
social groups

(1966: 28–30)

for Weber the concept of the prophet was taken

to mean a purely individual bearer of charisma, who by virtue of his
mission proclaims a religious doctrine or divine commandment . . .
the personal call is the decisive element distinguishing the prophet
from the priest. The latter lays claim to authority by virtue of his
service in a sacred tradition, while the prophet's claim is based on
personal revelation and charisma. . . . The priest, in clear contrast,
dispenses salvation by virtue of his office. Even in cases in which
personal charisma may be involved, it is the hierarchical office that
confers legitimate authority upon the priest as a member of a
corporate enterprise of salvation. But the prophet . . . exerts his
power simply by virtue of his personal gifts. . . . [Furthermore] the
criterion of gratuitous service also distinguishes the prophet from
the priest.

(1966: 46–7)

According to Fr Herbert McCabe 'the priest should *be* a revolutionary leader' because 'the revolution in its ultimate depths *is* the
proclamation of the Gospel' (1970: 989). Implicitly rejecting the
Weberian dichotomy, he argues that:

the business of the priest is to be one jump ahead of the Christian
life of his age; it is his job to be constantly representing to the
Christian people and to the world the evangelical, revolutionary
significance of their Christian, secular lives. It is every Christian's
task to be critical and interpretative of his world; it is the ministerial task to be interpretative of the Christian life, to see through it
to the Gospel that it more or less adequately embodies. It is to seek
out and re-present to men the Christianness of their Christianity,
the evangelical character of their lives. This is what promulgation
of the Gospel means . . . the 'credibility' of the Church [or parish]
is to be judged, not according to whether it is a community in
which we can begin to satisfy our personal need for human warmth

and kindness and decent personal relations, but according to whether it is an effective force in the revolutionising of the world.

(1970: 991–2)

In spite of this aspiration, it is tentatively suggested here that what evidence there is supports the Weberian distinction. Thus, while the Church's Canon Law can be said to be exhortatory and not exclude prophetic witness according to Gospel injunctions, in practice Canon Law can be seen to emphasise the role of the parish priest as an authorised office-holder in a hierarchical organisation, subordinate to the legal-rational authority of the bishop, and charged with the promotion of the institutional Church's goals of security and growth. In the main the concrete sociological reality is also that parish priests place a considerable emphasis on the maintenance of 'harmony' and 'balance' in their parishes, stressing the values of 'community' and 'consensus'. Conflict is almost universally abhorred and avoided by strategies of withdrawal and techniques of neutralisation. Thus there is a general tendency to avoid or play down the importance of the issues of justice and peace because they are known seriously to divide Catholics. Controversial issues are frequently labelled as 'political' rather than 'religious' and therefore as illegitimate areas of concern (and legitimate areas of unconcern!). The effect is the stifling of prophecy by an unholy alliance of timid priests and stubborn, lazy, and comfortable lay people.

According to Jan Kerkhofs, reflecting on the situation in Holland at the end of the 1970s,

Many senior Church leaders want a ministry which is liberating for those who exercise it and for the communities in which they serve. However, many senior Church leaders keep quiet for three reasons: they are hampered by ideas about the quasi-unanimity of the College; by the expectation that the Roman Church should be uniform; and by the fear of polarising a part of their own flock. . . . The scope for plurality is kept as limited as possible for fear of polarisation. The ideal policy becomes one of immobilism, which both rejects many living forces and excludes potential believers, especially young people. This is clear in the case of the silting up of ecumenism, and also in the fight to the death over the widening of the scope of the ministry.

(Grollenberg et al., 1980: 18)

Something of the reality of the 'immobilism' at the parish level is indicated in the following comments by a frustrated justice and peace activist in the north of England in the mid-1980s.

> I still have problems over the parish priest. . . . While intellectually he supports all the ideas of justice and peace and in a general discussion he's all for it, in actual practice he's terrified of offending people. And so he's always wanting to take the middle ground and he doesn't like conflict. I think he ducks the issue all the time; he wants everything to be nice and happy. I know it's very hard and he's got a Conservative councillor and a Labour councillor, and he's always got to be between the two. In the past few weeks all the readings at Mass have been about riches and poverty, Lazarus, and readings from Amos, and so on, and we've had some good sermons from him, in one sense excellent. But he just steps back from the brink of actually saying to people what it means in practice. He says we've got to be concerned with political action but he never actually says what he means. And I think he does it deliberately because he knows that if he started to say 'you've got to write to your M.P.s' about this or that or the other, it would cause conflict and people wouldn't like it. So I find it very frustrating. I think he needs to give practical examples to people. . . . All his sermons recently have been great but it seems too pious or abstract and the priority in the parish this year has got nothing to do with J & P; we're having a version of RCIA (Revised Christian Initiation of Adults) called 'Journey into Faith'. And that's really where his heart is and where his priority is, getting more people to become Catholics and understand the Catholic faith.
>
> (Taped interview, 1986)

What we have indicated in this section is the tension between the priestly and prophetic functions (in Weber's sense) in the contemporary parish. It reflects some of the dilemmas of the institutionalisation of religion resulting from the 'process of concretisation' of ethical insights and the 'routinisation of charisma'. These require the development of 'workable compromises between spontaneity and creativity on the one hand and a defined and stable institutionalised context for human activity on the other' (O'Dea, 1970: 254). Meanwhile there are signs in studies of French priests that a traditional monolithic Catholicism is dissolving with a greater emphasis on social involvement as a major characteristic of an emergent 'invisible Catholicism' (Hegy, 1987).

THE PRIEST IN A TRADITIONAL PARISH

In an analysis of the state of the priesthood in the United States shortly after the end of the Second Vatican Council, Andrew Greeley described well the normative expectations of the pre-Vatican Church which

> stressed loyalty, the certainty, and immutability of answers, strict discipline and unquestioning obedience, a comprehensive Catholic community, suspicious of the world beyond the Church, the avoidance of the re-examination of fundamental principles, and clearly defined models of behaviour that were appropriate for the various levels of the Church structure. . . . It left little doubt as to what was appropriate behaviour for either parish priest or for the layman. The priest visited the sick, buried the dead, prepared young people for marriage, moderated parish organisations, tried to straighten out 'bad' marriages, tried to reclaim 'fallen away' Catholics, provided some sort of minimal instruction for those who were going to public [i.e. state] schools, spent his day off with clerical classmates, made sure there was somebody always 'on call' in the rectory, and, if it was a particularly progressive parish, greeted the people in the back of the church after Sunday Mass.
>
> (1972)

Many Catholics look back to the pre-Vatican times with a fond nostalgia. All the same the apparent stability of that period was predicated on notions of obedience and deference to the 'sacred' figure of the priest and it is likely that the coercive authoritarianism of the 'benevolent' and the 'petty tyrants' (McLeod, 1974: 74) led to a great deal of alienative compliance on the part of lay people (Archer, 1986: 165–6). It is also important to recognise the general truth that compliance does not necessarily entail normative consensus (Fox, 1985: 112). It is clear from contemporary cases, however, that such authority styles persist and are sometimes manifested when new priests are appointed to parishes. Old customs are often quite arbitrarily stopped. At the National Conference of Priests in 1987, Fr Gerry Hughes told the story of the priest who stopped the monthly collection for Third World causes without effective opposition from the parishioners who only rose in revolt when he changed the beer in the mens' club! (Hughes, 1987: 11). In another parish, flowering ecumenical collaboration which had been carefully nurtured over many years was undermined by a new priest. Pastor Ignotus in his monthly parish diary in a recent issue of *The Tablet* (26 March 1988) voiced his alarm at 'an unaccountable new breed of young priest' who had recently become his assistant, and

> his penchant for ceremonial, for antique vestments, and for long forgotten sacerdotal privilege . . . his voiced dislike of Sisters functioning as pastoral assistants, women readers, special ministers, Folk masses and every conceivable type of parish committee.

One respondent was critical about 'a kind and generous' parish priest who nevertheless behaved as a 'benevolent dictator' over the sale of some parish land in an urban area.

> Originally it was a marvellous idea; we were going to sell it to a Housing Association and we were going to be involved with the management. But because of the lack of money through the Housing Corporation, it fell through. Then the next thing we knew was that the land had been sold to the architect who was going to design the original sheltered housing (for elderly people) and that he was going to build town houses on it to be sold privately. Now, behind the church, we have ten appalling houses that the architect has obviously made a vast profit out of, that are just for private consumption and probably very expensive in an area where sheltered housing would have been fantastic. Our priest did that without consulting anyone. He didn't say to the parish, probably because he knew we wouldn't like it: 'I'm going to sell it privately to the architect because the parish needs the money.' It wasn't for any altruistic purpose that they sold the land! I still feel angry about that. I don't know whether I'd ever be able to say to him how angry I feel.
>
> (Taped interview, 1986)

It has sometimes been said that in the pre-Vatican parish, if the role of the priest was 'to teach, sanctify and govern', the role of the laity was 'to sit up, shut up and pay up'! These expectations on the part of both the priest and fellow parishioners is apparent in the above interview extract and the informant explained that the parishioners were a lot of people with an Irish background who very much want 'Father' to be involved in everything; nothing is right unless 'Father' is there. If you're having a discussion group and Father's not there to give you the answers, nothing is right. And though he [the priest] doesn't like it, he finds himself falling into this role. This is all part of it; he makes decisions without consulting anyone.

This interview raised several issues about the pastoral practices of the Church which are of interest here: the exercise of power by the parish priest and the extent to which decision-making on parish matters is shared with parishioners, whatever the rhetoric of the 'People of God' theology; the trained submissiveness of lay people in the face of a powerful priest; the fear of conflict within the parish, particularly over justice and peace issues and especially where there are significant political differences within the Catholic body, and the assumption that an avoidance of these issues or a balanced harmony concerning them is the appropriate stance; and the gap between the theory and the practice, the rhetoric of community or participation and the everyday reality.

In his study of resistance to the changes emanating from the Second Vatican Council John Leslie described how

in his reading of pastoral letters or his communication of ecumenical events in the notices the parish priest has effectively blocked change. The Pastoral Congress and the bishops' message afterwards were potentially damaging to traditionalism. By cutting their influence in public meetings, which he managed directly himself, and by limiting discussion of them to established parish societies, he was able to limit their 'damage' and de-emphasise their significance. . . . Resistance to change in the parish certainly involves distorted communication; a strong feeling on the part of stable parishioners for the customs, practices, to which they have become attached, but more fundamentally on a deep-seated conception of the sacred person and the sacred place.

(Leslie, 1986: 464, 466)

In his research, Leslie described how a traditional priest in a north midlands parish in England attempted to control the forces of change in a number of complementary ways. First of all he removed the pamphlet rack and stopped the sale of Catholic papers in the

church (1986: 12). 'By careful control of the process of transmitting
. . . and filtering information from outside, the priest is able to de-
emphasise events and contacts he considers threatening' (1986:
22–4) such as the National Pastoral Congress, the Remembrance
Sunday service, the maintenance of contacts with a national Catholic
organisation, prayer groups in the parish, or even the influence of a
bishop's pastoral letter. The liturgical practices in the parish, an
outline of which was given in the previous chapter, stressed the maintenance of social distance between the priest and lay people. While
Mass was said facing the people, 'there remain few opportunities for
lay participation' and communion in the hand was preached against
as irreverent. The degree of autonomy, involvement and initiative
allowed to lay people was strictly limited. In general terms, in the
traditionalist parish the accepted view which determines every aspect
of parish life, priestly behaviour and the expectations of lay people, is
that 'Father knows everything and Father knows best'.

With hindsight it is clear that such assumptions, which were
common up to the Second Vatican Council, had begun to break
down as a result of social change in the post-war period. Joan
Brothers first documented the growing challenge to the previously
unquestioned authority of the parish priest in Liverpool by the pupils
of the extra-parochial grammar schools by the early 1960s (1964:
73–87). But with other Catholics and in stable enclaves, such as John
Leslie's parish in the North Midlands, traditional priests were able to
maintain to a considerable extent pre-Vatican styles of authority,
retain a monopoly of decision-making over every aspect of parish life,
and expect the deference and obedience of a docile laity.

Finally, two examples from the Notre Dame study of Catholic
parish life give something of the flavour of traditional parishes in the
United States. David Leege first observes that in some parishes
'Vatican II never really happened. The Mass is in English and the
celebrant faces the people . . . but other elements of the celebration
and parish life are about as they were in the 1930s' (1986b: 9). In Our
Lady's working-class ethnic parish in an economically stagnant mill
town,

> the pastor admits to being conservative and tradition bound. He
> aims the Mass at people over 50 with an eighth-grade education
> [equivalent to a school-leaving age of 14]. Liturgists describe it as a
> privativistic Mass, one that does not celebrate the community.
>
> (1986b: 9)

In another parish, St Paul's, the pastor had ministered for over three decades until his death. He

> predated Vatican II and did little to change his style of leadership in the years thereafter. All who recall him use the term 'autocrat'. The bishop said he had to establish a parish council. [He] did — for one week. He introduced the liturgical changes he liked from Vatican II — but never taught parishioners why the new procedures were desirable.
>
> (Leege, 1986b: 16)

THE PRIEST IN A PROGRESSIVE PARISH

In his book *Parish Alive*, Fr Brian O'Sullivan (1979) outlined in general terms how in a parish in the outer London commuter belt he and his parishioners endeavoured to articulate the reforms of the Vatican Council in concrete pastoral practices:

> We have tried to work out practical ways in which all the gifts that our parishioners have may be used for the building up of God's Church. The gift may be a very simple and humble one, the gift of being willing to scrub the church floor or weed the church garden. It may be something much more dramatic, an ability to speak, to lead discussions, to proclaim the gospel by word of mouth. But whatever it is, it is a service to the community and the essence of ministry is service.
>
> (1979: 16)

Thus the leadership of the priest has to be enabling or facilitating and empowering, 'a leadership that brings out all the gifts and qualities that our people possess' and helps to develop them to their full potential. In his account of the development of these ideas he discusses the work of the elected parish council with full responsibility being 'given to the councillors for whatever area of parish life they were commissioned'. This involved the transfer of responsibility to qualified parishioners, for example in the areas of financial administration, the maintenance of the parish churches and hall, the social life of the parish, the undertaking of specific projects for CAFOD (the Catholic Fund for Overseas Development), youth work, and so on.

An outline description of the liturgies in this parish has been given in the previous chapter. These liturgies are planned and co-ordinated by a Liturgy Committee under a lay chairperson. They not only plan the regular worship of the parish, selecting hymns, responsorial chants and bidding prayers to suit the major themes in the liturgical cycle of the Church, and arrange the rotas of welcoming stewards at the church entrance, servers, readers, special ministers and groups responsible for the construction of the Sunday bidding prayers, but also the liturgies for special occasions such as First Communion Sunday or a visitation from the bishop or an ecumenical occasion with the local Anglican and Methodist Churches. Thus unlike the pre-Vatican parish where the priest expected to initiate everything and simply tell the choir what to sing, in the post-Vatican parish a much greater load of co-ordinated planning is carried by a liturgical team on which the parish priest is a key but not the sole decision-making member. Beyond the regular Sunday worship, parishioners are also encouraged to initiate or participate in the planning of special liturgies, for example with a Justice and Peace Group in the planning of special themes at First Friday Masses, or vigils before the major feasts or special jubilee celebrations, and so on. In this way a very large number of parishioners is actively involved even in this most 'sacred' area of parish worship in contrast to the pre-Vatican parish where liturgy would have been regarded as the sole concern of the priest who claimed exclusive expertise and authority in this area.

Apart from the area of liturgical planning, the handing over of financial responsibility to qualified lay people (1979: 18–19) also represented a substantial transfer of decision-making power. Whereas in the pre-Vatican parish the priest had total control over the financial affairs of the parish and maintained an almost complete veil of secrecy over all financial matters and total discretion in his use and allocation of the available resources, in the progressive parish there is some move towards sharing financial decision-making. This might include, for example, arrangements for the payment of an appropriate allowance or salary to the priest for his own private use, the purchase of a parish car and its periodic replacement, and some provision for his pension. In this parish the counting and banking of all collections and the development of covenant and planned-giving schemes will all be undertaken by lay people. As Fr O'Sullivan observes: 'the amount of work that has been taken off my shoulders by this innovation has meant that I have had considerably more time to devote to the work for which I was ordained' (1979: 19). This indicates the shift of emphasis from maintenance to ministry and mission which is an attribute of a post-Vatican parish.

It is sometimes objected that such major changes from the way priests used to administer their parishes in the pre-Vatican period can only operate in suburban parishes where there is a large number of articulate and qualified parishioners with professional or managerial qualifications. It seems that this objection might simply provide an ideological justification for those who wish to leave things as they have always been. Certainly there are some interesting developments, for example in East London, where there is a growing awareness of the untapped reservoir of skills and resources among working-class Catholics (which previously might have been channelled into trade union activism, for example). Programmes which concentrate on the raising of the consciousness of ordinary Catholics, on enabling and 'empowering' them both within the parish and in their everyday lives are strongly promoted in post-Vatican parishes.

An interesting and poignant example is St Agnes parish in Belfast which during three weeks in Lent 1988 was chosen for the funerals of two of the three people killed in Gibraltar. One of the parishioners was killed at this funeral by a would-be paramilitary and it was at his funeral that two British soldiers were killed. Vicky Cosstick has described how this parish

> offers a paradigm of parish development: an active pastoral council, over forty parish organisations, long-term planning, involvement in a range of local social issues. The latest project is a near-complete £500,000 pastoral centre . . . [and with a] glossy parish magazine that is distributed free to all 1,732 homes, . . . Lenten study programmes and detailed pastoral plans.
>
> (1988: 580)

Other activities include a family ministry, 'a support group which discusses problems like single parenthood, the handicapped child, and so on', and there is a teenagers' drop-in club at the parish centre. The parish was the first in Northern Ireland to introduce planned giving. Laity weeks have been organised and house groups established on every street, 'developing awareness and meeting the needs of the bereaved, the unemployed, the young and the old, and developing a family ministry'. There are over forty lectors and the same number of eucharistic ministers.

Now the parish organisations include a Justice and Peace group

SPRED for the handicapped, the core group for the pastoral plan, a ministry to the divorced and separated, an advice centre for those receiving social security benefits. The local equivalent of Manpower Services, ACE (Action on Community and Employment), has an office in the parish centre.

(1988: 581)

This parish, with its core pastoral team around and with the parish priest, approximates closely to the ideal-typical post-Vatican parish. It should, however, perhaps be pointed out that the development of paid parish assistants and specialised staff is nowhere like as developed in Britain as it is in the United States.

Another example which illustrates the point that there can be working-class parishes in the post-Vatican mould is that of the black parish of St Mary's in the United States illustrated in the recent Notre Dame study of Catholic parish life. Although the parishioners are poor, and some barely literate, they have built and crafted their own church to express Vatican II theology. According to Leege:

empowerment came in the planning process. Fr. Joe acted more as a consultant, encouraging the parishioners to express what their house of prayer should be. They asked him for his viewpoints, too, for they respect him. He is no shrinking violet: his homilies are forceful expressions of both the Catholic understanding of life and our obligations as co-creators of the world God made. No solace. All challenge. Being God's own means being called to a lot of work. The religious education classes are deadly serious matters and there is no shortage of volunteers for both works of mercy and political witness. And the parishioners enjoy the fellowship of church dinners. Both Fr. Joe and the Gospel he preaches and lives told these people they are somebodies. They find dignity in their *common* efforts. Their building is *theirs*.

(Leege, 1986b: 4)

This case study provides a good description of the process of the 'empowerment' of parishioners, the facilitative role of the priest and the close and friendly, collegial but not subordinate, priest-lay relations which are said to characterise the post-Vatican parish. It also demonstrates that the post-Vatican parish does not have to remain the prerogative of middle-class, suburban Catholicism, but infused with an appropriate theology of liberation, can transform and dignify the lives of poor and deprived people.

142

Finally, in the post-Vatican parish with the growth of multiple ministries, the role of the priest in 'overseeing and co-ordinating' is not devalued provided that '(1) it creatively interacts with other ministries and (2) it is integrated into the traditional concern of the priest with the salvific movement of God' (Greeley *et al.*, 1981: 181–2).

CONCLUDING REFLECTIONS

There is general agreement that the role of the priest as the religious leader in the parish is crucial to pastoral outcomes, whether or not there has been a shift in the dominant models of Church, parish, and priest espoused by the participants. Thus Bishop Butler, reflecting on the experiences of change in the decade and a half after the end of the Second Vatican Council observed that 'experience has shown that the parish clergy are the key element in any attempt to change the direction of Catholic thought and action' (1981: 204). In the United States and Canada, too, Greeley and his colleagues, on the basis of their study of young Catholics at the end of the 1970s, concluded that:

> the importance of the priest cannot be overemphasised. A sensitive parish leader who prepares meaningful sermons and relates well to his parishioners strengthens their spirituality. More than anyone else the priest seems to be the person who fosters in young Catholics closeness to the Church as a whole.
>
> (Fee *et al.*, 1981: 29)

From the relatively meagre research data and impressionistically, it seems to be generally the case that while there is no evidence of serious anti-clericalism in Anglo-Saxon countries such as is sometimes experienced in continental Europe, relations between priests and most lay people are more distant and polite than close and warm. Some of the tolerant attitudes expressed towards priests seem rooted in an older deference to the 'man apart' and a docility more appropriate in the era of the immigrant and defensive Church. The point has been made and must be stressed again that lay compliance to clerical authority cannot be interpreted to mean normative consensus or affirmation.

In this chapter we have drawn attention to the changing social context within which parish clergy must live out their role. The world of the 1990s is quite different from the world immediately after the

Second World War. The officially approved model of the Church was radically changed at the Second Vatican Council. Inevitably the type of priest required to provide religious leadership at the parish level has also changed. Authoritarian styles of leadership are no longer as effective, and at least an active core of parishioners expects to participate more in every aspect of the life of the parish — from liturgical planning to financial accounting, and from catechesis to the maintenance of the plant.

As we enter the 1990s, a quarter of a century after Vatican II, it is apparent that the parish is still in a transitional period of revolutionary change between the pre-Vatican paradigm and the post-Vatican paradigm (Kuhn, 1970). The empirical reality reflects this and is untidy and multifarious. We have noted cases which approximate closely both the pre-Vatican and post-Vatican models of parish clergy. Where a pre-Vatican priest serves in a traditional parish with a stable population insulated from recent social and religious ideas and influences, the result may be a peaceful but dead parish (Leege, 1986b: 9). Where a priest and his parishioners do not share the same orientation to Vatican II, there is likely to be conflict which may transform a parish as well as divide its parishioners. Conflict is not necessarily harmful and may indeed generate needed change (Coser, 1956). A high threshold of tolerance among lay people for a wide variety of priestly styles, the passivity of the laity, and their strategies of resistance, from polite neglect to downright sabotage, and the conflicts between traditionalists and progressives among the laity themselves, all contribute to the wide variations between parishes (see Leege, 1986b, for a number of American examples). It is not surprising, therefore, that some have argued that within-Church theological differences are often greater than those between different denominations (Ranson *et al.*, 1977: 4, 165).

In spite of the untidiness of the present transitional period, a number of general pointers to the future might be noted on the basis of the research evidence. Firstly, following a review of parish life in the United States in the early-1980s, the staff director of the Committee on the Parish of the US National Conference of Catholic Bishops identified the crucial importance of the parish priest (pastor) in his list of thirteen theses:

There is no one style of good pastoring, yet there are some common qualities. Good pastors seem to have a confident sense of direction. Aware of their own abilities and of their own weaknesses, they have a very good notion of what a parish can be. Second, good pastors care about their people. They show respect for the experience and abilities of people and are as ready to listen as to speak. They listen carefully and really hear what people are saying. Third, good pastors are able to share decision-making and leadership. Their strength evokes the strengths of others. Weak pastors evoke the weaknesses of others, their tendency to dependency, pettiness or divisiveness. Fourth, good pastors seem to be interested in both the developments in theology and the life of the larger Church beyond their parishes.

(Murmion, 1982: 314)

Like Greeley, Fr Murmion stresses that 'nothing has such a broad effect as the Sunday Mass and preaching'. He also warns against the 'rather romantic notion of community' and emphasises that the creation of good personal relationships within parishes requires both hard work and endurance as well as continuing reflection and the development of new skills.

Second, in a small study of leadership styles in two London parishes at the beginning of the 1980s, Lane (1980) argued that though there were differences in ideology between the traditional priest in one parish and the progressive priest in the other, both typically 'scolded' their flocks and retained social control and power. The older, traditional priest complained because personal confession had fallen into disuse and explained that they were just 'simple folk', in ways reminiscent of Cardinal Heenan (see Kenny, 1986: 185, 187; also Archer, 1986: 10, 14, 156). On the other hand the self-designated 'team leader' in the 'progressive' parish talked in an egalitarian fashion but scolded his flock for preferring to paint the church rather than attend a meeting in preparation for the National Pastoral Congress, explaining it in terms of their Irish immigrant status. Lane concluded that in spite of the 'changes', nothing had really changed and the priest still retained his dominant power in the parish. In other words, even if the style of its achievement and the nature of its legitimation have changed, ultimate control still remains firmly in the hands of the clergy.

Having reviewed aspects of the changing nature of the religious leadership of priests in the parishes, we will move on to consider in the next chapter how parish clergy see their role in the parish at a time of transition from a pre-Vatican paradigm to a post-Vatican paradigm.

Chapter Seven

THE EVERYDAY LIVES OF PRIESTS IN PARISHES

INTRODUCTION

In the previous chapter we looked in general terms at the changing role of the parish priest over the past few decades. Two ideal-typical models were considered: the pre-Vatican and the post-Vatican priest. A review of the relatively scanty research evidence indicated that a quarter of a century after the ending of the Second Vatican Council empirical examples could be found which approximated to both types in Britain and the United States.

In this chapter a review will be given of the everyday work lives of priests in parishes based on the accounts given by fifteen priests interviewed in four English parishes in the mid-1970s: an inner-city and a commuter or suburban parish in both the London and Preston areas. The parishes had been selected to reflect both regional and social class variations and the priests included men with a very wide range of experiences (Hornsby-Smith, 1980b). It is worth noting that a significant proportion of priests working in parishes are members of religious orders whose seminary experiences will have differed from those of the diocesan clergy in some respects. In their accounts, which will be quoted from freely, the priests provide important insights into their professional socialisation in the seminaries and comment critically on some of the consequences of the process. They then indicate their responses to recent social and religious changes, reflecting in particular on the debate over contraception and authority in the Church and on liturgical and other pastoral reforms since the Second Vatican Council. In their observations on the everyday work lives of priests, particular attention is paid to their experiences of professional-bureaucrat conflict and the generation gap

147

between parish priests and their assistants, the pervasive problem of loneliness and its relationship to the celibacy issue, and the questions of appropriate pastoral styles and strategies, risk-taking, and parish visiting. It is suggested that the richness of these priests' accounts of their everyday lives provides valuable insights into the priests' 'definition of the situation' in the parishes and their different ways of adapting to recent changes.

THE SOCIALISATION OF PRIESTS

In the parishes' sample of fifteen priests nearly all of them described their home backgrounds as fairly or very religious and several had a life history of activity as altar servers and so on, so that, as one put it, 'the religious life was just part of the air we breathed in the home'. In the case of ten of the priests, both parents had been Roman Catholic and family prayers were an everyday routine: 'it was like doing the washing-up and leaving it until after the TV programme; it was inevitable'. For four of the priests one parent had been a convert to Roman Catholicism. One priest was himself a convert and former Anglican clergyman. About one-third of the priests came from large families with seven or more children and at least four had one or more brothers who were also priests. Just under one-half had attended junior seminary, in some cases from the age of 11. Apart from the convert priest, one other man had been a late vocation. The priests had attended a range of seminaries in England, Ireland, and continental Europe.

Becoming a priest seemed for most priests a natural process in their life-history. A sense of conscious choice or decision was rarely mentioned. For example, the late vocation commented that his life had increasingly appeared to be somewhat aimless so that he was 'firing on only one cylinder' and had come to see the priesthood as the most likely way of improving things. Only one other priest indicated that a conscious choice of alternatives had been made:

> I was very much involved with a girl whom I had known since we were at school . . . together . . . I loved her and she loved me. It would have to be a thing that we would have to test over a period of courtship which I didn't have time to do. I wasn't prepared to give the time because I felt that at the back of my mind I had to give the priesthood a try. That was the great thing about [the seminary]

because you came from this very strict life to complete freedom and you made a lot of mistakes and it clarified things for you.

Other priests added that their mother or the prayerful atmosphere of their home had been influential factors in their decision and one priest gave the impression that status-aspiration — being recognised by deferential and respectful children saying 'Hullo Father' — was an attraction.

The reactions of the priests to their seminary training varied considerably. Some enjoyed enormously the opportunities for sport and guided recreation in an isolated public (private) boarding school type of environment. Some were aware of the sacrifices made by their parents to ensure that they conformed to the rather middle-class norms of boarding schools:

My father couldn't really afford it but he . . . bought everything on the list that was given and he had to pay for it on hire purchase. But he said he was determined I wouldn't feel deprived when I went there. They made a lot of sacrifices that way. I discovered later that half the stuff was unnecessary.

Most priests were highly critical of the rigidity of the seminaries they had attended, usually for about six years. They were seen as highly bureaucratised organisations for producing priests. For example, one priest suggested that his seminary 'produced priests like . . . Heinz factories produce so many tins of baked beans; they just kind of spill out at the end and off they go into parishes'. Others complained that their seminaries had been rigid, traditional, unthinking, bound by frustratingly petty rules like only walking to the college gates and back and only going out in threes. One priest observed:

I was immensely happy at [my seminary] in the last stages, but I couldn't help having second thoughts about the whole system, as so many priests do, really. You are taught certain virtues: community and obedience, at the cost of initiative. I think I lost a lot of initiative at [my seminary].

This criticism of being treated as immature boys was made by several priests:

I felt that we were treated as little boys and that then suddenly on the day of ordination we were expected to be men.

The main trouble was that in the Sixth form at [the junior seminary] we'd had a lot of freedom and a lot of responsibility and we felt that going to [the senior seminary] that . . . we'd have even more. But, in fact, we were treated in the same way that we'd been treating kids in the years below us. We were not allowed to go out except in threes — only to go for a walk. . . . We used to make jokes about taking the wrong turning . . . when we were in the security wing of [the local prison]. It came as a big shock to us. We couldn't believe that human beings of our own age could be treated like that.

Not surprisingly, in a period of rapid change, the consequences were often painful, if not disastrous. Fr Brian O'Sullivan records some of the effects:

As priests we still suffered from the effects of our training and could not be close to one another in any way. So there I was at the age of thirty, spiritually dead and emotionally barren. I could no longer pray anything but the formal prayers of the liturgy; I went through the motions of doing my work, and on the surface it appeared to be well done, but I knew the emptiness at the heart of my ministry.

(1979: 2)

In his autobiography Anthony Kenny also gives a detailed account of his own training in the junior seminary at Upholland and then at the English College in Rome. Looking back twenty-five years after his ordination he is 'astonished at the thinness of the intellectual under-pinning of a lifetime commitment to the service of the Church', at the inadequacy of the emotional investment by itself for a life of priestly fidelity, and what he regards as the element of make-believe that characterised his position at that time (1986: 23–112).

Not surprisingly, seminarians developed their own strategies for coping with authoritarian regimes. One priest described his strategy as 'keeping his nose clean' while other priests admitted that they

bent the rules as much as we could . . . we rejected a lot of the traditions that made it almost like a public [high-status private] school. We were mainly from working-class families [and] didn't want to pretend we were anything else.

The younger priests referred to the relaxation in the seminary regimes in the years following the Second Vatican Council. Most expressed a strong preference for the greater openness but one did voice reservations about the changes:

There were several crises at [the seminary]. Whether you mean the Rector's influence and authority over the seminary at the time or it happened to be the general changes within the Church which were traumatic experiences, I was very much in the conservative or traditional camp . . . I was against such a rapid 'over to you and your own responsibility' philosophy, particularly from 1965 to 1968. . . . One had been told 'you do this and that' up to that time. I felt that there was still a certain amount of room for some of that, perhaps not in the small niggling ways we had it up to then, but I didn't feel that 'from two o'clock to seven o'clock you have got to get your studies in and it really is up to you how you place it', I didn't think we were quite ready for that and I think there is a bit of both which ought to come in. There is what I would call applied discipline and this brings obedience and all the rest of it and I felt that that was rather being chucked out of the window too rapidly.

Several priests were critical of various aspects of the seminary curriculum. The priest who had been a late vocation observed that the Moral Theology course had been particularly poor and had seemed to bear no relationship to the world of real human problems which he had experienced both in the services and at work. He bemoaned what he regarded as the terrible waste of time and energy expended on useless things such as learning everything in Latin. Priests trained in Irish seminaries commented that nothing was done to prepare them for the pastoral scene either in Britain or in Australia and the other countries to which they were sent. The seminary training 'wasn't sufficiently pastorally orientated' was a general view. Several of the Irish priests suggested there were class-based antagonisms between Maynooth and the other Irish seminaries:

I never wanted to be a priest in Ireland . . . because I think one of the main requisites for being a priest in Ireland is the ability to pay the bills at Maynooth perhaps, and I wouldn't have had the intellectual qualifications.

The selection of an English diocese by the Irish also seemed to be a rather haphazard affair. One priest commented that he resented his diocese even before he came and contrasted the 'long-winded' and 'unrealistic' pastoral letters of one bishop with the 'pithy little ones' of another bishop. There were criticisms, too, of the slightness of the contact between the seminarians and the bishop of the diocese they were going to:

> Then when he came himself with his entourage of monsignori it used to be a bit of a joke in the College. The high fliers are coming and you would be interviewed for one minute and he would have nothing important to say to you, just a word of encouragement, but showed no interest in your personal life or anything.

While it may seem at times that the isolated seminary with its strictly controlled regime, hierarchical authority structures, and pervasive systems of routines, regulations and rituals, shares many of the characteristics of a 'total institution' (Goffman, 1968), it is clear from the responses of these priests in the mid-1970s, that their definitions of the situation varied widely, that they adapted to their seminary regimes in widely different ways, that they evolved a range of coping strategies designed to ensure their successful graduation, but also that they expressed in a variety of ways, covert forms of resistance to the more coercive aspects of seminary life. The remark of Fichter about seminaries is apposite:

> A training program that sets out deliberately to keep a person in a perpetual state of childlike dependence cannot possibly develop a professional who exhibits initiative and responsibility.
>
> (1966: 112)

Brief reference might be made here to a number of suggestions which have been made from the perspective of lay people on the matter of the appropriate formation of priests for their special role of leadership at the parish level in the light of recent social and religious changes, including the changing needs of lay people and their expectations of priests. To a very considerable extent lay people do not challenge the religious leadership of the parochial clergy but they do, to an increasing extent, expect it to be exercised in a consensual rather than an authoritarian manner in all areas of parish life. Lay people have not yet seriously insisted on the community-recognition and affirming dimension of 'vocation' but they do increasingly see the task of their priest to be a man of prayer, to preach, to preside at their eucharistic celebrations and to co-ordinate the work of a multitude of lay ministries in the parish. These requirements should determine the nature of the training of priests (Hornsby-Smith, 1983; 1984; 1988a).

RESPONSES TO CHANGES

From their survey of a sample of 412 priests from three Roman Catholic dioceses in England in the early 1970s, Hinings and his colleagues found that, unlike the beliefs of comparative samples of Church of England clergymen and Methodist ministers,

> Roman Catholicism is a unified belief system within which theological nuances are relatively few. . . . We found considerable uniformity in the manner in which priests expressed their theological cosmology, a uniformity of style and tone unparalleled in the other Churches: the certainty of 'knowing' their Church to be the one, true, authentic Church as founded by Christ. . . . Priests present no clear and distinct categories of doctrinal belief, no differentiated theological cosmologies.
>
> (Ranson *et al.*, 1977: 49, 51, 154)

This uniformity of belief is attributed to the effort made to achieve a consensus in the theological socialisation of the priests and the fact that very high proportions of them are trained in their local seminaries (1977: 50, 154). While the theological belief systems of the priests appeared more unified than was the case in the other two denominations, these conclusions need to be treated with some caution. In the first place the views of this sample of priests on several controversial matters were by no means uniform. Thus wide differences of opinion and emphasis are reported on the relationship between Rome and the national Churches, the centrality of liturgical matters and on various proposals for reform suggested by the Laity Commission (1977: 49–50, 115–25). Second, under one-half of the sample of priests responded to the mail questionnaire, much less than was the case with clergy and ministers. It is likely that this resulted in a reduction of the variations between priests. Third, three-quarters of this sample were aged 40 or over and had therefore been socialised in seminaries before the influence of the Second Vatican Council. In contrast eight of my sample of fifteen priests were under the age of 40 and had experienced some of the changes arising from the Council. Not surprisingly, therefore, the evidence of variations in beliefs and attitudes is stronger in the focused interviews than in the mail questionnaire of Hinings and his colleagues.

Contraception and authority

This can, perhaps, best be illustrated by the comments made on contraception, pastoral responses since the publication of the papal encyclical *Humanae Vitae*, and the matter of papal infallibility. Thus one priest considered that:

> The Church is so much imprisoned by past pronouncements and . . . desperately needs to regain a bit of credibility. Its credibility has been terribly damaged by *Humanae Vitae*, but how can the Church do anything about what it has already said?

In an observation on marital difficulties another priest observed:

> that difficult period when they begin to have more pregnancies than they want and that I imagine must be a source of great trial for the faith, especially if they have a confessor who regards it as an intrinsically grave sin ever to use artificial contraception. That must be a thing that drives people out of the Church but I haven't experienced that very much.

A third priest explained his own response to ambiguity in a way which demonstrated the priority that he gave to institutional maintenance:

> I would underwrite completely all the things that were said at the time of the *Humanae Vitae* business. I never wrote nor did I put signatures at the bottom of letters. Many of those who did now aren't functioning as priests. Now it may be that I hadn't quite the guts to join the flag-wavers but, in fairness to myself, it might also be that I felt it didn't help to rock the boat completely. At a time when there was a great unease and unhappiness that it was God's work to keep what stability could be kept. So my own practice has been never to pull my punches privately — and I might add no matter to whom I had been speaking — but not to preach outright in a way that would provoke a storm. And this could be described as dishonest. There you are, that's life . . . but it is nevertheless a path, I think, which an awful lot of clergy have taken.

When prompted to give his views on *Humanae Vitae*, the same priest volunteered:

My view is that I cannot see and I do not believe that contraception is intrinsically wrong. I believe that a person can be selfish in sexuality, obviously, and that insofar as he is selfish, he is sinful. But I believe that a full sexual relationship is for most people a vital necessity in marital life and nowadays when you can have four babies in four years quite comfortably and inevitably, what does happen for the rest of your married life?

He went on to contrast this situation with that experienced by his grandmother, only six of whose thirteen babies lived to adult life. He also referred to a rebuke he had been given when at the seminary only sixteen years ago, for suggesting the importance of preaching on the infertile period. He did not rule out the choice of periodic abstinence by a married couple but added:

I just wouldn't be dogmatic to the point of saying that contraception was intrinsically wrong and I certainly wouldn't say to a married couple who had problems in this matter 'it is venial' because it seems to me that to say to someone that it is only venial at moments when they are closest to each other is almost criminal.

He continued to suggest that although the issue had been defused

by the universal clerical approach, which is to say 'well, if there are good reasons, it is only venial' . . . there are an awful lot of Catholics who are still carrying a great burden of guilt in this matter. I think it can greatly harm their lives.

One priest, in response to a question asking his views on authority in the Church, said:

Well! I really find it difficult to believe — this is lining myself up for the firing squad — that the Pope is infallible in faith and morals — full stop! I am very happy to hear an infallible statement about the Trinity or things of this sort. But when it comes to morals I think you have got to do your social homework. I don't think you can pull a solution out of the hat. I think you have got to look at the world as it is. Now if you have got a commission sitting on, talking about contraception for a good many years and, if after having expanded the commission because it looked as if it was coming out with the wrong answer, if at the end of all that you wind up with a view that there is nothing intrinsically wrong in contraception, I really cannot see that it is within the competence of the authority of the Church to go clean against it. I don't think it is a matter of revelation. It is not revelation. I think you have got to look at the evidence. Now, if authority pronounces on the matter in a sense which is clearly contrary to the evidence which has been examined, it seems to me that authority has lost its authority.

He went on to say that he recognised that the Pope was talking to the whole world and that many parts of the world did not hold with contraception. Again, he was talking in a historical situation in which popes had been expected to pronounce on all sorts of topics. But he opposed the waving of authority 'with a big A' in cases like this. In his view the overwhelming majority of priests were treating contraception as 'only a venial' matter and he thought that the bishops were of the same mind, adding:

I think we are, in large part, saving face at the present time . . . I believe that it can be a person's duty to practise contraception — absolute duty — for the sake of the marriage in every sense. And the only difference between me and the absolute orthodox person is that the absolute orthodox person will say 'Oh well! it is only a venial — not much wrong — it is the less perfect way'.

Commenting on an earlier draft one of the priests doubted if the quote 'on the infallibility of the Pope would find many echos' and a second urged that 'to keep the balance it would be good to have the views of a priest who is just as explicit about the orthodoxy of the Pope's teaching, i.e. myself!' A third priest observed that by the mid-1970s his

impression from the Deanery meetings . . . is that the issue seems less of a problem. I would like to think that priests generally accept *Humanae Vitae* as being the present moral position and merely interpret it with great compassion [elasticity?]. Some would agree with Cardinal Hume: 'the last word has not been said on this'.

Post-conciliar changes

A second area which illustrates the range of beliefs held by Catholic clergy relates to their responses to the Second Vatican Council and to changes emanating from it. Far from being uniform and agreed, the fifteen priests expressed a variety of views ranging from enthusiastic support but some frustration at the slowness of change or a desire for more thoroughgoing change, to opposition but conformity in obedience to authority or thinly disguised hostility. One priest expressed reservations about 'this preoccupation with the Church as a community within itself' and thought it was time to say that:

> the effect on the Catholic Church in this country so far, of the Vatican Council, has been to make us more 'churchy' than the Church was before the Vatican Council came along. [There was a] great preoccupation with liturgy and the parish community and the humanism and all those things of Church concerns and a certain loss, I think, of a sense of responsibility for the world outside, the secular order and secular structures etc.

This view, which interestingly predates the similar analysis expressed in the Chicago Declaration of Christian Concern (Barta, 1980: 19–27), was echoed by another priest who thought the Church

> should become more daring in its involvement . . . it needs to be much more overtly caring . . . far more involved in the problems, far more of the visible force for Christ.

Against this view, another priest who had been amongst the pioneers in the promotion of house Masses, expressed reservations about recent liturgical changes though he said he accepted them 'because the Church says so'. In his view most people would have preferred the old ways and he pointed to a decline in the number of conversions in his parish to only one-twelfth of the level of fourteen years earlier as evidence that the changes had not been self-evidently successful. This again can be contrasted with the observation of a priest who was 'bubbling over with the new liturgy' but who realised that at the parish level 'the Vatican Council had to filter through [and] it is still a long way from filtering through in some places'.

On the whole the priests in the four research parishes had accommodated to the liturgical changes by the mid-1970s without undue difficulty. Some of the young assistant priests felt frustrated at the fact that the 'boss' (i.e. their parish priest) reserved final decision-making to himself and sometimes was not prepared to innovate as rapidly as they would have liked over matters such as the introduction of the 'sign of peace' or the saying of Mass during the week in small day chapels. On the whole, however, they recognised a preparedness on the part of the senior priests to accommodate and adjust to new ideas. At the same time there was, among some priests, a recognition that liturgical change by itself was not sufficient to change the nature of Christian commitment. In other words there was no support for a sort of 'liturgical determinism'. Rather it was suggested that 'the changes in the Mass remain sterile unless there is the whole spirit of the parish which is more dynamic'. Another priest observed:

> I never saw this as being a solution to the problems. It is just a thing that I thought ought to be done that the Mass had become a pure ritual, something that was done by the priests and the people were just there. . . . Now there have been tremendous difficulties [with liturgical reform]; people got used to a passive way of carrying on, on the one hand. On the other hand, many older priests have found it very difficult and have just substituted one ritual for another . . . it was brought in far too quickly. . . . On the other hand, you do occasionally pick up from people: one woman said to me 'we have a lot more of the Bible read to us now'.

This same priest went on to observe that different liturgies were required in different settings: 'a House Mass is not the sort of thing you would put in a cathedral and the cathedral liturgy is not for the small parish church.'

The most 'traditional' of the priests interviewed in this research commented that some of the critics of the Church in the mid-1960s were

> an insult to our parents and grandparents. . . . In other words there was tremendous criticism of what was done in the past rather than see that this was a development of the past; the present and the future must go on developing. In my eyes the Vatican Council cannot be seen in terms of change when we mean a change of expression. The essence of the Church does not change and did not change at the Vatican Council. I think I would have objected to a thought-pattern in people's minds where we get the impression that this was the idea of the Vatican Council and now there was something fresh but not something new.

This priest was opposed to the model of the priest as 'a glorified social worker', had a strong sense that the parish priest 'is the boss', was opposed to anything 'gimmicky in the way that one would approach the sacrament of reconciliation', accepted a form of liturgical pluralism at different Sunday Masses though he was not very keen on folk Masses, and was suspicious of the charismatic movement though 'rather like all things in the Church from St Bernadette to everything else, it will be proved in time'.

These selections from our taped interviews with fifteen priests from four research parishes in England in the mid-1970s, dealing with such issues as *Humanae Vitae*, papal authority, and liturgical change, indicate a greater variety of theological positions than was suggested in the study by Hinings and his colleagues (Ranson *et al.*, 1977). They demonstrate that considerable transformations in the authority structures in the Church have taken place. For several of these priests there are clear indications of a shift away from the legal-rational forms of authority appropriate for a 'mechanistic' organisation. There are instances, notably in the case of contraception, where independent decision-making is emerging. Rather than regarding this as a process of 'Protestantisation' it seems more appropriate to interpret it as one of 'normative convergence' in a predominantly secular society (Hornsby-Smith, 1987: 216). It appears to indicate clearly the selection of the option of accommodation rather than intransigence in a pluralist society (Berger, 1973: 156). It also illustrates again that formal compliance with official norms in many cases does not entail normative consensus (Fox, 1985) but is rather a coping strategy, involving various 'techniques of neutralisation' (Matza, 1964), employed by relatively powerless officials in an organisation which continues to retain strong bureaucratic features enshrined for example in Canon Law.

THE WORK LIVES OF PRIESTS

In the course of our interviews, the priests discussed, among other things, various aspects of their work roles, areas of role conflict, the fragmentation of their work lives and the constraints on them, and their relationships with other priests and with housekeepers in the presbytery. In addition, they were invited to comment on the conflict between the priest as an official in a hierarchically structured institution where the parish priest was the superior of the assistant priest, on the one hand, and the fact that they were both professional colleagues with specialised role skills obtained after prolonged training, on the other.

Bureaucratic official and professional colleague

In his study of *Religion as an Occupation* (1966), Fichter analysed some of the basic conflicts inherent in the role of the priest as a key official in the religious organisation but also as a professional. There is a major literature on the nature of professional-bureaucrat conflict (e.g. Blau and Scott, 1966) which focuses on the different control structures. Briefly, the bureaucrat is controlled by his superior in a vertical hierarchy of offices and his loyalty is directed towards the organisation. The professional, by contrast, tends to be controlled by his colleague peer group and his loyalties are directed horizontally to his professional colleagues from whom he derives his values and standards of performance. Inevitably there are conflicts when a professional is employed in an organisation but typically a number of 'accommodative mechanisms' are devised to reduce the potential tensions (Hornsby-Smith, 1984: 158).

This type of conflict can be seen clearly in the case of the relationship between the younger assistant priest and the older parish priest. In organisational terms the parish priest is the superior official in the parochial structures of the diocese. As an official in a bureaucratically administered organisation (to follow Max Weber's ideal-type of bureaucracy; Weber, 1964: 329–41), the parish priest is entitled to issue instructions downwards to his subordinate, his assistant priest, who must then faithfully carry them out according to the standardised procedures of the organisation (i.e. in accordance with Canon Law). On the other hand, the assistant priest might well feel that he is a professional colleague, that he has undergone a lengthy and systematic training, and that on these grounds he is entitled to participate in joint decision-making on such matters as the liturgical style of the parish. This problem is perhaps exacerbated in the Roman Catholic Church where, as Hinings and his colleagues have pointed out, promotion is relatively slow and

> in general where relatively elderly people have been kept in positions of inferiority and subordination for long periods one might seriously expect to discover attitudes of dissent, resentment or disenchantment.
>
> (Ranson *et al.*, 1977: 24)

One very experienced priest did make a wry comment about his being the longest serving assistant priest in the diocese and did wonder if he would celebrate his silver jubilee in the priesthood before he obtained his first parish. He added:

> The interesting thing about a priest's life . . . is that you can get all sorts of jobs and find yourself back where you started. Here I am back as a curate almost as though the intervening years hadn't been there . . . most of us don't want to be a bishop or a dean . . . we don't have that ambition, so you are very much thrown back on faith. The only reason you do it . . . is because you believe in Jesus Christ; that's what it's all about . . . I could imagine that is why perhaps priests desire to become a monsignor or to become a canon, to receive some recognition of what they are or what they have done and in that way to fulfil ambition. You can't escape that in many ways you are going to suffer that kind of thing . . . 'why was he made a canon and why wasn't I?' and that sort of thing.

A sense of resistance to the intrusion of bureaucratic relationships among professional colleagues is also apparent in the frustrations expressed by one of the younger priests:

> I feel very strongly about the lack of sharing of responsibility. We started a weekly meeting here between the priests in the presbytery and after we got it established we wanted to involve others who work in the parish, teachers and all the different strata of parish society but the boss won't come to them. He escaped the first two and then he decided he wanted to do [outside visiting] work at that time. We wanted liturgical change. We want to ban confessions on a massive scale. We want baptisms changed and many others. But all these things he says you can't change overnight and it is very frustrating and leads to an awful lot of tension. There is more tension inside the house (presbytery) than outside. You could say it is a generation gap; there is certainly a clash of temperaments. You can't choose who you are going to live with; you are just sent. We are responsible men . . . but you are still treated like you are . . .

Presbytery relations and the generation gap

A parish priest was sympathetic to the problem and suggested that one difficulty was that

> a priest has all his eggs in one basket: his work life, his home life, his whole life is in one particular area and activity . . . if he doesn't

survive, the work doesn't survive and I think it is particularly vulnerable there.

This situation is contrasted with that of a married professional man who had alternative spheres of emotional support, tension release and status in home and leisure activities outside the work situation. For the priest, however, where two or more professionals are living under one roof and where there has to be one coherent parish policy, for example in regard to liturgy:

> it is very difficult for a man to be . . . at least 40 before he is in a position of having the last say . . . I see it as inevitable . . . but I don't really think I have known of any parish situation where there wasn't a degree of tension. . . . If you look at any photograph of a class at a seminary, you've got there up to twenty jolly nice people who, by and large, are jolly generous but it can well happen [that] by the time they have weathered the storm of fifty years, they are pretty difficult, edgy, crusty old chaps.

One assistant priest who had had several parish priests commented on the difficulties and isolation of a young priest with some parish priests:

> We never had a row but there was always a tremendous distance because we had nothing, really, in common. He was more elderly than his years and never moved out and knew only a very small clique and he had no interest at all in the parish. It was really a terribly deadening experience for a person who was groping with himself and felt that he could not get any help at all and no understanding or friendship.

A retrospective view was provided by a retired parish priest who argued that

> like married life [the relationship between priests in a presbytery] needs a lot of hard work to preserve an even, loving relationship because you know when you work close to a person you are very alive to their defects and these are a cause of irritation. But there is a difficulty now that my curates used the argument with me: they said 'You don't expect me to live cooped up in this house. Isn't it much better for me to spend my evenings with people, families?' So I said there was a lot in that but I tried to furnish a very nice common room and have a colour television with a view to offering

them something like a pleasant kind of community life in the evening but encountered this argument. And I don't know how you resolve that one. I am old-fashioned enough to think that people can't preserve celibacy without being a community of bachelors, but if you are a community of bachelors it rather restricts your social life and there is no doubt about it, that these visits of priests to families who welcome them does a lot of good to both parties. It provides a substitute for the female companionship they sacrifice and it also acquaints them with the attitudes of people because they are the 'good' Catholic families who want the priest usually . . . I don't know what the answer really is. Of course, you can [create] community life over the dinner table. Another thing is that the generation gap has been usually very much exaggerated because of the changes in the liturgy and the reluctance and frank dislike of old priests for changing everything. It worried them and distressed them and to find young priests who are enthusiastic about it all and want it to go further even would very likely produce contention in the house. I think with an effort life at the presbytery can be very pleasant but it is awfully difficult when it is two, one older priest who claims authority and one who is much younger. I have never had that. I have always had three [priests in the parish] and that is much easier because you can discuss with your fellow curate the idiosyncrasies of the other man and they often soften your attitudes.

Against the view of the bachelor community, a young assistant priest explained how he and a second young priest used to enjoy visiting friends in the parish and found the constraints of the traditional model of the socially-distant priest irksome:

We were the two lads . . . [We] believe in enjoyment in having our own friends. We resented very much the idea that a priest must mix with his other priests and play golf on Mondays. We resented that whole concept of the priesthood, at least on the social side. We also resented that when it was the parish dance we stood at the back of the hall being nice to everybody. We got in there and danced and we had enough confidence in our relationship with the people to accept us as human beings. We liked racing and we used to go off to race meetings. Because we combined so well we became efficient in missing people from Mass. People were very flattered that we missed them whether they just didn't go or whether they were sick.

Generally there is a considerable body of research evidence of a generation gap among priests. Thus in an in-depth study of an American archdiocese it was reported that

> pastors [parish priests] stress the importance of maintaining and expanding church structures, meeting financial obligations, and administering the parish effectively, while curates want to devote more time and energy to community development and their own personal growth.

(Hall and Schneider, 1973: 60)

Similarly in a study of priests in the Wellington diocese in New Zealand in 1973, it was reported that 'increased age and higher status within the Church hierarchy (at least somewhat related to age) are . . . the biggest contributors to traditionalism' (Reidy and White, 1977: 237) in attitudes to involvement in the parish community, morality and priestly life-style, modernisation of the Church, ecumenism, and the relaxation of the traditional Sunday Mass obligation. In a survey of members of the Society of the Divine Word (Pro Mundi Vita, 1973) 8 per cent of the 25–35 age group expressed pre-Vatican theological orientations compared to 57 per cent of the over-65s. Forty-seven per cent of the younger group selected post-Vatican theologies compared to only 5 per cent of the oldest age group and it was reported that age was a major distinguishing variable, more so than region or continent.

Reidy and White in New Zealand (1977) and Reilly in a study of all priests in one American diocese (1975) both found that younger priests gave more emphasis to 'prophetic' activities than administrative duties. Seminarians at Wonersh tended to emphasise the 'prophetic' rather than the 'priestly' aspects of the role (Hornsby-Smith, 1980a), at least in terms of the distinction made by Weber (1966) who regarded priests as specialised functionaries who claimed authority by virtue of their service in a sacred tradition in contrast to the prophet who proclaimed a religious teaching based on his own personal revelation and charisma. That the generation gap could be bridged, though, was attested to by one of my respondents who indicated that 'the PP couldn't have been a nicer companion. We did look on each other as companions and colleagues, even though he was so much my senior.'

These examples illustrate strategies for coping with the loneliness of the priest. Given this loneliness it was a surprising finding that in none of the four presbyteries did the priests appear to come together in the house for prayer. There seemed to be no attempts made at shared prayer for God's guidance in their search for solutions to the pastoral problems of the parish including, for example, their need to reconcile their frequently acute differences over the liturgical style of the parish. Occasionally attempts were made to read the Office or rosary together in a formal way:

At one time we had the family rosary here and, incredible as it sounds, it broke down because of the utter impossibility of finding the necessary quarter-of-an-hour . . . doorbells would go, telephones would go, in and out, so by the end of the rosary hardly any of the congregation were left!

One can, perhaps, only speculate about the reasons for this lack of a communal, spontaneous, prayer life within the presbytery. It seems likely that the broad pattern of a seminary education in the past prepared the priest for subsequent independence and isolation (Kenny, 1986) so that he had a 'trained incapacity' to pray easily with other priests. In the parish situation the stress on the bureaucratic official rather than the professional colleague relationship was also not conducive to the development of an easy, shared prayer life between a parish priest and his assistant priest. One of the priests who agreed with this interpretation subsequently wrote that:

it has been my experience that there is very little forward planning by the clergy in a parish as a team, possibly, and in fact ideally, involving the laity. What I mean is something along the classic lines of identifying problems or problem areas, e.g. Where are we now? Where are we going? How do we get there? Obviously I do not expect fool-proof solutions, but there might just emerge more of a sense of direction.

Loneliness and celibacy

The late Fr Bob Bogan, interviewing twenty priests in the south of England in 1971, interpreted his data in terms of Seeman's five dimensions of alienation (1959). Apart from their sense of powerlessness, meaninglessness, normlessness and self-estrangement, he reported a considerable measure of isolation and loneliness on the part of these priests which created tensions for them in relating to other people. Celibacy contributed to this loneliness 'not only because the priest remained single, but also because he had not learned how to relate deeply'. This was expressed poignantly by one of his respondents:

> Celibacy does bother a lot of priests; not lack of a sexual outlet but lack of companionship, which is not supplied by deep relationships with other people. I was so lonely I got a canary — but put not your trust in canaries.
>
> (Bogan, 1973: 201)

The question of loneliness is clearly related to the question of celibacy and a married ex-priest observed that 'companionship made me a fuller person and it improved my personality . . . I resented the fact that I had to leave the priesthood to get married'. For several priests celibacy was something they tolerated as part of the job specification. Several priests referred to a long process of decision-making between a girl with whom they were developing a close social relationship and the completion of their seminary training. Others 'regarded it as a price to be paid to become a priest' while one observed:

> I accepted the fact that there wouldn't be marriage; this was part of the package deal. But if you ask me whether I believe I would be more effective in my job, vocation, whatever you are going to call it, as a married man, I believe that I would be more effective.

Another priest did, however, argue that celibacy was important while admitting: 'nothing in the priesthood itself . . . says you must be celibate. The whole vocation to the priesthood is a call to complete commitment and I think celibacy is an aid to that commitment.'

Pastoral risks

One of the most interesting comments made in the course of the interviews concerned the question of the priest's relationships with women and the consequent elements of risk attached to aspects of his pastoral role. One young assistant priest observed that:

> You get into many, many risky sorts of situations, especially with women. I don't seem to be able to avoid this. I certainly don't desire it at times, but nevertheless it happens. The great thing is

that I can come down in the morning and say my Office and say my prayers and I feel confident to face the day . . . I go to the [parish club] and about three-quarters are lapsed, not the bad lapsed, but those who are just lazy and have dropped off. I can see most of my pastoral work there [and] I have quite a few converts. It is pastoral work of a nature, being able to sit down and have a drink and talk and even get up and have a dance, which still raises eyebrows. But nevertheless, how I justify this, perhaps it is not justified every time by no means, is that Our Lord went down into the hovels of the people too. He was happy with them. They were His people and it was their way of enjoying themselves, what they looked forward to. The difficulties are there but you are still very conscious of being a priest and that you are doing a job. People have accused me of really enjoying myself and they don't realise that I am still working. . . . Many a time I have conversations with women. . . . The dangers are that some people then start calling you by your first name and while in one sense I don't mind . . . it does automatically drop barriers which I prefer to be up when I am trying to do a job, and so there are difficulties that way.

My big difficulty comes with women, especially in this parish. It is very difficult to let them know . . . the most difficult part is dropping them gently . . . there are quite a few that I've had problems with. I don't think they look at me as a priest at all. They do in a sense; they won't touch me. They just see the man, I think, and it makes things very awkward at times. The difficulty is to keep them coming on, coming to Mass, showing them their responsibilities towards their children, and yet not get too close, too involved, because it impedes you.

Other young priests similarly stressed the importance of seeking out people where they were:

We made sure we danced with everybody, grannies and everybody, so it wasn't that we were after the nice bird, and once people saw that they were quite flattered to be danced and the men saw us as no threat. . . . We used also to go into pubs as well. . . . We were very conscious that the Church was unrealistic and that preaching or standing about or hearing confessions was one side of things, but that we weren't where the people were. And especially in an Irish population . . . we wanted to be where the people were, which a lot of the time was in the pub. Again, we made sure not to be spending all our time; it was a conscious policy. We would meet, for example, at lunch time . . . I would go in and have a beer and meet half-a-dozen people, fellows that were [working locally]. There were no great conversions. I don't think they got an opportunity to talk and we made sure, as well, to wear our collars in the pubs and it became acceptable. And then 'Where were you last week? I didn't see you', and we got very well 'in' with the managers of the pubs. This had the effect that we always got a bottle of whisky at garden fête time, and you got the licence for the dance bar, and in some places we arranged for a catechetical course for the kids over a pub, and we would hear confessions upstairs in a pub and things like this. Again we were very wary of that because sometimes you get people at an unfair advantage. But we did it by appointment when they were sober and it must be at the beginning of the night, not towards the end of the night. We were very conscientious like that.

Visiting and relating

Given this attempt by priests to develop new pastoral approaches more in tune with contemporary needs, the observed decline in the level of parish visiting is striking. The consequence is that priests do not have such a high profile in the family life of parishioners, and particularly the younger generation, as they had in the days of the fortress, immigrant Church. One consequence is a reduction of the opportunities to cultivate the close friendships between priests and young people which is likely to be necessary if parishes are to grow their own priests (Hornsby-Smith, 1988a). None of the four research parishes approached the level of home visiting every six weeks which was reported in the Liverpool parish of St Catherine's in the 1950s (Ward, 1965: 47). This is a matter where there appears to be a considerable gap between the ideology of close personal relationships between priests and parishioners and the actual pastoral practice. In consequence priests either express guilt at their failures in respect of parish visiting or else construct an elaborate structure of excuses (Scott and Lyman, 1968: 47) to explain the impossibility of regular visiting in the light of recent social changes. Some of these responses are reflected in the observations made by three priests:

My own visiting record is abysmally poor. By and large I visit those where there is a specific matter to be dealt with. I do realise, and I do believe, to see people at home is of paramount importance, but one way or another, I am never doing anything.

[Visiting is] very important. Unfortunately, in practice it is very difficult. [This parish] has a lot of people coming at evening time, lots of meetings, committees. [Yet] the only time, apart from the old people, is to visit in the evening time, try to visit husband and wife and children, but at that time you are involved in meetings . . . I like visiting but at the practical level . . . one doesn't have the opportunity.

Often visiting in those [tower] blocks . . . I wonder now why should I keep on going to these flats [apartments] where nobody is interested in me and I am not really welcome, and I am not invited in. Is there any good going round and round them? And yet this is what that kind of apostolate means that you try very hard offering them goods even if they refuse you many times.

Several priests broadened the discussion and stressed the importance of being available at the crisis points in the lives of their parishioners:

I began to preach the idea that the job of the Church was to go to people where they were. It was useless trying to get people to Church until they could see something of the relevance of the Church in their lives. Now there are certain times, and this is where visiting and the priest knowing his people and being in contact is so important, where there are certain areas in their lives in which religion is going to touch them. The obvious one is death, there is sickness, trouble and so on. And that is the place where they see the Church, they can see the point of the priest as someone to whom they can open their hearts, someone to whom they can give their complete confidence, who is with them in their present difficulties. In other words it is what the priest is. He is seen as someone who has a meaning in their lives at those points. There is still something there that they recognise and hold on to.

I am a people's friend. Even if you can't do anything about it, if you are with them, with the sick, the people in distress, if you haven't done a useful thing by utilitarian standards, you will be amazed . . . how grateful they are . . . (there is) nothing to take the place of real steady visiting of your people.

This priest, however, admitted that he was not successful at visiting his parishioners in their homes, pointing out that many mothers are now working. People did not return home from work until late, and with that and various other regular responsibilities, for example hospital visiting, he had lost the rhythm of regular home visiting. A young assistant priest, however, saw this as evidence:

> that priests are out of touch with people. For example, there is not much point in visiting people at four o'clock in the afternoon . . . when they are getting their tea or Saturday afternoon when there is sport on. I think the reason is that priests are out of touch and don't know when is the right time to visit people. Also because there are so many stupid set-ups in the parishes they can only visit at certain times because they have to be back for a meeting in the parish that about a dozen people in the parish will come along to.

This priest saw no point in returning to the presbytery through rush-hour traffic for an inflexible evening meal time and often invited himself out for supper with a family he had got to know. In his judgement 'one good night's visiting is better than visiting twenty people in one road for five minutes to talk about pleasantries'. Finally a senior priest articulated the view of the priest as a father of his parishioners and sharply distinguished his role from that of the social worker:

> A priest is involved in society . . . but he is not expected by any Catholic to be a social welfare expert. They will come to him for difficult things and he knows where to send them if he listens to them. If they know they have got his sympathy and compassion, that is what they want.

A flavour of the fragmentation of the working lives of priests was given by the same priest in his description of an evening's work:

> Somebody the other night came [when] I was doing confessions by myself. The front door went; I had to run down quickly, answered the phone: 'can you give me ten minutes?' I went back and finished off confessions, dashed into the waiting room and this poor girl told me her trouble, marriage trouble, drinking trouble, and she talked for three-quarters of an hour. There was nothing I could do. She knew I couldn't do anything [but] she was most grateful and when she went off she said she would come back. I suppose I did help her in one way. That's what they (the people) want a priest for and you get examples of that day after day. . . . Whenever I am

going around the parish in my car [there are kids] on every corner. This is being a priest, being a father of the kids. There is no disgrace in being a father. It's not being paternalistic . . . if you get a priest . . . who goes about his work with insensitivity and ruthlessness, trying to be professional, he has missed the notion of what a priest is. A priest can't be ruthless or be insensitive. He has got to be in tears with his people. He has got to have that much sympathy that he can identify himself with their problems; they are not for the social worker.

CONCLUSIONS

The purpose of this chapter has been to let priests in parishes speak for themselves about their everyday experiences of parish life. Because the expectations which priests have of their role were largely the product of the long processes of professional socialisation, we first reviewed their reflections on their training in the seminaries. We noted a much greater degree of differentiation among the fifteen priests interviewed in the four research parishes than had emerged from the structured questionnaire survey of Hinings and his colleagues. Generational differences seemed to be significant, a finding which reflected research findings in the United States and elsewhere. The interviews with the priests demonstrated the inadequacies of any simple structuralist explanations since, in the main, the priests in the parishes in the mid-1970s had been quite creative in devising coping strategies in order to survive what they often regarded as coercive seminary institutions.

In a review of priests' responses to the social and religious changes of recent decades, two areas in particular were identified for special consideration. Priests clearly differed not only in their responses to the papal encyclical *Humanae Vitae* but also in their interpretations of the limits of legitimacy on issues of religious authority. One is left with the strong impression that the pastoral approaches of many priests on the matter of contraception are undogmatic and pragmatic, if not casuistic. On the wider issues of changes in the Church since the Second Vatican Council, the fifteen priests showed a variety of responses from frustrated enthusiasm to suspicious obedience. Most had accommodated themselves to liturgical change but here, in the larger parishes where there were two or more priests, generational differences between more cautious parish priests and their more innovative assistant priests, sometimes emerged.

In the course of the focused interviews priests had talked about various aspects of their work lives in ways which do not appear to have been recorded previously in Britain in such detail. Five areas in particular were noted. First, there was good evidence, at least among some of the priests in these parishes, of the conflict between the perspective of the parish priest as the superordinate official in the Church bureaucracy and that of the assistant priest who regarded himself more as a junior professional colleague and hence expected to play a larger part in pastoral decision-making in the parish. Second, there was evidence that this conflict spilled over on occasion into relationships within the presbytery. Third, this issue was related to the important issue of loneliness and its association with the celibacy rule. Fourth, the notion of pastoral risk was introduced, especially by young priests when referring to their problems of relationships with women. There was evidence of very different views as to what were appropriate pastoral strategies and relationships between priests and parishioners, especially those who might be regarded as deviant or dangerous in terms of the official norms of the institutional Church.

Finally, the issue of visiting was considered in the context of promoting closer relationships between priests and lay people. Most priests expressed guilt at what they regarded as their failures in this regard or constructed elaborate excuses for them. In practice there was evidence that priests' lives were structurally fragmented so that fundamental structural reform would be necessary if priests were seriously to concentrate more on the task of developing genuinely close and deep relationships with the parishioners in their care. This might include, for example, the systematic delegation of large areas of pastoral responsibility, in the pre-Vatican parish regarded as the exclusive concern of the ordained priest, to lay ministers legitimated by their fellow parishioners. The extent to which lay people might be in a position to respond to such revolutionary changes and challenges will be considered further in the next chapter.

Chapter Eight

THE COMPLIANCE OF PARISHIONERS

INTRODUCTION

This chapter is concerned with the parishioner, the 'lower participant' in the parish seen as a religious organisation. Given the primary focus of this book on the Catholic parish in a process of 'revolutionary' transition (Kuhn, 1970) from a pre-Vatican model to a post-Vatican model, particular attention will be paid to the changing nature of parishioner compliance within the institutional Church at the parish level. Following Etzioni, the concept of compliance

> refers both to a relation in which an actor behaves in accordance with a directive supported by another actor's power, and to the orientation of the subordinated actor to the power applied.
>
> (1961: 3)

As is well known, Etzioni distinguished three kinds of power: coercive, remunerative and normative, and three kinds of orientation of the lower participants to the organisation as a power or control system, that is alienative, calculative and moral involvement in the organisation. He also postulated three congruent types of organisation but allowed for the possibility of incongruent types, for example as a result of the exercise of different kinds of power (1961: 11–13). Thus parishioners might be physically coerced to comply to officially prescribed norms or do so because of the normative obligations imposed on them by a close-knit socio-religious community and its recognised clerical leadership. Their involvement or commitment would then vary correspondingly from the alienative to the moral and might also be based calculatively on their assessment of the rewards and costs of this-wordly pleasures and indulgencies as well as their expectations of other-worldly salvation or damnation.

At the end of Chapter 6 the suggestion was made that in spite of the changes emanating from the Second Vatican Council and in consequence of the social transformations in the post-war world, and despite priestly adaptation to these changes and their adoption of new styles of leadership in the parish and new forms of legitimation of their priestly authority, social control still remained securely in clerical hands. The suggestion was that far from there having being an end to a rather coercive enforcement of lay compliance and the domestication of lay people in all-embracing forms of religious socialisation and highly effective means of ideological control, and a shift towards collaborative processes of formation and religious praxis, all that had changed was the sophistication of the clerical strategies for maintaining control of the laity and ensuring their incorporation into the institutional Church.

In this chapter we will explore this hypothesis further and consider whether and in what ways the nature of the social relationships between priests and lay people and their compliance with the clerical leadership in the Church at the parish level might be changing. In previous chapters we have seen that there has been an emergence of new paradigms of the Church, the parish and the parish clergy in recent decades. Here we aim to explore further the extent to which there has been a corresponding emergence of a post-Vatican parishioner to replace a pre-Vatican model. As before we will be using the Weberian ideal-type methodology and then looking at some available evidence to discern the extent to which the empirical reality approximates more-or-less closely with one or other model. The attempt will also be made to review parishioners' religious interpretations of their everyday lives (Hornsby-Smith, 1988b, 1989), their lay roles in the Church, particularly as they experience it at the parish level, and the nature and extent of social interaction, shared values, mutual support and aid, and ecumenical collaboration at the parish level. At a time when many of the traditional indicators of religious practice, such as attendance at Sunday Mass and adult receptions into the Church, have been declining, what evidence is there that new forms of institutional involvement or religious commitment are emerging? We will also attempt to indicate something of the enormous variations both between and within parishes.

In Figure 8.1 a summary of ideal-typical pre-Vatican and post-

Figure 8.1 Models of pre-Vatican and post-Vatican parishioner

Characteristic	Pre-Vatican	Post-Vatican
Institutional status:		
	devoted adherent to passive conformist	active participant
	subordinate assistant sponsored helpmate dependent follower	partner in team collaborative minister independent initiator
Lower participant characteristics:		
a) involvement	alienative/calculative to moral	moral
b) subordination	high; tight	low; loose
c) performance	low	high
Institutional orientations:		
a) to religious authority	loyal, dutiful obedience uncritical loyalty	critical collaboration loyal critic
b) to parish clergy	distant, deferential	close, collegial
c) to action:		
i) in Church	passive spectator	active participant
ii) in world	disciplined cadres/cells under hierarchical control	self-acting leaven with interest group support
Decision-making stress:		
a) in parish	acceptance of priest's decisions	collegial contribution
b) personal morality	obedience to rules and instructions	appeal to informed conscience
c) social morality	follower of papal encyclicals	contributor to ecumenical collaboration

Vatican parishioners has been given. It will be seen that these are consistent with the models of the pre-Vatican and post-Vatican Church, parish, and priest which have been discussed in previous chapters. Thus there is a fundamental shift in the nature of the status of the parishioner in the two models. In the pre-Vatican parish the priest regarded the parishioner as an assistant subordinate in every respect to his decision-making. While some core parishioners were sponsored by him to be his special helpmates, most parishioners were expected to follow the priest as sheep follow their shepherd. They were socialised to a dependent role in the parish and this status was reinforced by near-total processes of socialisation into the dominant clerical ideology in the parish and associated institutions such as the parish school. By contrast the post-Vatican parishioner in a 'People of God' Church and parish was regarded as a partner with skills and talents to contribute to the pastoral team of the parish. In this sense s/he had the status of one who also ministered as a collaborator of the priest, the presidential leader. Given this colleague status, the parishioner was able to initiate action independently rather than simply remain a passive and reactive follower.

In his analysis of different types of lower participants, Etzioni distinguishes between parishioners, members and devoted adherents in terms of three dimensions: involvement in terms of direction (that is with or against the purposes of the organisation) and intensity, the extent of the subordination of the lower participants, and the expected performance obligations (1961: 16–20). In the pre-Vatican model of the parish, the expectations of at least the core group of parishioners was that they would be devoted adherents, scoring high on all three dimensions. Otherwise the expectations were for passive conformity to the minimum performance obligations of the Church in a situation of high subordination. In the post-Vatican parish, on the other hand, the performance obligations are if anything greater than in the pre-Vatican parish even though there is a greater stress on the parishioner's self-motivation rather than simply conformity to coercive pressures or normative obligations as in the pre-Vatican parish. The active participant in the post-Vatican parish represents an extension to Etzioni's typology (1961: 20). This can be seen also in a comparison of lower participant characteristics in terms of Etzioni's dimensions. Thus because of the coercive elements of clerical power and the strong emphases on divine retribution for wrong-doing in the pre-Vatican parish, parishioner involvement varied from the alienative and calculative to the moral. With the looser form of subordination in the post-Vatican parish, the involvement of the parishioner was more likely to be moral.

In the pre-Vatican parish the parishioner was expected to be dutifully obedient to clerical authority and to give the priest, as the 'man apart', an uncritical loyalty. Because of the fundamental status differences between priests and lay people, direct relationships with priests were limited and distance was maintained while the parishioner remained deferential to his or her religious superordinate. In the post-Vatican parish, in contrast, the relationships between priest and parishioners are much closer and collegial in the sense of the recognition of complementary skills and talents. The orientation of the parishioner to religious authority is correspondingly one of critical collaboration. These contrasts are evident also in the orientations to action both within the parish itself, for example in determining liturgies or pastoral strategies, and to the secular world of home, neighbourhood, work, and politics. Within the parish the role of the parishioner is that of the passive spectator in the pre-Vatican parish but the active participant in the post-Vatican parish. Catholic Action in the pre-Vatican parish is firmly under the direct control of the clergy whereas in the post-Vatican parish, the emphasis is rather on forming and empowering lay people for their independent task of acting as a leaven in the secular world and of providing some social support but also recognising the validity of other sources of support and inspiration.

Finally, there are significant differences, too, in the nature of decision-making by the two types of parishioner. Whereas in the pre-Vatican parish there is an unquestioned acceptance of the authority of the priest on all matters from the placing of flowers and the mending of roofs to the choice of liturgical styles, in the post-Vatican parish all such decisions are the result of collegial decisions by all those concerned, including the priest, but not necessarily allowing him a veto-power. Again, in matters of personal morality, such as contraception or marital breakdown, the relevant criterion in the pre-Vatican parish is obedience to the rules and ecclesiastical instructions as interpreted by the priest. The post-Vatican parishioner appeals to his or her 'informed conscience' in such matters and feels entitled to consult a variety of priests in coming to a decision. On social matters, too, there is a subtle difference between the loyal and uncritical following of the papal social encyclicals by the pre-Vatican parishioner and the more open and questioning approach of the post-Vatican parishioner who will also take into account not only other writers on controversial issues such as liberation theologians but also ecumenical contributions and climates of social and political opinion in the secular society generally.

Before proceeding to a comparison between empirical examples of parishioners, we will first note some aspects of the considerable differentiation between parishioners which exists empirically.

SOCIAL AND RELIGIOUS DIFFERENTIATION

It is important to recognise that just as there are large differences between parishes and between priests working in parishes, so there are huge variations between parishioners. Since the heterogeneity of English Catholics has been the subject of an extensive review in previous work (Hornsby-Smith, 1987: 47–66), only a brief summary will be given here. First, evidence from the 1978 national survey

> led to the conclusion that crude sex differences are not of great consequence . . . but that women other than housewives are more likely than other groups to diverge from the official teaching of the Church on such issues as birth control, divorce, belief in hell and eternal punishment, the significance of missing Sunday Mass and the infallibility of the Pope. . . . Women were more likely to be . . . members of parish organisations (than men).
>
> (1987: 56–7)

Second, age differences are particularly striking. In general 'Catholics are more likely to be critical of the institutional Church or of its authorities or of its official teachings or regulations the younger they are' (1987: 58–9; Hornsby-Smith and Lee, 1979: 130–1). Third, while

> social class differences in religious belief and behaviour are not as significant as might have been expected . . . there is evidence of a tendency for the higher social classes to be more involved in the associational life of the Church than the lower social classes. . . . Tentatively . . . the Roman Catholic Church in this country is disproportionately attractive for the middle classes and . . . reforms stemming from the Vatican Council, the increased participation of the laity from liturgical reading to membership of parish councils or national commissions and so on, favour the educated and articulate middle class. This last group is happier with the changes which have emanated from the Vatican Council, more involved in associational activity and is more approving of the Church's belief and value systems. By contrast, working-class Catholics are less happy with recent changes, suspicious of the shift of emphasis from ritual to participation, defensive about their loss of a privatised autonomy, and suspicious of proposed new forms of ministry, possibly because they represent new and alternative sources of

authority to which they will be expected to respond.
(Hornsby-Smith and Lee, 1979: 126–8; Hornsby-Smith, 1987:
60–1; Archer, 1986)

Fourth, the level of educational attainment appears to be an important variable, though its effect does not appear to be linear. The national survey data showed that

> those with the most education rated their priests much less highly than other groups . . . [and] scored highest not only in terms of church commitment but also in terms of actual or potential institutional innovation, for example, new-style activism and new-style ministries. In contrast those with the least educational experiences were the most traditional, in terms of their sexual orthodoxy, their favourable evaluation of priests, their stress on papal authority and the salience of religious sanctions and in their conformity to institutional identity.

> (Hornsby-Smith, 1987: 62)

However, it is difficult to disentangle the effects of education, social class and age and

> there does not appear to be any simple relationship between educational experiences and religious attitudes and practice. What does appear to be indicated is that those respondents born in the two decades after the Second World War and leaving school in the 1960s and 1970s at the age of fifteen or sixteen, were particularly disaffected with institutional Catholicism.

> (1987: 63)

Fifth, because the number of Catholics from ethnic minorities in the national sample was too small for separate analysis, little attention has so far been paid to ethnic differences between Catholics or parishes other than in the case of the Irish. In the early 1980s there were around 170 Ukranian or Polish priests or chaplains to over twenty different foreign immigrant communities in England and Wales. The Ukranian Exarchate had around a dozen parishes and served over fifty centres in Britain and there were around seventy Polish parishes with some autonomy from the diocesan bishop. A few parishes also have special arrangements for the pastoral care of Italians while other parishes have regular Masses for other foreign language concentrations such as the Spanish. There are no parishes specifically for black Catholics, for example from the Caribbean. Estimates from the 1981 Census Country of Birth tables suggested that there were around 115,000 first generation black Catholics in England and Wales (Hornsby-Smith, 1986b). What evidence there is from the Westminster archdiocese suggests that their experiences in the parishes have not been very happy and there were complaints of 'racism within the institutional structures of the Church and in the attitudes and practices of individual white Catholics' (Hume, 1986, ix).

Sixth, apart from heterogeneity of Catholics associated with demographic differences, variations of both belief and practice are reflected in considerable differences in both communal and associational involvement in the Church (Lenski, 1963: 22–4). In his classic study Fichter (1954) distinguished between parish leaders and nuclear, modal, marginal, and dormant parishioners in terms of a number of indicators of religious practice and belief. Nearly four decades after his work some clarification of the criteria differentiating between the different types and some modification of his typology is necessary. One problem is that he regarded ordinary weekly Mass attenders as a 'modal' type. Statistically this is not the case for English Catholics in the 1980s. A second problem is that he substantially ignores the self-identifying Catholics who do not regard themselves as parishioners. In England and Wales around one-third of Catholics do not attend church or regard themselves as attached to a parish. This is likely to result in an over-optimistic evaluation of the religious vitality of parishes and it seems preferable to regard such Catholics as dormant.

The national survey of English Catholics in 1978 showed just how complex the situation really is. In an analysis of variations of identity, belief, practice, parish involvement, and sexual morality, ten distinct types of Catholics were identified and described (Hornsby-Smith, Lee and Turcan, 1982). The institutionally involved orthodox attenders (Types A and B), or parish activists, appear to correspond to Fichter's nuclear parishioners. The non-involved traditionalists and other regular attenders (Types C, D and E) correspond to Fichter's 'modal' Catholics, though, since the term is statistically incorrect, it would be better to refer to them as passive attenders to distinguish them from the nuclear parishioners who are members of parish organisations. The irregular attenders (Types F and G) can be regarded as marginal while the remaining three types, the non-

Table 8.1 Demographic and religious characteristics by type of parishioner (%)

Characteristic	Dormant (H,J,N-I)	Marginal (F,G)	'Modal'* (C,D,E)	Nuclear (A,B)	Core (Officers)
Sex: Male	46	40	49	33	41
Social Class: AB	10	8	14	19	19
Age: under 35	55	54	33	13	18
TEA: 19 and over	5	8	9	9	8
½ or more friends R.C.	28	41	54	78	90
Convert	6	9	8	26	30
Parish: v. sorry to leave	21	24	44	72	72
Prayer: daily	26	40	71	83	82
Papal infall. true	36	62	85	97	96
Allow Caths divorce	90	80	46	28	46
N = 100%	333	243	279	93	31

Source: Adapted from Hornsby-Smith, Lee and Turcan, 1982.

*Passive attenders.

attenders and the baptised but non-identifiers, approximate to Fichter's dormant parishioners.

An indication of the demographic and religious variations between the different types of parishioner has been given in Tables 8.1 and 8.2. In Table 8.1 it can be seen that nuclear parishioners are disproportionately women, middle-class and in the older age group, converts but finding their friendships mainly among fellow-Catholics, with a 'local' orientation in the sense of having a high attachment to their parish, religiously orthodox and with a high level of prayer. Core or leader Catholics are very similar to nuclear Catholics. Dormant Catholics, on the other hand, are much more likely to be 'cradle' Catholics in the younger age group and are much less likely to have had a further or higher education. They have been less involved in the communal and associational life of the parish and are much less orthodox in terms of religious beliefs and practices. Table 8.2 shows similar variations when comparing those who are not attached to a parish with those who are attached and those who are members of parish organisations. In addition comparable data for the lay delegates to the National Pastoral Congress have been given. These demonstrate clearly the extent to which the delegates were a highly selected group of educated middle-class activists who were in many respects much more 'progressive' than Catholics generally

(Hornsby-Smith, Procter, Rajan, and Brown, 1987). Parish activists with regard to organisational memberships, on the other hand, were much more traditional in terms of their openness, for example to married or women priests, than the delegates. In a previous chapter reference was made to the 'greedy' parish consuming all the discretionary time and energy of parishioners. This effect of multiple memberships and obligations is experienced only by the parish activists or nuclear parishioners and especially the core leadership group.

This section has demonstrated that parishioners are extremely heterogeneous in terms of their demographic and social characteristics and their religious attributes. It is necessary to take account of this when generalising about pre-Vatican and post-Vatican parishioners.

Table 8.2 Demographic and religious characteristics by associational involvement (%)

Characteristic	Not attached	Parish attached	Organis. member	NPC lay delegate	All Caths. (RCO)
Sex: Male	48	44	32	55	44
Mar. Status: Single	22	20	5	30	19
Social Class: AB	17	17	23	68	11
Age: under 35	55	41	1	27	42
TEA: 19 and over	6	7	8	47	7
½ or more friends R.C.	29	4	69	75	44
Convert	6	9	22	15	10
R.C. Type:					
Involved orthodox attender (A + B)	0	0	99	74	9
Non-invol. orthodox attender (C + D)	3	39	0	24	22
Irregular attender (F + G)	13	37	0	1	24
Non-practising (H + J + Non-identifying)	83	14	0	1	32
Scale Scores (% high):					
Doctrinal orthodoxy	31	55	77	na	52
Sexual orthodoxy	27	48	65	73	43
Evaluation of priests	6	19	38	48	18
New style activism	15	39	75	96	36
New style ministries	50	35	23	63	38
N = 100%	317	560	125	959	1036

Source: Adapted from Hornsby-Smith, 1987: 218–21, 223–4.

PRE-VATICAN PARISHIONERS

In St Catherine's parish in Liverpool, studied by Conor Ward (1965) in the 1950s, about one in every eight Mass attenders was involved in regular and continuous parochial activities. However, over half of these were concerned solely with fund-raising activities such as running the parish football pool. Only 2 per cent of Mass attenders were involved in 'apostolic' activities such as running the parish clubs, confraternities and sodalities, the catechesis of children, or social welfare work. Apart from singing in the choir and collecting the offerings, no other liturgical activities were noted. The response to appeals from the pulpit for volunteers tended to be negligible. Although face-to-face contacts with priests were frequent, nuclear parishioners criticised the apathy of most parishioners, while non-members of societies complained of cliquishness and newcomers referred to a general lack of welcome from established parishioners who directed their loyalty towards the parish rather than to individuals. Remarkably little in Ward's study related to the religious practices of parishioners or the meanings and significance they attached to them. In general the picture given of Liverpool parishioners in the 1950s was of a stable local religious identification, unquestioned deference to priestly leadership and initiative, ritual attendance at Sunday Mass, and private forms of devotionalism.

The accounts given by Anthony Archer's working-class respondents in a Newcastle Catholic parish in the north-east of England in the 1970s also give a picture of religion as essentially a private matter, with priestly authority pervading all aspects of parish life (even if lay compliance was not infrequently given only under protest), and a general Catholic suspicion of outsiders. 'Religion was an inheritance largely taken for granted' (Archer, 1986: 112). For these Catholics a rich variety of devotions, such as receiving communion on the first Friday of nine consecutive months, offered the promise of achievable paths to salvation.

Traditional Catholics regarded the existing state of affairs in the parishes as timeless. Thus they would sympathise with Cardinal Bourne's dismissal as unwise the proposal of eighty-seven prominent lay people sixty years ago for increased parochial co-operation between clergy and laity especially in areas of lay expertise such as finance, building, property, and relations with the secular authorities (Moloney, 1985: 149–50). The contemporary traditional parishioner

continues to be inhibited about taking any initiative whatsoever
without first 'asking Father's permission'.

In his study of a north midlands parish in the early 1980s, John
Leslie (1986) contrasted the traditional parishioners, who tended to
be both socially and geographically immobile and to have lived in the
parish most of their lives and who shared close kinship ties with each
other, who had internalised the traditional ideology of the present
parish priest, and who were strongly 'local' in their orientation and
loyalties, with the 'charismatics', most of whom had returned to
religious practice after a period of 'lapsation' following some sort of
conversion experience, and who were more mobile, more often 'newcomers' to the parish, and more 'cosmopolitan' in their openness to
external influences such as prayer groups with their uninhibited
manifestations of joy and friendship.

In this parish traditional parishioners had a very keen sense of the
boundaries between the 'sacred' and the 'non-sacred'. The church
was a sacred place so that 'relatively formal demeanour and interaction' was expected there with the discouragement of talk and other
forms of social interaction. This was also reflected in the ritual of
making the sign of the cross with holy water from the stoup in the
porch on both entering and leaving the church. Traditionalism was
reflected in the resistance to the admission of women to membership
of the Society of Saint Vincent de Paul (SVP), with its special concern
for charitable and welfare work with the needy, the disaffiliation of
the parish women's group from the Catholic Women's League seem-
ingly to insulate the parish from external and national influences, and
the suspicion of ecumenical occasions such as the annual Remembrance Day services, usually on the grounds of the priest's preferences. In this respect traditional Catholics were passive and accepting
of the maintenance of social distance from the priest, whom they
regarded as a 'sacred' person, a 'man apart', and who was to be
treated with special respect and deference whatever the personal
views of the parishioner. Similarly, religious matters were not
regarded as proper topics for discussion by lay people but were best
left to the priests. What was the point of discussion, anyway, since the
Church already had its authorised teachers with a divine mandate
and guarantee? Thus there were suspicions of proposals to consider
the preparatory materials for the National Pastoral Congress (1980),
and they justified this stance along lines suggested by their parish
priest in terms of his perceptions of the bishops' 'real' desires and in

the light of supposed threats from radical clergy and laity.

In this parish a traditional Catholic had asked the parish priest's permission to start a prayer group and had been refused. He was concerned that it would be disobedient to the parish priest if he attended one. Several traditional Catholics referred to the way they had been brought up to 'marry into your own kind'. Others expressed traditionalist conceptions of the Blessed Sacrament:

> when I was a boy . . . we were not allowed to touch the sacred vessels. . . . Now it seems any Tom, Dick and Harry can come along and start fumbling about on the altar. . . . You know we hardly dared touch the unconsecrated wafer . . . I still receive Communion on the tongue . . . I think it's far more pure . . . to come from the priest's hand . . . Communion in the hand . . . this is a very delicate matter. . . . You're receiving the body and blood of Jesus Christ. You leave home, you drive your car, you blow your nose . . .
>
> (Leslie, 1986: 452)

Leslie notes that 'even those in favour of a parish council see its task as primarily a financial rather than a liturgical one. The priest is the cultic specialist who alone can handle the sacred' (1986: 457). At the end of his study of the north midlands parish, he concludes:

> Resistance to change in the parish certainly involves . . . a strong feeling on the part of stable parishioners for the customs, practices, to which they have become attached, but more fundamentally on a deep-seated conception of the sacred person and the sacred place. . . . The predominant influences on their religious praxis, however, remained the traditionalist ideology, which merely served to reinforce their relative passivity.
>
> (1986: 466–7)

In all the studies we have considered there is evidence that traditionalist parishioners hold pre-Vatican conceptions of the Church, the role of the priest, the proper relationship which should exist between the parish priest and his parishioners, and responses to the 'sacred'. In these respects they approximate to the ideal-type of pre-Vatican parishioner.

POST-VATICAN PARISHIONERS

Post-Vatican parishioners are those who wholeheartedly espouse the vision of the Church as the pilgrim 'People of God' always on the move and ready to face the forever changing contingencies of every-day life in the contemporary world. While continuity with established ways of doing things may be important, it is not the primary concern of the post-Vatican parishioner. A critical questioning of traditional ways in the light of the Gospel imperative to 'bring the Good News to the poor', for example, might lead to the emergence of new liturgical styles, changing pastoral emphases, more ecumenical openness, the more self-conscious promotion of 'community' and search for those in need, a radical shift in the way parishioners relate to the leadership of the priest, and so on.

Examples of such parishioners are to be found among the contributors to the series on 'The Everyday Lives of Lay People' in *Priests and People* in 1987/88. Thus James McEvoy, retired after a life in management, describes his growing disenchantment with the official Church structures and 'a growing alienation from the ordained ministers of the Church'. In his life ' "Muscular Christianity" has replaced the old intellectual interests' (1987: 261) and he describes his growing contentment in work with the SVP. Barbara Wood, a busy housewife, describes how an ecumenical group of friends in a short period of daily shared prayer finds 'a special kind of togetherness and a deep sense of sharing which our parish Mass lacks'. She complains that:

> None of us feel the same acceptance within our parish acts of worship. The Church, despite its teachings about the importance of the family, does not make provision for the nurture of families within the framework of its liturgies. Worship is designed for adults. Our parish work is done without children or is frustrated by their presence. This fosters the feeling that children hinder one's spiritual life whereas we need to be encouraged and supported to see our children as a God-given part of our spiritual life and journey into faith.

> (1987/88: 301)

Similar instances of a critical reappraisal of traditional Catholic practices are provided by other contributors to this series. Thus David Ireson, a senior teacher in a comprehensive secondary school,

calls for change in the structure of the parish to facilitate participation. He advocates restructuring around small groups which
celebrate the Eucharist and only occasionally come together with
other groups in the parish for large celebrations, priests living 'like
everyone else and not set apart', inter-communion for inter-Church
families, and a more sincere effort to respond to the 'ecumenical
imperative' (1988: 24–5). Carol Burns, a justice-and-peace activist,
finds support mainly from like-minded friends, both Catholic and
non-Catholic, but believes it necessary to 'be involved in the parish if
you want to see what you believe in carried out' (1988: 87). While the
development of a deep prayer life and the pursuit of justice must have
priority, sometimes it is necessary to join with others in repairing the
church roof.

Accounts given in previous chapters described the extent to which
parishioners have been involved in a wide range of parish activities
which might once have been regarded as the special province of the
priest. In contradistinction with the traditionalist parishioners who
stress the 'sacred' status, power and rights of the priest, and a submissive deference to priestly authority, the post-Vatican parishioner
sees few barriers to the extension of his/her ministries within the
parish and assumes a participative style of leadership on the part of
the priest.

Some of the implications of this contrast can be seen in the comparison between the parishioners of St Catherine's parish, Liverpool,
in the 1950s, which we discussed in the previous section, and those in
the parish described a decade ago by Fr Brian O'Sullivan (1979).
Whereas in the former parish about 12 per cent of Mass attenders
were involved in regular and continuous parish activities and around
3 per cent in 'apostolic' activities of one sort or another, both the
proportions involved and the range of activities pursued are much
greater in the latter parish. In 1986 when this parish had just under
500 Mass attenders, over one-quarter of the parishioners were
officially listed as being active either as members of the Parish
Pastoral Council, or as one of the leaders recognised as such in the
annual parish directory, or on one of the rotas as stewards, readers or
special ministers, or on the telephone prayer team. Furthermore,
over one-half of these parishioners, or nearly 15 per cent of all Mass
attenders, were involved in more than one of these lists. For example,
the chairman of the Parish Pastoral Council was also involved in the
local Council of Churches and with ecumenical matters generally,

and was also on the rotas for stewards and special ministers, as well as on the telephone prayer link. If anything these figures underestimate the institutional involvement of post-Vatican parishioners since they do not take account of the fact that a substantial proportion of regular Mass attenders will be children.

Those parishioners with a post-Vatican orientation expressed their commitment in a number of distinct ways. First of all they stressed the full participation of the laity in the worship of the parish. They favoured the establishment of an active liturgy committee to plan the regular and special liturgies in the parish and they encouraged the introduction, acceptance, and development of the ministries of reading and lay distribution of communion under both kinds (consecrated host and the chalice). They also planned a number of special vigils and such innovations as regular justice and peace liturgies introduced by lay people on the first Friday of each month. Rotas of parishioners compose the Sunday bidding prayers each week while at daily Mass they encourage spontaneous bidding prayers. The parish choirs and folk group all stress the full participation of the congregation.

Second, post-Vatican parishioners encourage the development of strong community ties. This is reflected in the care taken to welcome newcomers, exchange the sign of peace warmly at Mass, promote the regular visiting of the sick, lonely and dying, annual parish days of prayer and socialising, and the development of neighbourhood or other support groups. Regular meetings of special groups such as mothers and toddlers or the divorced and separated aim to provide mutual aid and support.

Third, post-Vatican parishioners support the processes of renewal through the provision of regular adult education programmes and reflection. Lenten house groups for prayer, scripture study and discussion are increasingly arranged in collaboration with the other local Churches on an ecumenical basis. The promotion of self-awareness as the 'People of God' aims to encourage the full participation of lay people in the life of the parish and to reinvigorate its spiritual life.

Fourth, at least lip-service is paid to the importance of justice and peace issues and the need to interpret for themselves the imperative of bringing the Good News to the poor. In practice these issues have sometimes been controversial and have led to anger and conflict. The contribution of parishioners to a special collection at Christmas at the rate of 10 per cent of extra spending on presents, food and drink, was originally intended to benefit approved groups in Third World countries, but in recent years this has been modified to include distribution to favoured local charities and acceptable causes at home.

Fifth, the areas of healing and the ministry to the sick, lonely, dying, and bereaved has been steadily developed. Visits are often undertaken by special ministers who distribute Communion to the housebound. While some people originally found this threatening or distasteful, they are now generally grateful for this change of pastoral practice as evidence of the support and concern of the local Christian community.

Finally, post-Vatican parishioners not only contribute their skills and talents to the everyday running of the parish in such matters as financial accounting, building maintenance, and so on, but also expect to participate as members of a team in collaboration with their priest in the determination of the basic framework of pastoral policy for the parish. In ways such as these they are endeavouring to change the climate of opinion in the parishes and promote the acceptability of the full participation of lay people in the life of the Church.

Nevertheless, a note of warning is in order about the dangers of an excessive concern for institutional reform at the cost of transformative and evangelising goals. It is worth recalling here the fears which were first expressed more than a decade ago by the signatories of the Chicago Declaration of Christian Concern (Barta, 1980) that new forms of clericalism had emerged in the years since the end of the Second Vatican Council. This fear was discussed earlier in the analysis of the 'greedy' parish. It draws attention to the danger that the search for renewal in the Church, and especially at the parish level, might lead to an exclusive focus on 'churchy' concerns such as lay participation in the planning and execution of parish liturgies or in the new participatory structures such as parish councils at the cost of a relative neglect of the education and training of lay people to give prophetic witness in their everyday worlds of employment and politics, neighbourhood and home. It might be noted here that one-quarter of the lay delegates to the National Pastoral Congress in 1980 were not members of parish organisations (Hornsby-Smith and Cordingley, 1983: 52). It seems that at least some of the most committed lay people are primarily involved either with extra-parochial forms of organised Catholicism, such as the Catholic Institute for International Relations (CIIR) or the Catholic Fund for Overseas Development (CAFOD) or Pax Christi, or were articulating their religious commitment through secular agencies such as the pressure groups working on behalf of the poor, homeless, or unemployed, or those subject to racial discrimination.

PARISHIONER PARTICIPATION

In the two preceding sections we have given brief empirical accounts of the parishioners in two very different English parishes in the 1980s. The early results from the Notre Dame study of parish life in the United States also point to considerable variations in the participation and commitment of parishioners both within and between parishes. They also indicate the importance of the unique historical development of the parish, the social class and ethnic composition of the parishioners and their relative social and geographical mobility, the urban, rural or suburban nature of the parish, the divergent styles of clerical leadership experienced, and so on. The general picture is that empirically there exists a wide variety of parishioners, some of whom approximate to the pre-Vatican model and others the post-Vatican model. In this section we will return to the concerns with which we began this chapter: the extent and nature of parishioner compliance to clerical authority within the parish.

In the traditional parish studied by John Leslie (1986) there were numerous instances where the pre-Vatican priest used coercive forms of veto-power to suppress the intrusion and dissemination of views and even episcopal decisions and communications with which he disagreed. Young people were also refused Communion in the hand, the selling of Catholic papers at the back of the church was suppressed and the pamphlet rack limited to a narrow range of materials, a bishop's pastoral letter was quoted only selectively and through a strongly antagonistic interpretative filter, parishioners were forbidden to start prayer groups in their own homes and were allowed to discuss the preparatory documents for the National Pastoral Congress only under protest and only in a carefully planned setting under the direct and close control of the priest. According to Etzioni (1961) the congruent form of parishioner involvement would have been alienative, that is strongly negative and oppositional. In practice parishioners reacted differently:

> It is evident from the observational data . . . that a small but influential group of parishioners support the parish priest's resistance to change in many areas. Nevertheless it is also clear that a less

coherent group have experienced dissatisfaction with existing structures. Their objections were channelled into requests for modest changes in the provision of activities and groups to serve particular needs . . . many of those who wanted change did not feel sufficiently confident or knowledgeable to challenge either the parish priest, or other parishioners, directly.

(Leslie, 1986: 324 – 5)

This clearly indicates not only that some parishioners have internalised the pre-Vatican models of Church, parish, priest, and parishioner, and collude with the priest in their own state of dependency and passivity, but also that others resist this subordination to a greater or lesser extent and demonstrates that compliance does not necessarily imply that these models were normative.

In the progressive parish we have considered in this book there has been no necessary congruence between priestly power and parishioner involvement. From Etzioni's analysis (1961: 12) we would have anticipated that a shift to normative forms of power based upon persuasion and processes of resocialisation to internalise the emergent norms of the post-Vatican Church and community pressure to conform, would have led to 'moral' involvement on the part of the parishioners. In fact the empirical evidence indicates a variety of parishioner responses in terms of commitment and involvement. As Fr O'Sullivan has testified (1979) the emergence of post-Vatican manifestations in his parish was greatly facilitated by the existence of active laity who had possessed *de facto* influence in the two areas prior to their being united on the formation of the new parish. These post-Vatican parishioners performed as 'moral entrepreneurs' (Becker, 1963: 147) who both actively advocated and worked for a post-Vatican parish with high levels of lay participation corresponding to their own vision of the Church, and also provided strong leadership support and encouragement to the priest, especially in the early years of its implementation and development.

Again, as in the case of the traditional parish considered earlier, not all parishioners were happy with these developments. It is true that there emerged relatively high levels of parishioner involvement in the extending range of parish activities. Empirically the total number of 'nominal' Catholics in the parish is simply not known but if national survey evidence is taken as a guide, only one-third or fewer Catholics in the parish are likely to be regular Mass attenders. As we

191

have noted above, only around one-quarter of these are likely to have a recognised formal role in the parish. The remaining parishioners tolerate to a greater or lesser extent the dominant characteristics of liturgical worship and styles of priestly authority and lay participation which have emerged. As we have noted before, compliance does not necessarily imply normative consent. Indeed some former parishioners have 'voted with their feet' and gone to other parishes which they find more conducive or less demanding. This might mean a much more traditional liturgy, much less emphasis on lay participation, more traditional forms of clerical authority, and so on. At the same time there has been an in-migration of people who have been attracted by the general ethos of the parish in preference to their previous one. One of the characteristics of the parish in the 1980s is that it is very largely voluntaristic and chosen by parishioners as conforming more or less closely to their own preferences for challenge or the quiet life.

An example of the general orientation of some post-Vatican parishioners from this parish can be gleaned from their response to the open invitation from the Committee for Ministerial Formation of the Bishops' Conference of England and Wales to comment on the consultative document on lifelong priestly formation *Ministry and Mission* (1987). In the first place they challenged the imposed limits to the consultation implicit in the assumptions that priests must be male and celibate and that their training should in the main be in seminaries. Second, in spite of the social and religious changes of the past few decades, they regretted the general decline of parish visiting on the grounds that 'without such visiting there is no opportunity to cultivate the close friendships with priests' which they considered essential if parishes were to grow their own priests. Third, they stressed their vision of the priests as the 'key religious leaders in the local community' who ought to be 'relating people' with an enabling and facilitating style of leadership. They believe:

> the role of the parish priest is of immense importance in stimulating, initiating, encouraging, co-ordinating and sustaining the Christian life of the parish as a community. To do this properly we believe the priest needs to be a person of transparent holiness, deeply spiritual, familiar in his conversation with God, able to convey that familiarity in the prayer life of the parish, in the care and respect with which he presides at the Eucharist, in his familiarity with the

needs of his particular community and in his ability to reflect on these in his teaching in the light of scripture. We expect our priests to be humble people who recognise that they cannot undertake all the work of the busy parish but who encourage lay people to play their proper part in the life of the Church and in its mission in the world. We also believe that a major concern of the priest should be his forming of his parishioners for their lay roles in their everyday lives. In our judgement this task has been sadly neglected since the Council as the focus of renewal has tended to be on more parochial issues.

(Hornsby-Smith, 1988a: 192)

It might reasonably be inferred from this extract that post-Vatican parishioners manifest a new confidence in their status and talents as members of the 'People of God' and in their right to express loyal dissent in matters which impinge on their everyday lives as lay people and as parishioners. They are respectful, critical and active rather than resentful, submissive and passive. At the same time this does not signify an anti-clericalist stance but rather a plea for facilitative and collaborative styles of religious leadership on the part of priests if the renewal process is to be more fully realised.

There is an enormous variability in the formal structures of lay participation at the parish level. Some parish priests refuse to have parish councils and regard them as 'talking shops' or an irrelevance, given their own powers in Canon Law. Others allow them under protest following pressure from the bishop, other priests or parishioners, but do all they can to sabotage their effectiveness. In the Notre Dame study, one instance is quoted of a reluctant priest submitting to pressure from his bishop to set up a parish council only to disband it within a week (Leege, 1986b: 16). Parish priests may select the members of the parish council and restrict the range of matters they may consider or they may simply emphasise their advisory rather than decision-making functions. Some parishes have experimented with parishes-in-council rather than representative parish councils in an effort to promote maximum parishioner participation. No comprehensive study of parish councils in England has yet been carried out, as far as is known, but one might anticipate that they will differ little from other voluntary organisations and that they have the same problems of power differentials and oligarchic tendencies, and from pre-emptive decision-making by priests or their surrogates and their

subtle use of strategies of co-optation of radicals or awkward dis-
senters or critics. An interesting case study would be the degree to
which there was genuine consultation and freedom of choice for
parishioners in diocesan-wide programmes for renewal.

An example of a very open form of parish pastoral council with
very wide terms of reference, including not simply building maintenance and the organisation of social events but also the development of the parish liturgy, the detailed financial management of the
parish and the co-ordination of care for the needy, is given by Fr
Brian O'Sullivan (1979: 15–22). Ten years later it is worth recording
that it has become much more difficult to find parishioners willing to
serve on the PPC in this parish. It may be that representative bodies
such as parish councils become less salient in the life of the parish
when large numbers of parishioners are involved in the proliferation
of groups and activities in the post-Vatican parish. The danger, however, is that a new and powerful parish priest might then once more
be in a position to operate unilaterally rather than collaboratively
with his parishioners in pastoral decision-making.

This leads us to the consideration of the vulnerability of parishioners to a sudden change of priest with an autocratic style of leadership.
The observations of a senior English priest are pertinent:

> the structure still gives the priest total control over everything and
> everybody in his parish. He can be as democratic as he wants to be
> or he can be as autocratic as he wants to be. There are no legal
> restraints on him at all. Canon Law only insists that he has a
> Finance Committee; it doesn't tell what the Finance Committee
> can do or what authority it has . . . only what the priest or the
> bishop cares to give to the Committee. Canon Law doesn't insist
> that there should be a Parish Council at all; it insists on a Finance
> Committee but it does not insist on a Parish Council [Cans.
> 536–37]. Again, there are no guidelines as to what authority or
> control a Parish Council has; it can have as little or as much as the
> parish priest is prepared to give it. The structures favour the priest
> having total control over everything and, even if he has a Parish
> Council . . . he can have a sophisticated style of dictatorship,
> really, in which the Parish Council rubber-stamps his decisions in
> one way or another.
>
> (Taped interview, June 1988)

Sociologically, therefore, the situation is one of asymmetric power distribution and prone, one might suppose, to inherent conflict. In practice overt conflict is relatively rare and traditionally has been managed by socialising parishioners into a dependent relationship to the 'sacred' man-apart model of the priest. Even in the pre-war years, however, high status laity claimed some share of decision-making. With the raising of the average educational level of the Catholic laity and the gradual dissemination of the 'People of God' theology in the post-Vatican years, parishioners have increasingly challenged auto-cratic styles of decision-making by the priest and have legitimated this by reference to *Lumen Gentium*. While there is relatively little evidence, yet, of the laity's use of the 'power of the purse' (except possibly in a reduction of contributions to Peter's Pence following the scandals at the Vatican Bank), occasionally they have 'voted with their feet' and withdrawn from a parish led by a priest who does not satisfy minimum levels of consultation with the people whom he is supposed to serve. A senior priest illustrated this where a new parish priest is appointed:

> He can undo, literally overnight, everything that his predecessor may have built up and can totally change the whole attitude and style of the parish. He can in fact, destroy a parish overnight and I've seen it happen . . . [in] a parish which had two priests in two years and both of them literally destroyed what had been a happy, thriving, friendly, growing parish. They halved the Mass attend-ance in two years simply because there's simply no control what-ever on what they can do. And so they came in and simply changed everything without the slightest consultation with the parishioners even on such sensitive issues as, for instance, they came in one Sunday morning and found the tabernacle had gone from the high altar and was stuck on a side altar. Now that is a major issue, a very emotive issue, and he just did this off his own bat and without any consultation whatever and, of course, immediately alienated about two-thirds of his parish overnight. I think the structures are too much in favour of the autonomy and autocracy of the parish priest. This can go to the head of a parish priest.
>
> (Taped interview, June 1988)

Finally, brief reference will be made to the analysis of types of religious commitment to a socio-religious community. Towler has distinguished between *local* commitment where the salient context is the parish or neighbourhood, *party* commitment where the salient focus of loyalty is the denomination, and *pragmatic* commitment characterised by detachment and non-involvement (Towler, 1974: 161–71). Using data from the 1978 national survey of Catholics in England and Wales, it was shown that those with a *local* commitment were disproportionately in the oldest age groups, women, working class, and converts. They had the highest Mass attendance rates and levels of sexual orthodoxy. They were nearly twice as likely as Catholics generally to be members of parish organisations and to give their priests high ratings. Nearly two-thirds of them reported that half or more of their friends were also Catholics. Yet one-quarter of them had also attended an ecumenical service within the previous two years. One-fifth of them, or twice the proportion of Catholics generally, were involved orthodox attenders (Types A and B) and very few were non-practising. Two-thirds of them described their parish as active (Hornsby-Smith, 1987: 196–9). These figures suggest that English Catholics who are 'local' in their religious orientation and strongly attached to their parish tend to score relatively highly on their conformity to the traditional indicators of Catholic belief and practice. This is less true of those who are less attached to the parish, *per se*, but more 'cosmopolitan' in their religious loyalties.

CONCLUSION

This chapter has provided evidence that there may be considerable divergence from Etzioni's congruent types of parishioner compliance. This is partly because parishioners have access to a variety of strategies for coping with a variety of types of clerical power. These include not only alienative, calculative and moral involvement, but also withdrawal, migration, avoidance or lack of involvement, and passive conformity without normative consent. Given the asymmetries of power between parish priests and parishioners which are enshrined in Canon Law, there is always the potential for conflict. However, it seems to be an empirical fact that in practice conflict is rarely manifest and open. Rather it tends to remain suppressed and latent. In the case of those with low levels of commitment it is managed by processes of avoidance and withdrawal. For highly committed parishioners, on the other hand, it is controlled by processes of bargaining and negotiation and relatively high levels of accommodation by both priests and committed parishioners as they each learn to adapt to the new expectations of the post-Vatican Church.

Chapter Nine

PERSISTENCE AND CHANGE IN A TIME OF TRANSITION

METHODOLOGICAL RECAPITULATION

The main focus of attention in this book has been the Roman Catholic parish, particularly in England, a quarter of a century after the ending of the Second Vatican Council which provided the theological foundations for a thorough-going process of renewal in the Church in a period of global transformations following the traumatic events of the Second World War, the discovery of nuclear weapons, the ending of the colonial period and the enormous advances in communications. It has been suggested that the transformation in the Church can be likened to that of a scientific revolution (Kuhn, 1970) from one dominant paradigm to another but that the transitional period is characterised by conflict between the stubborn adherents of the traditional paradigm and the enthusiastic proponents of the emergent paradigm. This conflict is manifested at every level in the Church, including the parish level which is the particular concern of this present book.

In approaching this task we have employed the methodology of contrasting ideal-types in attempting to draw out some of the implications of the transformation from what we have called the pre-Vatican paradigm to the post-Vatican paradigm. It is important to recall that these ideal-types, in the Weberian sense, do not purport to be descriptions of the empirical situation but are, rather, analytical constructs developed to facilitate the generation and testing of hypotheses, the making of comparisons and the understanding of social and religious change. As a result of post-war social change and post-conciliar religious change it has been suggested that there has been a paradigm shift from a pre-Vatican Church to a post-Vatican

Church. In Figure 1.1 the characteristics of these two Churches in terms of contrasting organisational features, legitimating ideologies and external relationships were specified.

It has been suggested that the paradigmatic shift in the nature of the Church has been manifested at every level. Thus in Figure 2.1 we have compared pre-Vatican and post-Vatican models of the parish in terms of its membership characteristics, organisational features and prevailing liturgies. Similarly in Figure 6.1 we compared models of parish priests in terms of their personal characteristics, theological orientation and pastoral practice. Finally, in Figure 8.1 we considered ideal-types of pre-Vatican and post-Vatican parishioner in terms of institutional status and lower-participant characteristics and orientations and decision-making emphases.

Having set up the four pairs of contrasting ideal-types taking into account both the nature of post-war social changes, especially in England, and the sociological implications of the theological shifts of emphasis articulated at the Second Vatican Council, and especially in the key Dogmatic Constitution on the Church, *Lumen Gentium*, the next task was to investigate the extent to which the empirical situation in the parishes approximated to one or other set of ideal-types. In the main this has been done by contrasting evidence from the traditional-ist parish in the north midlands of England which was studied by John Leslie (1986) and the relatively 'progressive' parish in the outer-London commuter belt which was described by Fr Brian O'Sullivan (1979), its first parish priest. In the latter case more recent data from a participant-observation study in the same parish have also been drawn upon. A number of priests, including fifteen priests from four research parishes in the London and Preston areas, were also inter-viewed about the changing role of the parochial clergy and their everyday work lives, some on more than one occasion.

Apart from these studies, reference has been made to comparative research from continental Europe and Australia and particular atten-tion has also been paid to the early findings from the Notre Dame survey of Catholic parishes in the United States (Leege *et al.*, 1984–88; Dolan, 1987). Unfortunately no such survey of a repre-sentative sample of parishes in England has yet been attempted. The evidence from the two parish studies in England does seem to indicate that, in the 1980s, there are empirical cases which converge on the two ideal-types of pre-Vatican and post-Vatican parishes. We can conclude, therefore, that in the transitional period following the

Second Vatican Council, there is evidence of a considerable variability among English parishes in terms of their response to the call to
renewal. The comparative data also suggest that these findings have
much wider relevance.

SUMMARY OF FINDINGS

The parish is a major, possibly *the* major social institution for most
Roman Catholics. Despite its critics who claim, not without reason,
that it is too large to offer high levels of social interaction between
people who know each other intimately and so can celebrate the
Eucharist together meaningfully, it remains the main focus of contact
and often religious identity for the majority of those who retain their
Catholic allegiance. Its importance is underpinned by the Canon Law
of the Church and it is the major starting point for a great deal of the
pastoral activity of the Church. Inevitably, however, its social
functions have changed strikingly as a result of the social changes
which have transformed the Roman Catholic community since the
Second World War. A significant trend has been the movement out
of the traditional, largely Irish, working-class, inner-city areas and
into the new suburban estates populated by the upwardly-mobile
skilled working class and new middle class. Similar evidence of group
embourgeoisement can be discerned in the United States and
Australia with the successful assimilation by or integration of
Catholic immigrant groups to their host societies. With these processes the parish is no longer required to provide for the basic survival
needs of the bulk of its members. As Catholics have moved out of the
ghetto, the functions of the parish have changed significantly. In
England, although there has been a significant decline in many of the
traditional sacramental indicators since the 1960s and in the number
of priests, the ratio of parishioners to priests is still very low by international standards.

As a result of these social changes, there has been a gradual
emergence of a more educated and self-confident Catholic laity.
Relationships between priests and parishioners have inevitably been
transformed as lay people have become less ready to defer passively to
clerical authority. As the defensive walls which once surrounded the
fortress Church have been dissolved in the solvent of post-war social
change and as ecumenical relationships have softened following the
Second Vatican Council, all the indicators of communal involvement

have declined sharply. Catholics are now much less likely to marry fellow Catholics and find their friends mainly among other Catholics than a generation ago. For the Catholic parish the challenge is to balance the need to develop new and more relevant processes of socialisation so that its members will successfully penetrate the dominant institutions of the society as a Christian leaven, with the dangers of becoming introspective and 'greedy', consuming all the discretionary time and energies of its most active members. A brief review of the parish especially in the United States, Europe, and Australia, suggests that the trends we have indicated are general and not peculiar to the situation in England.

A legitimating claim often made on behalf of the parish is that it is a major source of 'community'. This claim was subject to close scrutiny in Chapter 4 in terms of three defining characteristics: the existence of shared beliefs and values among its members, high levels of inter-action between them, and the provision of reciprocal social support and mutual aid to each other. It was argued that with regard to these three criteria there is little evidence what parishes do or, given their size, could do to create community-like experiences in the modern world with its high rates of social and geographical mobility, its emphasis on individual achievement as a basis of employment allocation, and the strong emphasis on individualism in its dominant culture. Thus, in spite of the strong emphasis on community-building in the contemporary Church, it is important to recognise that the sociological reality falls a long way short of the official ideology. This is not to say that many parishes, and many individual parishioners, do not strive mightily to provide a great deal of support and comfort for those in social or physical need, but to stress the limits of what is realisable in a Church with an inclusive and heterogeneous member-ship emerging out of the ghettos and entering the mainstream of society. Among the minority of Catholics who constitute the core group of committed activists, however, there is a danger that they will be consumed by the greedy demands of their fellow-parishioners and clergy and occupied totally and exclusively by 'churchy' concerns, whether driven by a sense of guilt or by a view of the role of lay people or of participation in the Church which is excessively ecclesiastical.

The parish liturgy, the public ritual expression of communal worship by the parishioners, holds a central place in the everyday activities of the Church. In the contemporary theology of the Church it both expresses and contributes to the creation of a sense of community on the part of the participants. Given the significance of the liturgy for its members, it is perhaps not surprising that it has been the focus of some of the most violent manifestations of conflict between those who wish to retain the essential features of the Tridentine Mass and those who have enthusiastically embraced the spirit of the reforms in the post-conciliar period. The evidence suggests that the overwhelming majority of Catholics have either welcomed the reforms or adapted to them without undue difficulty. It is also clear that the near-uniformity of liturgies in the pre-conciliar period has been replaced by considerable variations in liturgical styles both between and within parishes. In the struggle over liturgies, the parish priest remains a key figure.

The parish priest is the official religious leader in the parish and has clearly defined responsibilities and powers enshrined in Canon Law. At the same time he has had to adapt to radical shifts in expectations of his role in the past few decades. Some have welcomed the changes and encouraged more participatory styles of collaboration with lay people. Many have adapted with some reluctance to the reforms while a few have attempted to sabotage them in their own parishes. In England, priests continue to be rated relatively highly by their parishioners on the whole. To some extent this reflects a continued passivity on their part. Elsewhere there have been long-standing struggles between priests and active groups of parishioners who contest autocratic forms of decision-making. In general terms the pre-Vatican model of the sacred 'man apart' is gradually being replaced by a more facilitative and enabling style of religious leadership which encourages the fuller participation of lay people in the various ministries in the parish. Having said that, it still appears to be the case that the priest retains his position of dominance and power in the parish.

Over the past two decades large numbers of priests have left the priesthood and this has fuelled the notion that the priesthood is in a state of crisis. In Chapter 7, therefore, we let parish clergy speak for themselves. They described their socialisation in the seminaries, often critically and unfavourably. Five areas of particular interest concerning their everyday work lives were addressed. First of all young priests expressed considerable frustration in their subordinate status in the parishes and argued for a greater say, as professional colleagues with their parish priests, over decision-making. Second, there were sometimes generational conflicts between young assistant priests and

Vat II ?

the older parish priest which made presbytery relations extremely tense. Third, there is evidence of much loneliness on the part of isolated priests which may be related to the question of celibacy (and, in all probability, alcoholism). Fourth, there are elements of risk involved in searching out the lost sheep. Young priests in particular referred to the risks involved in their pastoral role, especially with women. Fifth, all priests complained about the difficulties of visiting as a result of recent social changes, such as the higher levels of employment of married women and the pervasiveness of television-viewing in the evenings. Finally, in their reflections on questions of authority in the Church many were critical of the papal encyclical *Humanae Vitae* (1968). Priests differed widely in their interpretations of the limits of legitimacy on issues of religious authority.

It was also clear from the interviews with priests that their work lives were extremely fragmented as they struggled to respond immediately to the unexpected sick calls, funerals, or the urgent pleas for counselling help. This led to the consideration of the structural reforms which would be necessary if priests were to concentrate more on developing close and deep relationships with their parishioners. These might include the systematic delegation of large areas of pastoral responsibility to lay people. However, while a minority of progressive activists in the parishes advocates such changes, there is little evidence that the majority of parishioners shares their enthusiasm. On the whole they prefer the quiet life.

This led finally to the consideration of the nature of parishioner compliance to priestly authority in the parishes. Clearly the situation varies widely. It was found to be necessary to modify Etzioni's congruent types of compliance in a number of ways. In a Church with an inclusive membership which is extremely heterogeneous in its social and religious attributes, parishioner involvement and compliance varies considerably. It has been suggested that parishioners have access to a variety of strategies for coping with a variety of types of clerical power. Thus compliance may range from the alienative, in the case of autocratic clerical power, to moral in the case of congruence between a priest with a facilitative style of leadership and progressive active parishioners. But while there is often the potential for conflict between the wielders of clerical power and parishioners as the lower participants, in many, perhaps the majority of instances, such conflict remains latent and is suppressed. In these circumstances the response of parishioners is likely to be one of passive conformity without normative consensus but increasingly it is also likely to include complete withdrawal as parishioners vote with their feet and find a parish or priest more suited to their own image of the Church.

The conclusion to which we have been driven in the course of this study, then, is that a quarter of a century after the Second Vatican Council, the situation in the parishes is extremely uneven. Parishes have responded to the call for renewal in a variety of ways and with greater or lesser degrees of enthusiasm. There is no necessary match between the traditional or progressive characteristics of the priest and his parishioners. Consequently there is considerable potential for conflict between those whose definitions of the Church and of clerical authority differ widely. On the whole, however, this conflict remains latent rather than manifest, largely because the level of commitment of many Catholics is low and because many of the contested issues do not have great salience for them in their everyday lives. This is likely to remain the case as long as Catholicism continues to operate as a 'Church', that is with an open-door or inclusive and undemanding membership policy allowing considerable heterogeneity of commitment, rather than as a 'sect' with much more demanding membership obligations.

In Figure 9.1 a summary has been given of our discussions of both pre-Vatican and post-Vatican models of the Church, the parish, the parish priest, and the parishioner. The situation in the parishes is, as we have seen, one of both the persistence of the pre-Vatican ways in many respects and the changed ways resulting from the reforms legitimated by the Second Vatican Council. In the first of our two major case studies we noted both the persistence of a traditional model of the hierarchical Church, with the priest as the sacred 'man apart' who alone had the right to determine pastoral policy and practice, and the predominantly passive and deferential parishioners, and the gradual emergence of a post-Vatican model with lay challenges over such issues as open participation in discussions in the run-up to the National Pastoral Congress, Communion in the hand and the sign of peace at Mass, and attendance at charismatic prayer meetings or ecumenical services. Similarly, in the second of our two major case studies, the attempt to operationalise the post-Vatican model of the Church does not necessarily imply that the compliance of the majority of parishioners reflects a normative consensus. It seems likely that many parishioners, especially the many newcomers in an area of high mobility, either like or simply tolerate the way

203

Figure 9.1 Persistence and change in the Catholic parish

Characteristic	Persistence	Change
Church:		
organisational features	hierarchical	'People of God'
legitimating ideology	static uniformity	dynamic pluralism
external relationships	segregated, suspicious	ecumenical, open
Parish:		
membership	ascribed identity	voluntary religious affiliation
a) community character	socio-religious sub-culture	limited but greedy
organisation	coercive hierarchical	normative collaborative
a) parish council	non-existent	elected members
b) special groups	none or recognised Catholic organisations	plurality
liturgy	uniform ritual	spontaneous pluriformity
a) planning	no lay participation	lay participation
b) lay ministries	minimal (servers)	numerous
c) devotions	traditional	emergent pluralism
Parish priest:		
personal character	obedient, man apart	confident co-worker
a) prerogatives	juridical official	general presidency
theological emphasis	certainty	pilgrim quest
a) orientation	closed to change	open to change
pastoral practice	maintenance	mission
a) leadership style	authoritarian	democratic
b) relations with laity	superior	collaborative
Parishioner:		
status	passive subordinate	active partner
involvement	dependent	independent
orientation	uncritical loyalty	loyal critic
a) to priest	deferential	collaborative
b) to action	passive follower	lay leaven
decision-making	recipient	participant

things happen to be but find that they do not necessarily have great salience for them in their everyday lives.

In sum, all parishes are likely to contain elements of both persistence and change at the present time in relative proportions which reflect their unique histories, the characteristics of their priests over many years, and the characteristics of the parishioners, especially their relative stability or mobility, their ethnic and social class composition, and the serendipitous emergence of key charismatic leaders. When it is realised that the pre-Vatican model of the Church had overwhelming dominance for several centuries, it is not surprising that the transformation to a new post-Vatican model is contested and is likely to take several generations to form deep roots. Perhaps the sociologically important question is not so much 'why has the process of reform taken so long and been resisted so much?', but 'how can we explain the fact that so many parishes, priests and parishioners have been converted to the post-Vatican paradigms so quickly?' This raises further questions such as 'whose interests are served by the espousal of each paradigm? What are the social bases of both those who resist change and those who advocate the new paradigms?'

Apart from the themes of persistence and change, this study has also drawn attention to the co-existence of both conflict and accommodation. It has been suggested that conflict over the competing paradigms is endemic in the parishes but that whether or not it becomes manifest is contingent upon a whole range of social and religious circumstances and the particular local histories of the parishes. At the core is the dispute over rival interpretations of ministry, of the priest but also of lay people generally, in the mission of the Church. For most Catholics it is the parish which is the focal point of their lives in the Church but, for the reasons which have previously been discussed, only a small minority of activist Catholics is intensely concerned with the outcome of the struggle. For many, perhaps most Catholics, their religion is 'customary' (Hornsby-Smith, Lee and Reilly, 1985) and is the product of a formal early religious socialisation as a Roman Catholic, which has, over the intervening years, become subject to trivialisation, conventionality, apathy, convenience, and self-interest.

For those for whom these matters are salient, the struggle concerns two contrasting visions of the laity. On the one hand there are those who regard them as 'sheep' to be guarded and guided by the priest as shepherd. For the priest who sees himself as the sacred 'man apart', the laity should be subordinate, obedient, and conforming. The sociological consequence of this model is a passive and dependent laity. On the other hand, for those who regard the laity as the Christian leaven in the wider society, parishioners are seen as collaborating ministers, active and committed to their own participation in the mission of the Church, and properly and critically independent in their own contribution.

Apart from the key conflict over the respective roles and statuses of priest and lay person in the actions of the Church at the parish level, the parish also offers opportunities for alternative forms of status and power at the local level and among those who generally live in a geographically defined neighbourhood. This has not been a major concern of this book but it can be said that such struggles for power and status seem to be intrinsic to the human condition and are to be found in most parishes, in petty disputes over the control of the choir, who arranges the flowers best, who controls the prayer groups or dominates the social functions in the parish, officiates in parish organisations, and so on. For people whose lives are drab and unrewarding or whose work lives are alienating, or who, for whatever reason, are little regarded in their domestic or work situations, the parish, like other voluntary organisations, offers some opportunities for enhancing a sense of self-worth and status.

Even so, it is likely that the overriding conflicts between the classes, generations, and sexes in the wider society will only be attenuated to a limited extent in the Catholic parish. Thus there is little evidence that the Catholic parish is generally able to stem the tide of disaffection and alienation from institutional religion expressed by many young Catholics. Similarly the Church can hardly claim to be in the vanguard in the struggle for greater gender equality. While it is true that women are disproportionately involved in parish activities and in caring concerns in the parishes, there is also evidence that they are not so prominent in decision-making positions and in the key liturgical and presiding roles. Again, while in the early defensive stages of immigrant assimilation there might have been close contact between the social classes, there is a danger that this class-solvent function of the parish has been somewhat romanticised and exaggerated for ideological purposes. The reality, it is suggested, is less attractive. The likelihood is that social class divisions within parishes are as prevalent and impervious as they are elsewhere in society. In the English situation this is most apparent in the differential involvement in parish activities of Catholics from council (public housing) estates and those from owner-occupied estates within the same parish.

These social cleavages are also carried over into the debates about the relative emphasis to be placed on 'this-worldly' as opposed to 'other-worldly' religious concerns. This bears not only on interpretations of the nature of mission and understandings about salvation, but also about the issues of justice and peace. It is in these areas that the cleavages in the wider society intrude most brutally. Two instances in the progressive parish considered earlier in this book illustrate the point: the angry comment of an ex-serviceman to a woman religious representative from Pax Christi after she had preached about peace and disarmament, that if she had been a man he would have punched her on the nose; and the bitter accusation from a man with business interests in Latin America, on the occasion of a petition against torture in that continent, that Amnesty International was a communist-front organisation. It is perhaps in the controversial areas of justice and peace, often labelled 'political' and not 'religious', that the problematic nature of creating a meaningful parish 'community' is most apparent. Thus Gannon (1978) notes the problem of reconciling the development of 'particularistic communal attachments' in the local parish with 'participation in the wider society', for example in the issues of justice and peace. This is an area which it is intended to explore further in a subsequent work.

EVALUATION OF THE CONTEMPORARY PARISH

It is time to attempt a balanced evaluation of the parish in the contemporary world, a quarter of a century after the end of the Second Vatican Council which invited the Catholic Church to renew itself, taking account of the changing world in which we live. What is the state of the parish as we enter the last decade of the second millenium?

(a) *institutional decline?*: the data summarised in Tables 1.1 and 1.2 give some credence to an interpretation of steady institutional decline. In terms of the sacramental and related indicators collected annually by the Catholic Education Council there is evidence that the institutional Church in England and Wales is declining. This can most obviously be seen in the decline in the Mass attendance by one-quarter since the late 1960s. The levels of child baptisms, first communions, confirmations, and marriages have declined by over two-fifths since the peak years, and adult receptions into the Church are only one-third of their level in 1960. In the post-war period the Catholic population had increased largely as a result of huge inflows of Irish and Poles in the 1940s and 1950s. In the four decades after the war the number of parishes increased by two-fifths but since the mid-1960s the number of priests has declined and the median age of the parochial clergy is increasing significantly. The changing demographic composition of the Catholic population is reflected in the steadily increasing

207

number of deaths recorded in the parish returns. Memberships of recognised Catholic organisations are also likely to have fallen sharply over the same period. In sum, the picture appears to be one of significant institutional decline. At the same time related institutions, such as the Catholic schools system, have also experienced a sharp decline following the fall in the birth rate in the early 1960s (Hornsby-Smith, 1978). Finally, social changes generally, such as the higher living standards, higher educational levels, better housing, universal television, and a greater range of leisure opportunities, have all resulted in the decline of the parish as a major focal point for educational and entertainment pursuits. With the dissolution of the boundary walls which previously defended the fortress Church (Hornsby-Smith, 1987) the parish is no longer required primarily to provide social support and identity to a religio-ethnic group with a distinctive subculture which it is committed to preserve.

(b) *emergent features:* Can the picture of institutional decline be accepted at its face value? There are, it might be suggested, good reasons to be cautious. In the first place parishes might be pushed to concentrate much more firmly on their more overtly religious functions, such as the transmission of the beliefs, practices and moral values of Catholicism. Second, the general level of their activities might be performed to much higher standards than hitherto. Thus there might be much more emphasis on scriptural teaching, adult religious education programmes, and the development of an independent, mature laity capable of grappling with the emergent moral issues at the end of the twentieth century. When this wider perspective is taken it can reasonably be claimed that there are signs of new life in the Catholic parishes. One measure of this would be the evidence from our two case-studies that a much higher proportion of parishioners in the progressive parish than in the traditional parish were involved in a much wider range of ministries. They were clearly participating in many activities formerly the sole preserve of the ordained clergy and they were participating in real decision-making in all areas from the planning of liturgies to the keeping of the parish accounts.

(c) *realistic judgement:* The overwhelming majority of Catholic parishes are recognisably different from their predecessors of thirty or forty years ago. Sometimes the changes are little more than cosmetic: the priest faces the congregation at Mass which he says out loud in English. But in many parishes the changes are more extensive. There are lay readers and special ministers, some of them women, there are bidding prayers and communion is given in the hand. Many parishes have a parish council with members elected by the parishioners and an annual general meeting at which there is at least some opportunity to discuss and even challenge some of the pastoral practices or decisions made by the priest. It may be that in most parishes the priest retains *de facto* control and only shares power over relatively trivial matters such as flower arrangements while retaining absolute power over such matters as the liturgical style of the parish and major items of expenditure. Informants have stressed that enormous variations can occur even between adjacent parishes. These may be due partly to the influence of the parish priest but also to differences in local circumstances or 'historical memories'.

A realistic assessment would be that there is clear evidence of a shift of paradigm in the life of the contemporary parish in England. This would also appear to be clearly the case on the basis of the first reports of the Notre Dame study in the United States. At the same time there are some adherents, both priests and lay people, who cling tenaciously to the old ways and do whatever they can to sabotage or slow down any changes. But in the main the responses of both priests and lay people to the new models of Church, parish, priest, and parishioner have been more-or-less enthusiastic or tolerant or resigned. Given a long historical perspective, this is probably no more than might have been expected only a quarter of a century after the Second Vatican Council for which the Church in England and Wales, at any rate, was quite unprepared. What seems to be certain is that the changes under way, however unevenly, are unlikely ever to be reversed. Once the participation of lay people is an expectation among all Catholics and once they have had a real experience of shared ministry *with* their priest in their parishes, there seems little chance that they will passively relinquish that share in the mission of the Church for which they will have been socialised. This is not to predict the ending of the distinction between priest and lay person but rather to suggest that there will be a general shift away from autocratic styles of clerical leadership to more facilitative and enabling forms.

Finally, the continued vitality of a great deal of parish life has relevance for the on-going debate about the processes of secularisation in society. It cannot be stressed too highly that the memberships of the new religious movements, which are the focus of such a large proportion of the research endeavours of sociologists of religion, are tiny in comparison with those of the mainline Churches. Thus in spite of the decline of Mass attendance in recent years, to which we have drawn attention, it remains a social fact that in England the number of Roman Catholics at Mass in their parishes each weekend is several times the total national attendance at the country's favourite spectator sport, soccer.

Karel Dobbelaere has suggested that secularisation is a multi-dimensional concept. In his formulation he distinguishes secularisation, meaning *laicization*, or the process of structural differentiation whereby 'institutions are developed that perform different functions and are structurally different', from *religious involvement*, which 'refers to individual behaviour and measures the degree of normative integration in religious bodies', and *religious change*, which 'expresses change occurring in the posture of religious organisations . . . in matters of beliefs, morals, and rituals, and implies also a study of the decline and emergence of religious groups' (1981: 11–12). In subsequent work Dobbelaere has distinguished societal, organisational and individual levels of analysis of secularisation (1985).

In this book on the changing nature of the Catholic parish, we have been concerned mainly with the organisational level and to some extent the individual level of analysis. We have noted that one of the characteristics of post-Vatican Catholicism is that of an emergent pluralism, of ideology, groups, liturgies, and popular devotions. According to Dobbelaere, such 'religious pluralism stimulates the stripping of religious qualities from social problems in order to reduce tensions and conflict, and . . . also promotes the development of a secular morality . . . (and hence) laicizes society' (1981: 112). Furthermore 'religious and cultural pluralism . . . stimulates the privatisation or individuation of religion' (1981: 116). Such a process is indicated at the parish level in the extension of personal choice of liturgical style either within or between parishes.

In Peter Berger's view, religious institutions confronted by a pluralistic situation have to select between the options of accommodation to the world or intransigence against it. This choice, which is related to the issues of the routinisation of charisma (Weber, 1964: 363–86) and the dilemmas of the institutionalisation of religion

(O'Dea, 1970: 240–55), is problematic. At the parish level there is the tension between, on the one hand, the sense of mission of activists who seek or even demand those high levels of membership commitment and exclusiveness which characterise voluntary sects, and on the other hand, the offering of pastoral comprehensiveness to a much more inclusive and loosely-defined membership. Such dilemmas are evident in the determination of sacramental policies. Thus different priests and different parishes will develop quite different responses towards the baptism of children or the marriage in church of non-practising parishioners.

It is suggested that the Second Vatican Council legitimated the option of accommodation and encouraged the Church to reorganise itself 'in order to make it "more relevant" to the modern world'. We have shown that this may involve much higher levels of lay participation as collaborating ministers at the parish level. The danger, however, as Berger points out, is that of 'subjectivisation' where 'subjective emotionality takes the place of objective dogma as a criterion of religious legitimacy' and the relativisation of the religious content (Berger, 1973: 156–9; Dobbelaere, 1981: 117).

Finally, Dobbelaere considers the relationship between secularisation and religious involvement. This leads him in particular to review theories which seek plausibility structures for institutional religions in local communities. Thus he quotes the findings of Roof (1976) and Roof and Hoge (1980) who argue that 'locals' are more committed to institutional religion than 'cosmopolitans'. As noted above in Chapter 8 (p. 196), this is supported by the data from the 1978 national survey of English Catholics (Hornsby-Smith, 1987: 196–9).

This study of the Catholic parish a quarter of a century after the end of the Second Vatican Council has shown signs of both persistence and change, intransigence and accommodation. Rather than interpreting the empirical evidence as unambiguously indicative of secularising processes, it is suggested that there are good grounds for distinguishing between (a) the evidence of laicization and the differentiation of the former diffuse functions previously performed only by the priest, (b) the decline of some types of religious involvement but the emergence of new types, and (c) clear evidence of religious change as the post-Vatican paradigms of the Church, parish, priest and parishioner struggle for supremacy over earlier pre-Vatican paradigms.

Appendix

PASTORAL REFLECTIONS

This book has endeavoured to describe and interpret the paradigm shift in the nature of the Catholic parish over the past few decades. It has drawn on empirical studies wherever possible in order to pursue its sociological purposes. While it is not the task of the sociologist to indulge in exercises of futurology, nevertheless in this Appendix a few reflections will be offered as to the implications for pastoral policy of the findings. These are offered in response to the invitation from two of my priest informants. Both suggested that if it is assumed that the direction in which the Church ought to be moving is that indicated by the post-Vatican models, then there were signs of hope and of development. This is undoubtedly the case. Parishes and parochial clergy are no longer where they were thirty years ago on the whole and, as we have seen, in some parishes the involvement of lay parishioners as co-workers with the priest as the facilitator, has been striking. All the same, a general impression, supported by the early findings from the Notre Dame study, is that the process of institutionalising the role of both paid and voluntary lay pastoral assistants in the parishes has gone a good deal further in the United States than it has in Britain.

It was suggested to me that one disadvantage of the methodology employed, that is the contrasting of case-studies and the use of ideal-types, was to give too static a snap-shot and that 'the reality is surely one of significant movement . . . I got a healthy sense of confusion from your text but would have liked a stronger sense of movement'. This again seems a fair point but it is not inconsistent with what has been written. To some extent it reflects the optimism, or possibly hopefulness, of a priest with a post-Vatican vision who finds some evidence that the pilgrim Church has started on its journey. Others might suggest with equal legitimacy that it has not yet gone very far! Perhaps that is not the point. As a Filipino saying has it: 'The greatest thing in this world is not so much where we stand as in what direction we are going.'

The practice of moving priests around is probably an inevitable aspect of the professional career structure of the parochial clergy. But given the power which the parish priest has in Canon Law, quite arbitrary decision-making by incoming priests can have horrendous consequences even for stable and mature parish communities as we have seen. It is surely the job of bishops to ensure that such tragedies are avoided. On the other hand, the legitimate right of parishioners to have some say in the type of parish priest they would like to have cannot be absolute. For one thing the number of available priests is finite and diminishing. More important, though, is the danger that extreme forms of 'congregationalism' might simply trap parishes into a cosy perpetuation of the way things are, corrode their vitality and leave them unable to respond to unanticipated challenges and out of touch with developments elsewhere in the Church.

In recent years there has been much discussion about the potential of small groups, possibly conceptualised as basic Christian communities. Some have argued that the parish as we know it is too large to provide a realistic sense of community which can then be celebrated in the liturgy. Much of this is true and in Chapter 4 we have been critical of the assumption that parishes are in fact communities in any sociological sense of the term. On the other hand it does not follow that the parish is inappropriate for the needs of the contemporary world. In particular the advocates of basic Christian communities have to face the related problems of remaining 'in communion' with the global Church and of continuity of religious leadership. In my view the parish is an appropriate intermediate and mediating body between the small neighbourhood or special interest groups and the diocesan Church under the leadership of the bishop. It is large enough to challenge with a certain membership heterogeneity and in a society where Catholics are in a minority it is a suitable size for the development of ecumenical relationships.

Having offered a warning about the assumption that basic Christian communities can replace the parish as we know it, I do believe that there are some very important lessons to be learned from the pastoral developments in such groups in Third World countries. On this point an intuitive reflection might be offered. If we have the imagination to recognise it, the global Church in the twenty-first century is likely to reflect a membership which will come overwhelmingly from Third World countries (Bühlmann, 1976). Catholics in western European countries and those countries resulting from the global migrations associated with the colonial period, including the United States and Australia, tend to be relatively complacent about the contemporary Church which is very largely constructed in their own likeness. Any visitor to the basic Christian communities in the Third World (in my case in the Philippines; see Hornsby-Smith, 1986a), however, can hardly fail to be excited about the vitality of the faith, the relevance of the vision, and the effectiveness of the methodology of the basic Christian communities in raising the religious consciousness of ordinary people who are often poor, deprived, and oppressed. In my view, while there are certainly signs of change and hope in some of the developments taking place in some parishes in western countries, change remains very much a 'top-down' phenomenon and ordinary parishioners are rarely genuinely involved in the processes of *conscientisation* and renewal. I believe that we have a very great deal to learn from the basic Christian communities in Third World countries.

Where, then, do we go in the light of our consideration of the contemporary parish? First of all there are important implications for bishops. There are indications that they are not as close to the everyday realities of life in the parishes as they should be if they are to perform their role as the chief shepherds in their dioceses. Thus harassed priests have sadly observed that their bishop is a stranger who has not sat down with them for a meal or stayed with them overnight as once they used to. Bishops need to reorder their priorities so that they are closer to their priests and the people in the parishes. Second, there are signs that priests are not being adequately educated and trained in the seminaries for the realities of everyday life in the parishes. Furthermore, the secular clergy seem to be notoriously unprofessional in not keeping up with the latest developments in scripture, moral theology, pastoral experiments, and so on. It is the task of bishops to insist on serious in-service training for priests and continuing education which is relevant for their increasingly demanding role of parish leadership.

Third, implicit throughout this book is the need for an enabling and facilitating style of religious leadership from the priests in the parishes. It cannot be stressed too strongly that no priest should feel that he is losing essential functions as he shifts from an autocratic to a facilitating style of leadership. Rather, the challenge to encourage the emergence of a mature and responsible laity is an exciting and demanding one but also a rewarding one. No one man can do everything in the modern parish and it would be lacking in humility to suppose it possible. But there is a multiplicity of talents and gifts in the 'People of God' waiting to be coaxed into a rich collaborative venture of worship, training, encouraging, caring, and healing. Furthermore, a major task of the parish priest is to train lay people to play their full part in the transformation of the world so that it is dragged ever more closely to the Kingdom values of justice and peace.

Fourth, there is a need for the laity to grow up too. For too long they have been happy to limit their involvement to the minimum required by Church regulations. One of the implications of the Second Vatican Council is that the 'People of God' have responsibilities. They are required not only to make their due contribution to the renewal of the Church but also to take as their special task the transformation of the social, economic, and political structures which oppress their fellow human beings both in their own society and indeed throughout the whole world. The parish is both an important location for struggling with these issues within the Church itself and also for preparing the lay person for his/her everyday vocation.

Finally, the warning about greedy institutions should be noted by all the participants. Bishops, priests, and lay activists in the Church are all caught up in the ever-expanding bureaucratic structures of participation. All need to reappraise their priorities to ensure that their discretionary time and energies are not consumed by incestuous 'churchy' deliberations. Committees have their place, and discussion by all relevant participants is essential if due concern is to be paid to the dignity of all the 'People of God'. But it is also important to ensure that there is a proper sense of priorities. These must include the creation of close relationships between bishops and their priests and between priests and their parishioners. And in the end all have to go out and preach the 'Good News to the poor'! The Gospel injunction not to be afraid is too often forgotten. One of my priest informants reminded me of this when he observed in connection with the untidyness of much of the situation in the parishes that 'frustration and failure is the last thing that the Easter People should be afraid of'. (The *Easter People* was the title of the response of

the bishops of England and Wales to the 1980 National Pastoral
Congress.)

BIBLIOGRAPHY

Abbott, W. M. (ed.) (1966) *The Documents of Vatican II*, London: Geoffrey Chapman.

Anon. (1981) *Liverpool 1980: Official Report of the National Pastoral Congress*, Slough: St Paul Publication.

Archdiocese of New York (1982) *Hispanics in New York: Religious, Cultural and Social Experiences* (2 vols), New York: Office of Pastoral Research.

Archer, A. (1986) *The Two Catholic Churches: A Study in Oppression*, London: SCM.

Barta, R. (ed.) (1980) *Challenge to the Laity*, Huntington, Indiana: Our Sunday Visitor.

Beck, G. A. (ed.) (1950) *The English Catholics: 1850–1950*, London: Burns Oates.

Becker, H. S. (1963) *Outsiders: Studies in the Sociology of Deviance*, New York: Free Press; London: Collier-Macmillan.

Beckford, J. A. (1973) 'Religious organisation: a trend report and bibliography', *Current Sociology*, 21(2), 7–170.

Bell, C. and Newby, H. (1971) *Community Studies: An Introduction to the Sociology of the Local Community*, London: Allen & Unwin.

Berger, P. L. (1971) *A Rumour of Angels: Modern Society and the Rediscovery of the Supernatural*, Harmondsworth: Penguin.

—— (1973) *The Social Reality of Religion*, Harmondsworth: Penguin (published in USA as *The Sacred Canopy*, 1967).

Bishops' Conference of England and Wales (Annual) *Catholic Directory*, Liverpool: Associated Catholic Newspapers.

Bishops' Conference of England and Wales and the National Conference of Priests (1973) *The Church 2000: An Interim Report offered by the Joint Working Party on Pastoral Strategy*, Abbots Langley: Catholic Information Services.

—— (1976) *A Time for Building: Report of the Joint Working Party on Pastoral Strategy*, Abbots Langley: Catholic Information Services.

Blau, P. M. and Scott, W. R. (1966) *Formal Organisation: A Comparative Approach*, London: Routledge.

Board, D. M. (1980) *Responses: An Account of the Correspondence which followed 'The Church 2000' and 'A Time for Building' — the two reports of the Joint Working Party on Pastoral Strategy*, Abbots Langley: Catholic Information Services.

217

Boff, L. (1985) *Church, Charisma and Power: Liberation Theology and the Institutional Church*, London: SCM.

Bogan, R. V. (1973) 'Priests, alienation and hope', *The Month*, 6(6) June, 195–201.

Boylan, A. B. (1980) 'The content of liturgical formation', Bishops' Conference of England and Wales: Liturgy Commission, Abbots Langley: Catholic Information Services.

Brothers, J. B. (1964) *Church and School: A Study of the Impact of Education on Religion*, Liverpool: Liverpool University Press.

Bryman, A. (1985) 'Professionalism and the clergy: a research note', *Review of Religious Research*, 26(3), 253–60.

Bühlmann, W. (1976) *The Coming of the Third Church: An Analysis of the Present and Future of the Church*, Slough: St Paul Publications.

Burns, C. (1988) 'The revolutionary patience of a housewife', *Priests and People*, 2(3) April, 83–8.

Burns, T. and Stalker, G. M. (1961) *The Management of Innovation*, London: Tavistock.

Butler, C. (1981) *The Theology of Vatican II*, London: Darton, Longman and Todd.

Cafferty, P. and McCready, W. C. (eds) (1985) *Hispanics in the United States: A New Social Agenda*, New Brunswick, Oxford: Transaction Books.

Canon Law Society of Great Britain and Ireland (1983) *The Code of Canon Law*, London: Collins.

Catholic Education Council, Summary of Pastoral Statistics (private communication).

Catholic Media Office (1986) *Synod 87: Summary of the Consultation 'Called to Serve'*, London.

—— (1987a) 'Ministry and Mission: Proposals for a National Policy for Lifelong Priestly Formation', *Briefing*, *17*, No. 17, 4 September.

—— (1987b) Synod Special 1, *Briefing*, *17*, No. 20, 9 October.

—— (1987c) Synod Special 2, *Briefing*, *17*, No. 21, 16 October.

—— (1987d) Synod Special 3, *Briefing*, *17*, No. 22, 23 October.

—— (1987e) Synod Special 5, *Briefing*, *17*, No. 24, 6 November.

Clark, D. (1977) *Basic Communities: Towards an Alternative Society*, London: SPCK.

Coleman, J. A. (1978) *The Evolution of Dutch Catholicism: 1958–1974*, Berkeley, Los Angeles, Ca: University of California Press.

Coman, P. (1977) *Catholics and the Welfare State*, London: Longman.

Comerford, M. and Dodd, C. (1982) *Many Ministries: Lay People in Neighbourhood Care: A Practical Guide* (S361) London: CTS.

Coser, L. A. (1956) *The Functions of Social Conflict*, Glencoe, Ill.: Free Press.

—— (1974) *Greedy Institutions: Patterns of Undivided Commitment*, New York: Free Press; London: Collier-Macmillan.

Cosstick, V. (1988) 'The Gospel and the gun', *The Tablet*, *242*, No. 7714, 21 May, 579–82.

Cumming, J. and Burns, P. (eds) (1980) *The Church Now: An Inquiry into the Recent State of the Catholic Church in Britain and Ireland*, Dublin: Gill & Macmillan.

Dinges, W. D. (1987) 'Ritual conflict as social conflict: liturgical reform in the Roman Catholic Church', *Sociological Analysis*, *48*(2), 138–57.

Dobbelaere, K. (1981) 'Secularization: a multi-dimensional concept', *Current Sociology*, *29*(2) Summer, 3–213.

—— (1985) 'Secularization theories and sociological paradigms: a reformulation of the private-public dichotomy and the problem of societal integration', *Sociological Analysis*, *46*(4) 377–87.

Dobbelaere, K. and Billiet, J. (1976) 'Community-formation and the Church: a sociological study of an ideology and the empirical reality' in Cauldron, M. (ed.), *Faith and Society* (Acta Congressus Internationalis Theologici) Louvain, 211–59.

Dolan, J. P. (1985) *The American Catholic Experience: A History from Colonial Times to the Present*, Garden City, New York: Doubleday.

Dolan, J. P. and Leege, D. C. (1985) 'A profile of American Catholic parishes and parishioners: 1820s to the 1980s', Notre Dame Study of Catholic Parish Life, Report No. 2.

Dolan, J. P. (ed.) (1987) *The American Catholic Parish: A History From 1850s to the Present* Vol. I. Northeast, Southeast, South Central; Vol. II Pacific States, Intermountain West, Midwest, New York, Mahwah: Paulist Press.

Dominion, J. (1968) *Marital Breakdown*, Harmondsworth: Penguin.

Douglas, M. (1973) *Natural Symbols: Explorations in Cosmology*, Harmondsworth: Penguin.

Droel, W. L. and Pierce, G. F. D. (1987) *Confident and Competent: A Challenge for the Lay Church*, Notre Dame, In: Ave Maria Press.

Dulles, A. (1976) *Models of the Church: A Critical Assessment of the Church in all its Aspects*, Dublin: Gill & Macmillan.

—— (1977) *The Resilient Church: The Necessity and Limits of Adaptation*, Garden City, New York: Doubleday.

Ellis, J. T. (1969) *American Catholicism*, Chicago: University of Chicago Press.

Etzioni, A. (1961) *A Comparative Analysis of Complex Organisation: On Power, Involvement and Their Correlates*, New York: Free Press; London: Collier-Macmillan.

—— (ed.) (1969) *The Semi-Professions and Their Organisation*, New York: Free Press.

Fee, J. L., Greeley, A. M., McCready, W. C. and Sullivan, T. A. (1981) *Young Catholics in the United States and Canada: A Report to the Knights of Columbus*, Los Angeles, New York and Chicago: Sadlier.

Fichter, J. H. (1954) *Social Relations in the Urban Parish*, Chicago: University of Chicago Press.

—— (1966) *Religion as an Occupation: A Study in the Sociology of Professions*, University of Notre Dame Press.

—— (1973) *One-Man Research: Reminiscences of a Catholic Sociologist*, New York, London, Sydney, and Toronto: Wiley.

—— (1974) *Organization Man in the Church*, Cambridge, Mass: Schenkman.

—— (1978) *Dynamics of a City Church*, New York: Arno Press.

Fitzpatrick, J. P. (1971) *Puerto Rican Americans: The Meaning of Migration to the Mainland*, Englewood Cliffs: Prentice Hall.

Flanagan, K. (1980) 'Sociological errors in liturgical thinking', Paper read to General Meeting of the Association for Latin Liturgy, 18 October.

—— (1981) 'Competitive assemblies of God: lies and mistakes in liturgy' *ISWRA Research Bulletin*, University of Birmingham, 20–69.

Forrester, D. (1980) 'The parish and the priesthood' in Cumming, J. and Burns, P. (eds), pp. 73–81.

Fox, A. (1985) *Man Mismanagement*, London: Hutchinson.

Fraser, J. (1987) 'Community, the private and the individual', *Sociological Review*, *35*, (4), 795–818.

Gannon, T. M. (1971) 'Priest/minister: profession or non-profession?', *Review of Religious Research*, *12*, 66–79.

—— (1978) 'Religious tradition and urban community', *Sociological Analysis*, *39* (4), 283–302.

Gibson, K. and Hornsby-Smith, M. P. (1987) 'Parish support in the early years of marriage' *Briefing*, *17*, (2), 23–32, London: Catholic Media Office.

Gilley, S. W. (1971) *Evangelical and Roman Catholic Missions to the Irish in London, 1830–70*, University of Cambridge, Unpublished Ph.D. thesis.

Goffman, E. (1968) *Asylums: Essays on the Social Situation of Mental Patients and Other Inmates*, Harmondsworth: Penguin.

Goldner, F. H., Ference, T. P., and Ritti, R. R. (1973) 'Priests and laity: a profession in transition', in Halmos, P. (ed.) *Professionalisation and Social Change*, Sociological Review Monograph No. 20, Keele, 119–37.

Greeley, A. M. (1972) *The Catholic Priest in the United States: Sociological Investigations*, Washington, D.C.: United States Catholic Conference.

—— (1976) *The Communal Catholic: A Personal Manifesto*, New York: Seabury Press.

—— (1977) *The American Catholic: A Social Portrait*, New York: Basic Books.

—— (1981) *The Religious Imagination*, Los Angeles, New York, Chicago: Sadlier.

Greeley, A. M., Durkin, M., Shea, J., Tracy, D., and McCready, W. (1981) *Parish, Priest and People: New Leadership for the Local Church*, Chicago: Thomas More Press.

Greeley, A. M. and Rossi, P. H. (1966) *The Education of Catholic Americans*, Chicago: Aldine.

Grollenberg, L., Kerkhofs, J., Houtepen, A., Vollebergh, J. J. A., and Schillebeeckx, E. (1980) *Minister? Pastor? Prophet? Grass-roots Leadership in the Churches*, London: SCM.

Hall, D. T. and Schneider, B. (1973) *Organisational Climates and Careers: The Work Lives of Priests*, New York and London: Seminar Press.

Hall, R. H. (1968) 'Professionalization and Bureaucratization', *American Sociological Review*, *33* February, 92–103.

Hegy, P. (1987) 'The Invisible Catholicism: Research Note', *Sociological Analysis*, *48* (2), 167–76.

Hervieu-Léger, D. (1986) *Vers Un Nouveau Christianisme? Introduction à la Sociologie du Christianisme occidental*, Paris: Cerf.

Hesser, G. and Weigert, A. J. (1980) 'Comparative dimensions of liturgy: a conceptual framework and feasibility application', *Sociological Analysis*, *41* (3) Fall, 215–29.

Hickey, J. (1967) *Urban Catholics: Urban Catholicism in England and Wales from 1829 to the Present Day*, London: Geoffrey Chapman.

Hornsby-Smith, M. P. (1975) 'Plural parish liturgies', *Clergy Review*, *60* (8) August 518–24.

—— (1978) *Catholic Education: The Unobtrusive Partner*, London: Sheed & Ward.

—— (1980a) 'Sociology for seminarians' *Clergy Review*, *64* (4) April, 135–41.

—— (1980b) 'In tears with his people: reflections on the role of the Roman Catholic clergy in four English parishes', *New Blackfriars*, *61*, December, 504–23.

—— (1983) 'Formation for the priesthood: reflections of a lay person', *Clergy Review*, *68*, (12) 434–44.

—— (1984) 'Priests, people and parishes in change: reflections of a sociologist', *New Blackfriars*, *65*, April, 153–69.

—— (1986a) 'The emergence of basic Christian communities in the Philippines', *Clergy Review*, *71* (10), 353–60.

—— (1986b) 'The immigrant background of Roman Catholics in England and Wales: a research note', *New Community*, *13*, No. 1, Spring-Summer, 79–85.

—— (1987) *Roman Catholics in England: Studies in Social Structure Since the Second World War*, Cambridge: Cambridge University Press.

—— (1988a) 'A lay response to "Ministry and Mission"', *Priests and People*, *2* (5) June, 190–3.

—— (1988b) *The Everyday Lives of Lay Catholics: An Exploratory Study*, Occasional Papers in Sociology and Social Policy No. 15, Guildford, University of Surrey.

—— (1989) 'Some pastoral implications of everyday lay lives', *Priests and People*, *3* (1) January, 3–7.

Hornsby-Smith, M. P. and Cordingley, E. S. (1983) *Catholic Elites: A Study of the Delegates to the National Pastoral Congress*, Occasional Paper No. 3, Guildford: University of Surrey.

Hornsby-Smith, M. P., Lee, R. M., and Reilly, P. A. (1977), 'Lapsation and ideology', *The Month*, *10* (12) 406–9.

Hornsby-Smith, M. P. and Lee, R. M. (1979) *Roman Catholic Opinion: A Study of Roman Catholics in England and Wales in the 1970s*, Guildford: University of Surrey.

Hornsby-Smith, M. P., Lee, R. M., and Reilly, P. A. (1985) 'Common religion and customary religion: a critique and a proposal', *Review of Religious Research*, *26* (3) March, 244–52.

Hornsby-Smith, M.P., Lee, R. M., and Turcan, K. A. (1982) 'A typology of English Catholics', *Sociological Review*, *30* (3) August, 433–59.

Hornsby-Smith, M. P., Procter, M., Rajan, L., and Brown, J. (1987) 'A typology of progressive Catholics', *Journal for the Scientific Study of Religion*, *26*, 234–48.

Hornsby-Smith, M. P. and Turcan, K. A. (1981) 'Are northern Catholics different?', *Clergy Review*, *66* (7) July, 231–41.

Hughes, G. (1987) 'The priests as pilgrim guide', Paper given to the National

Conference of Priests, Newman College, Birmingham.

Hume, B. (1986) *With You in Spirit? The Report of Cardinal Hume's Advisory Group on the Catholic Church's Commitment to the Black Community*, London.

Ireson, D. (1988) 'The ship of the Church: standby to put to sea . . . a Catholic teacher's view of the Church', *Priests and People*, 2 (1) February, 23 – 7.

Jackson, J. A. (1963) *The Irish in Britain*, London: Routledge.

Janowitz, M. (1967) *The Community Press in an Urban Setting*, Chicago: University of Chicago Press.

Jarvis, P. (1975) 'The parish ministry as a semi-profession', *Sociological Review*, 24, 911 – 22.

Kelly, M., Francis, M., and Johnstone, J. (1988) 'Coping as a single parent', *Priests and People*, 2 (5) June, 163 – 8, 174.

Kenny, A. (1986) *A Path From Rome: An Autobiography*, Oxford: Oxford University Press.

Kerkhofs, J. (1980) 'From frustration to liberation? A factual approach to ministries in the Church', in Grollenberg, L. *et al.* (1980) pp. 5 – 20.

Konstant, D. (Chairman) (1981) *Signposts and Homecomings: The Educative Task of the Catholic Community*, Slough: St Paul Publications.

Kuhn, T. S. (1970) *The Structure of Scientific Revolutions*, London and Chicago: University of Chicago Press.

Laity Commission (1971) *Report to the Laity: The Provisional Laity Commission Reports on its Work and Experience on the Completion of Its Five Years of Office*, London: Living Parish Pamphlets.

Lambert, Y. (1985) *Dieu Change en Bretagne: La Religion à Limerzel, de 1900 à nos jours*, Paris: Cerf.

Lane, R. (1980) 'Two parishes in London: a note on leadership styles', Paper read at BSA Sociology of Religion Conference at Birmingham University.

Leat, D. (1973) 'Putting God over: the faithful counsellors', *Sociological Review*, 21, 561 – 72.

Leege, D. C. (1986a) 'Parish organisations: people's needs, parish services, and leadership', *Notre Dame Study of Catholic Parish Life*, Report No. 8.

—— (1986b) 'Parish life among the leaders', *Notre Dame Study of Catholic Parish Life*, Report No. 9.

—— (1987a) 'The parish as community', *Notre Dame Study of Catholic Parish Life*, Report No. 10.

—— (1987b) 'Catholics and the civic order: parish participation, politics and civic participation', *Notre Dame Study of Catholic Parish Life*, Report No. 11.

—— (1988) 'Who is a true Catholic? Social boundaries on the Church', *Notre Dame Study of Catholic Parish Life*, Report No. 12.

Leege, D. C. and Gremillion, J. (1984) 'The U.S. parish twenty years after Vatican II: an introduction to the study', *Notre Dame Study of Catholic Parish Life*, Report No. 1.

Leege, D. C. and Gremillion, J. (1986) 'The people, their pastors, and the Church: viewpoints on Church policies and positions', *Notre Dame Study of Catholic Parish Life*, Report No. 7.

Leege, D. C. and Trozzolo, T. A. (1985a) 'Participation in Catholic parish life: religious rites and parish activities in the 1980s', *Notre Dame Study of Catholic Parish Life*, Report No. 3.

Leege, D. C. and Trozzolo, T. A. (1985b) 'Religious values and parish participation: the paradox of individual needs in a communitarian Church', *Notre Dame Study of Catholic Parish Life*, Report No. 4.

Lees, L. H. (1979) *Exiles of Erin: Irish Migrants in Victorian London*, Manchester: Manchester University Press.

Lenski, G. (1963) *The Religious Factor: A Sociological Study of Religious Impact on Politics, Economics and Family Life*, Garden City, N.Y.: Anchor.

Leslie, J. H. (1983) 'Lay conceptions of liturgical practice in the Roman Catholic Church', in Newton, D. (ed.) *Liturgy and Change*, IWSRA: University of Birmingham, 54–66.

—— (1986) *Resistance to Change in a North Midlands Parish*, Unpublished Ph.D. Thesis, Guildford: University of Surrey.

Lewins, F. W. (1978) *The Myth of the Universal Church: Catholic Migrants in Australia*, Canberra: Australian National University.

McCabe, H. (1970) 'Priesthood and revolution' in Cutler, D. R. (ed.) (1980), *The World Year Book of Religion: The Religion Situation Vol. II*, London: Evans Bros, 980–92.

—— (1985) *The Teaching of the Catholic Church: A New Catechism of Christian Doctrine* (Do 565), London: CTS.

McCaffrey, J. F. (1979) 'Politics and the Catholic community since 1878', in McRoberts, D. (ed.) *Modern Scottish Catholicism: 1878–1978*, Glasgow: Burns, pp. 140–55.

McCoy, A. W. (1984) *Priests on Trial*, Ringwood, Australia: Penguin.

McCready, W. C. (1975) *Changing Attitudes of American Catholics Towards The Liturgy: 1963 to 1974*, Collegeville, Minnesota: Liturgical Press.

McEvoy, J. (1987) 'Rock Climbing: reflections on a life in business', *Priests and People*, *1* (7) November, 259–61, 264.

McLeod, H. (1974) *Class and Religion in the Late Victorian City*, London: Croom Helm.

—— (1981) *Religion and the People of Western Europe: 1789–1970*, Oxford: Oxford University Press.

—— (1986) 'New perspectives on Victorian class religion: the oral evidence', *Oral History Journal*, *14* (1), 31–49.

Matza, D. (1964) *Delinquency and Drift*, New York: Wiley.

Merton, R. K. (1957) *Social Theory and Social Structure*, New York: Free Press.

Michonneau, Abbé (1949) *Revolution in a City Parish*, Oxford: Blackfriars.

Moloney, T. (1985) *Westminster, Whitehall and the Vatican: The Role of Cardinal Hinsley 1935–43*, Tunbridge Wells: Burns & Oates.

Moore, J. (1975) 'The Catholic priesthood', in Hill, M. (ed.) *A Sociological Yearbook of Religion in Britain*, *8*, 30–60.

Murmion, P. J. (1982) 'Parish renewal: state(ments) of the question', *America*, *146* (16) 24 April, 314–17.

Neal, M. A. (1970) 'The H. Paul Douglass lectures for 1970, Part I the relation between religious belief and structural change in religious orders: developing an effective measuring instrument'. *Review of Religious Research*, *12*, Fall, 2–16.

223

O'Brien, N. (1985) *Seeds of Injustice: Reflections on the Murder Frame-up of the Negros Nine in the Philippines*, Dublin: O'Brien Press.

O'Dea, T. F. (1970) *Sociology and the Study of Religion: Theory, Research, Interpretation*, New York, London: Basic Books.

O'Farrell, P. (1985) *The Catholic Church and Community: An Australian History*, Kensington, NSW: New South Wales University Press.

O'Leary, M. (1987) 'Parish support in early years of marriage', *Priests and People, 1* (5) September, 190–2.

O'Sullivan, B. (1979) *Parish Alive*, London: Sheed & Ward.

Paul VI, Pope (1968) *The Regulation of Birth (Humanae Vitae)*, London: Catholic Truth Society (Do 411).

Pittarello, A. (1980) *'Soup without Salt': The Australian Catholic Church and the Italian Migrant: A Comparative Study in the Sociology of Religion*, Sydney: Centre for Migration Studies.

Pro Mundi Vita (1973) 'Pluralism and pluriformity in religious life: a case study', Bulletin 47, Brussels.

Ranson, S., Bryman, A., and Hinings, B. (1977) *Clergy, Ministers and Priests*, London: Routledge.

Reidy, M. T. V. and White, L. C. (1977) 'The measurement of traditionalism among Roman Catholic priests: an exploratory study', *British Journal of Sociology, 28* (2) July, 226–41.

Reilly, M. E. (1975) 'Perceptions of the priest role', *Sociological Analysis, 36* (4) 347–56.

Rex, J. and Moore, R. (1967) *Race, Community and Conflict: A Study of Sparkbrook*, Oxford: Oxford University Press.

Roberts, R. (1973) *The Classic Slum: Salford Life in the First Quarter of the Century*, Harmondsworth: Penguin.

Roof, W. C. (1976) 'Traditional religion in contemporary society: a theory of local-cosmopolitan plausibility', *American Sociological Review, 41*: 195–208.

Roof, W. C. and Hoge, D. R. (1980) 'Church involvement in America: social factors affecting membership and participation', *Review of Religious Research, 21* (4), 405–26.

St Joseph's Parish (1984) *Parish Magazine*, Summer, Epsom.

St Julie Parish (1986) *Parish Silver Jubilee: 1961–1986*, Eccleston.

St Lawrence Parish (1987) *Synod on the Laity: A Parish Response*, Sidcup.

Schreuder, O. (1961) 'The parish priest as a subject of criticism', *Social Compass, 8* (2), 111–26.

Scott, G. (1967) *The R.C.s: Report on Roman Catholics in Britain Today*, London, Hutchinson.

Scott, M. B. and Lyman, S. M. (1968) 'Accounts', *American Sociological Review, 33* (1) February, 46–62.

Searle, M. and Leege, D. C. (1985a) 'The celebration of liturgy in the parishes', *Notre Dame Study of Catholic Parish Life*, Report No. 5.

—— (1985b) 'Of piety and planning: liturgy, the parishioners, and the professionals', *Notre Dame Study of Catholic Parish Life*, Report No. 6.

Seeman, M. (1959) 'The meaning of alienation', *American Sociological Review, 24* (6), 783–91.

Siefer, G. (1964) *The Church and Industrial Society: A Survey of the Worker-Priest*

Movement and its Implications for the Christian Mission, London: Darton, Longman & Todd.

Smelser, N. J. (1959) *Social Change in the Industrial Revolution*, Chicago: University of Chicago Press.

Stacey, M. (1960) *Tradition and Change: A Study of Banbury*, Oxford: Oxford University Press.

Stark, R. and Bainbridge, W. S. (1980) 'Networks of faith: interpersonal bonds and recruitment to cults and sects', *American Journal of Sociology, 85* (6) May, 1376–95.

Struzzo, J. A. (1970) 'Professionalism and the resolution of authority conflicts among Catholic clergy', *Sociological Analysis, 31* (2), 92–106.

Tanner, T. (1980) 'The Church and social responsibility' in Cumming, J. and Burns, P. (eds) (1980), 161–9.

Tomasi, S. M. (1975) *Piety and Power: The Role of the Italian Parishes in New York Metropolitan Area, 1880–1930*, New York: Centre for Migration Studies.

Tönnies, F. (1963) *Community and Society*, New York, Evanston and London: Harper.

Towler, R. (1974) *Homo Religiosus: Sociological Problems in the Study of Religion*, London: Constable.

Towler, R. and Coxon, A. P. M. (1979) *The Fate of the Anglican Clergy: A Sociological Study*, London: Macmillan.

Turner, D. (1983) 'The relevance of Christian values today', *New Life, 39* (4), 3–7.

Vallier, I. (1970) *Catholicism, Social Control and Modernization in Latin America*, Englewood Cliffs, New Jersey: Prentice Hall.

Vanier, J. (1979) *Community and Growth*, London: Darton, Longman & Todd.

Ward, C. (1965) *Priests and People: A Study in the Sociology of Religion*, Liverpool: Liverpool University Press.

Ward, M. (1949) *France Pagan? The Mission of Abbé Godin*, London: Catholic Book Club.

Weber, M. (1949) *The Methodology of the Social Sciences*, New York: Free Press.
—— (1964) *The Theory of Social and Economic Organisation*, Edited with an Introduction by Talcott Parsons, New York: Free Press; London: Collier-Macmillan.
—— (1966) *The Sociology of Religion*, London: Methuen.

Willmott, P. (1986) *Social Networks, Informal Care and Public Policy*, Policy Studies Institute Research Report 655, London.

Winter, M. M. (1973) *Mission or Maintenance: A Study in New Pastoral Structures*, London: Darton, Longman & Todd.
—— (1979) *Mission Resumed?* London: Darton, Longman & Todd.
—— (1985) *What Ever Happened to Vatican II?*, London: Sheed & Ward.

Wood, B. (1987/88) 'The everyday life of a Catholic housewife', *Priests and People, 1* (8) December/January, 297–302.

INDEX

226

dying, care of 81–2, 84, 131, 188–9

Easter People, The 11, 74–5, 215
economy, cooperative 67–8
ecumenism 133, 164
education 32, 53, 55, 66, 70, 74, 86,
    110, 124, 131, 165, 179, 182, 188–9,
    208, 214
elderly, care of 81, 84, 141
elites 45, 61–2, 109
Ellis, J. T. 48, 50
embourgeoisement 18, 199
empowerment 124, 142
encyclicals, papal 154, 171, 177, 202
endogamy, marital 26, 38–9, 43
English College (Rome) 150
enterprise, of salvation 119–20, 132
entertainment 6, 83
enthusiasm, frustrated 171
entrenchment, sect-like 123
entrepreneurs, moral 191
estates, housing 67, 104, 199, 206
ethnicity, salience of 50
Etzioni, A. 19, 30–1, 52, 92, 173, 176,
    190–1, 196, 202
eucharist 10, 12, 52, 74–5, 187, 192;
    celebration of 5, 75, 95–6, 199;
    commensal 67–9
evaluation 179–80; of parish 207–11
Exarchate, Ukranian 179
expectations 13, 56, 104, 112, 115, 129,
    135–6, 152, 171, 174, 196, 201, 209
experience 33, 48, 52, 61, 77, 103, 162,
    165, 209; conversion 184
experiences 50–1, 54, 105, 112, 127,
    143, 147, 171, 179–80; of black
    Catholics 80; community-like 51,
    200; religious 5, 51, 76; seminary
    147, 151
experiment, worker-priest 59
experiments, pastoral 214
experimentation 61, 124, 127
expertise 109, 118, 126, 140, 183

faith 13, 27, 56, 58–9, 75–6, 95,
    122, 131, 134, 155, 161, 186, 214
faithful 8–10, 14, 23–4, 27, 58, 68–9,
    74–5, 95, 122, 131; simple 29
families 70, 148, 150, 162, 186; inter-
    Church 187; problem 83
family 59, 124, 170
Family and Social Action (FSA) 85
fasting, regulations 37

father, priest as 171
'Father' 137
fear 133; of conflict 137
fears 189
feasts 140
Fee, J. L. 143
fellowship 74, 76, 130, 142
festivals 60, 104
Fichter, J. H. 47, 49–50, 53, 66, 70,
    115, 118, 126, 152, 160, 180
fidelity 87; priestly 150; religious 59
filter, interpretative 190
Fitzpatrick, J. P. 50
Flanagan, K. 107–9
flock 133, 145
follower, passive 175–6
following, uncritical 177
formation 8, 11–13, 91, 106, 131, 174;
    of priests 15, 152, 192
Forrester, D. 9, 131
Fox, A. 135, 159
fragmentation 19, 76, 159, 170
Fraser, J. 71, 92
freedom 150; of choice 194; of
    expression 112
Friday, first 183, 188
friends 68, 72, 79, 86, 130, 163, 169,
    186; Catholic 39–42, 196, 200
friendship 103, 162, 184
friendships 39, 42, 84, 181–2; between
    priests and parishioners 79, 192,
    between priests and young people
    168; Catholic 39–40, 68
frustration 156, 201, 215
functionaries, specialised 164
functions, loss of 6, 18, 66, 92, 124
funerals 62, 202

Gannon, T. M. 71, 93, 127, 207
gap 62; opportunity 86; between parish
    priests and assistants 147–8, 161–5;
    between priests and people 56, 168;
    between theory and practice 137
gatekeeper 123
Gaudium et Spes 1, 36, 73, 119
gemeinschaft (community) 71–2
generation, younger 168
generations 7, 206
gesellschaft (society) 71–2
ghettos 199–200; Catholic 28; Irish
    25
Gibson, K. 86
gifts 87, 119–20, 132; of lay people 78,